Managing Country Risk

A Practitioner's Guide to Effective
Cross-Border Risk Analysis

"Many important areas of modern finance lack that one solid, unbiased book that tells both the novice everything he or she needs to know about the subject, brings a coherent structure, and important, fresh insights to seasoned practitioners. Daniel Wagner has brought the world the go-to book on country risk analysis. *Managing Country Risk* provides a broad, deep, and accurately detailed analysis of country risk analysis tools and techniques in a volume unlike any I have read before. It is both timely and likely to enjoy a long shelf life."

Jeffrey Christian, Managing Director, CPM Group and author of Commodities Rising

"Daniel Wagner has written an excellent, thought provoking, and well-crafted book that speaks directly to the needs of financial professionals tasked with navigating the complex world of cross-border risk analysis. Investment managers, commercial lenders, risk managers, and members of senior management will all benefit from the insights in this book, which provide the tools needed to make stronger, better, and more holistic global investment decisions."

Peter Went, Vice President, Global Association of Risk Professionals Research Center

"Wagner carefully sorts through the fundamental principles of country risk management, adding context with examples from his quarter century as a political risk insurance underwriter, country risk manager, and advisor. The chapter on political risk insurance is the best comprehensive description of the product that I have seen. This book is an invaluable tool for the scholar and practitioner alike in understanding country risk and the techniques available to international investors and traders to address those risks."

Frederick E. Jenney, Partner, Project Finance & Development Group, Morrison & Foerster

"I found great value in Daniel Wagner's approach of combining 101 subject matter with graduate level country risk concepts, and was fascinated with the practical examples he used to drive the points home. I would think that this book would be of great value to a widely varied audience, including CEOs, CFOs, risk managers, directors of multinational boards, insurance underwriters and brokers, academics, and public sector practitioners."

Rod Morris, Vice President of Insurance, Overseas Private Investment Corporation

"The first book that combines easily understood text, insightful analysis, and effective strategies to minimize the risks inherent in cross-border business transactions. I consider this book a must read for anyone charged with managing country risk."

Mark T. Williams, Executive-in-Resident/Master Lecturer, Boston University School of Management, and author of Uncontrolled Risk: The Lessons of Lehman Brothers and How Systemic Risk Can Still Bring Down the World Financial System

"This book is a marvelous exploration of a mind trained to integrate all information on all subjects into a coherent viewpoint that produces a business decision. After a long career practicing this kind of thinking in both the public and private sectors, Wagner's approach, and this book, are a treasure."

Dr. Paul Armington, President, World Institute for Leadership and Management in Africa

Managing Country Risk

A Practitioner's Guide to Effective Cross-Border Risk Analysis

Daniel Wagner

CRC Press
Taylor & Francis Group
Boca Raton London New York

CRC Press is an imprint of the
Taylor & Francis Group, an **informa** business

A PRODUCTIVITY PRESS BOOK

First published in paperback 2024

First published 2012 by CRC Press
2385 NW Executive Center Drive, Suite 320, Boca Raton FL 33431

and by CRC Press
4 Park Square, Milton Park, Abingdon, Oxon, OX14 4RN

First issued in hardback 2019

CRC Press is an imprint of Taylor & Francis Group, LLC

© 2012, 2019, 2024 Taylor & Francis Group, LLC

Library of Congress Cataloging-in-Publication Data

Wagner, Daniel.
  Managing country risk : a practitioner's guide to effective cross-border risk analysis / Daniel Wagner.
     p. cm.
   ISBN 978-1-4665-0047-1 (alk. paper)
   1. Country risk. 2. Investments, Foreign. 3. Economic forecasting. I. Title.

HG4538.W244 2012
332'.042--dc23   2011037293

ISBN 13: 978-1-46-650047-1 (hbk)
ISBN 13: 978-1-03-292269-0 (pbk)
ISBN 13: 978-0-42-925316-4 (ebk)

DOI: 10.1201/b11601

Visit the Taylor & Francis Web site at
http://www.taylorandfrancis.com

and the CRC Press Web site at
http://www.crcpress.com

I dedicate this book to my spouse, family, and friends, who have all been an incredible source of love and support over the years. Thank you for being there throughout the ongoing journey.

Contents

List of Tables

List of Figures

List of Maps

Preface

Almost any event can increase a trader's, investor's, or lender's cross-border risk. An unexpected resignation, a terrorist act, or a currency collapse can completely transform the political and economic landscape of a country, a region, or the world. Since the advent of globalization, politics and economics have been forever entwined, sometimes resulting in calamitous outcomes. There have been several sobering examples over the past two decades, including the collapse of the Thai baht in 1997. The sudden and dramatic collapse of the Thai currency set off a chain of events that ultimately led to the economic meltdown of many of Asia's economies, resulted in the overthrow of the Indonesian government, and sent gyrations across the rest of the world.

One of the disadvantages of globalization and instant communications is that the impact of such change is felt instantaneously. Today there is less time to react before someone else does; we may be sleeping while others are reacting. Perhaps the impact of localized economic and political events would not be so dramatic if the international marketplace were not so interconnected—if currency and stock trading did not occur and information were not broadcast 24 hours per day. The trend toward seamless international financial transactions has continued at an even more breathtaking pace over the past decade.

One action or event that may be forecast to have a certain outcome at a certain point in time may end up having a completely different or unanticipated outcome years later. For example, when former US President Carter granted ownership of the Panama Canal to Panama in 1978, who would have imagined that, in 1999, when ownership was actually transferred, a Hong Kong company (Hutchison Whampoa) would spread enough money around the power brokers in Panama City to buy control over the ports at both ends of the canal? As a result, some would argue that China instantly gained the potential ability to influence the flow of global trade. On the flip side, by granting the concession to operate the ports to Hutchison, Panama, which has no national army, virtually guaranteed that US military influence would be present in the country for decades to come. This, in turn, will impact how future US military budgets are allocated and how US tax dollars are spent.

Consider also the impact that Turkey's possible accession to the European Union may have on Europe and beyond. Turkey has tried to join the EU for more than a decade, but strenuous objections from Greece and other members kept it from succeeding. Yet today, Turkey looks like the bastion of stability and conservatism compared to the economic "basket case" that Greece has become. Turkey and its political model—a pragmatic blend of civilian and military influence—have enormous political influence throughout the Arab world. What impact might the EU have in the Arab world today if Turkey had been admitted to the EU a decade ago? Today, Turkey is less interested in joining.

The impact of political change on businesses is as significant as it is on individuals—perhaps even more so. At stake are trillions of dollars of revenues derived from trading and investing abroad. For a business, the risks associated with political change are multifaceted. In general, an international investor often faces the risk of expropriation of assets when a new government takes power or an existing government adopts a negative orientation toward foreign investment. The risk of not being able to convert local currency into hard currency or to transfer hard currency out of a country because of a shortfall in the national foreign exchange supply or a change in law is ever present. And depending on where an investment is located within a country, the risk of damage to a facility or an interruption of business operations because of political violence can arise without warning.

For international traders, political risks are every bit as real. Imagine exporting goods to a government buyer only to discover after the fact that it has not been paying its bills, the United Nations has just imposed an embargo on the country, or your own government has just rescinded your export license. Cross-border partnerships can be unexpectedly tested as unanticipated events may unravel promising business prospects. These types of events happen all the time—even in times of peace. Political change only accentuates the political risks inherent in trading or investing abroad.

This book is about how to identify and manage the plethora of risks associated with conducting business abroad and how to think outside the box to be able to anticipate the impact of change on business operations. By reading this book, you will come to know more about country risk management than virtually all of your peers. You will also be able to add value to the risk management processes in your organization, even if you are not formally part of a risk management unit. If doing so helps your organization become smarter about how it does business abroad and enhances its ability to make a profit, all the better, because in the process it will be contributing to development, job creation, and improving the lives of people around the world.

Daniel Wagner
Norwalk, Connecticut

Acknowledgments

Over the course of the past quarter-century I have worked with a lot of really talented people, a number of whom were particularly influential in helping me better understand the nature and practice of country risk management. In the realm of political risk insurance underwriting, Christophe Bellinger of the Asian Development Bank, John Hegeman of Chartis, and Christina Westholm-Schroder of Sovereign Risk Insurance provided unique working-level insight based on their own in-depth experience and perspective. Luis Dodero, formerly general counsel of the Multilateral Investment Guarantee Agency (MIGA), and Srilal Perera, formerly chief counsel of MIGA, enabled me to better appreciate the impact of legal and regulatory risk on cross-border investment. It was a privilege to work with each of them. I also want to thank the many individuals I worked with along the way who helped me learn so much about managing country risk while I lived and worked in Asia, Europe, and North America. Doing so enabled me to amass the knowledge I am now sharing in this book.

I want to thank Professor Alexis Papadopoulos of DePaul University, Professor Mark T. Williams of Boston University, and Mark Yim of GAMCO Investors for providing their insights and comments on a draft of this book.

Finally, I wish to thank everyone at Taylor and Francis, who has been a joy to work with. In particular, I wish to thank Kris Mednansky, who first embraced the book and has been a great source of support and guidance, as well as Judith Simon, the book's very capable and patient editor. Thanks for recognizing the book's potential to influence our ever-changing world and helping to make it a reality.

The Author

Daniel Wagner is the founder and CEO of Country Risk Solutions (CRS), a cross-border risk consultancy based in Connecticut, and Director of Global Strategy with Political Risk Services. Prior to founding CRS, Daniel was senior vice president of Country Risk at GE Energy Financial Services, where he was part of a team investing billions of dollars annually into global energy projects. Daniel was responsible for advising senior management on a variety of country risk-related issues, strategic planning, and portfolio management. He created a Center of Excellence for country risk analysis in GE and led a team that produced a comprehensive automated country risk rating methodology.

He began his career underwriting political risk insurance (PRI) at American International Group (AIG) in New York and subsequently spent 5 years as guarantee officer for the Asia region at the World Bank Group's Multilateral Investment Guarantee Agency (MIGA) in Washington, DC. During that time, he was responsible for underwriting PRI for projects in a dozen Asian countries. After serving as regional manager for political risks for Southeast Asia and greater China for AIG in Singapore, Daniel moved to Manila, Philippines, where he was guarantee and risk management advisor, political risk guarantee specialist, and senior guarantees and syndications specialist for the Asian Development Bank's Office of Cofinancing Operations. Over the course of his career, Daniel has also held senior positions in the PRI brokerage business in London, Dallas, and Houston.

Daniel has published hundreds of articles on risk management and current affairs, is a nonresident scholar at the Institute for Near East and Gulf Military Analysis in Dubai, and a regular contributor to foreignpolicyjournal.com, *The Huffington Post,* and the International Risk Management Institute (IRMI). His editorials have been published in such notable newspapers as the *International Herald Tribune* and the *Wall Street Journal.* His first book, *Political Risk Insurance Guide,* was published by IRMI.

Daniel holds master's degrees in international relations from the University of Chicago and in international management from the American Graduate School of International Management (Thunderbird) in Phoenix. Daniel received his bachelor's degree in political science from Richmond College in London. He can be reached at daniel.wagner@countryrisksolutions.com or through www.countryrisksolutions.com.

Abbreviations

ADB	Asian Development Bank
AID	Agency for International Development (of the United States)
AIG	American International Group
ASEAN	Association of Southeast Asian Nations
BCA	Brazil Cooperation Agency
BI	Business Interruption
BIS	Bank for International Settlements
BMI	Business Monitor International
BRIC	Brazil, Russia, India, China
BRICS	Brazil, Russia, India, China, South Africa
CCP	Chinese Communist Party
CDB	China Development Bank
CEND	Confiscation, expropriation, nationalization, deprivation
CF	Contract frustration
CI	Currency inconvertibility/nontransfer
CIRC	China Insurance Regulatory Commission
CNOOC	China National Offshore Corporation
CNPC	China National Petroleum Corporation
EBRD	European Bank for Reconstruction and Development
ECA	Export Credit Agency
ECGD	Export Credit Guarantee Department (of the United Kingdom)

ECI	Export credit insurance
EIU	Economist Intelligence Unit
EU	European Union
EXIM	Export–import
FARC	Revolutionary Armed Forces of Colombia
FDI	Foreign direct investment
FSA	Fuel supply agreement
FTA	Free trade agreement
G20	Group of 20 (finance ministers and central bank governors)
GDP	Gross domestic product
GOI	Government of Indonesia
HDI	Human Development Index
HIPC	Highly indebted poor country
IADB	Inter-American Development Bank
IBRD	International Bank for Reconstruction and Development (World Bank)
ICSID	International Center for the Settlement of Investment Disputes
IDR	Indonesian rupiah
IFC	International Finance Corporation
IIF	Institute for International Finance
IMF	International Monetary Fund
IPP	International power project
LC	Letter of credit
LEU	Low-enriched uranium
LNG	Liquefied natural gas
M&A	Mergers and acquisitions
MBPD	Million barrels per day (of oil)
MDBs	Multilateral Development Bank
MENA	Middle East and North Africa
MIGA	Multilateral Investment Guarantee Agency
MNE	Multinational enterprise
MOF	Ministry of Finance
MW	Megawatt
NATO	North Atlantic Treaty Organization
NEXI	Nippon Export and Investment Insurance (of Japan)
NKW	NKW Holdings
ODA	Overseas development assistance
OECD	Organization of Economic Cooperation and Development
OFDI	Outward foreign direct investment
OPIC	Overseas Private Investment Corporation (of the United States)
PDVSA	Petroleos de Venezuela
PLN	Perusahaan Listrik Negara (of Indonesia)
PNG	Papua New Guinea

PPA	Power purchase agreement
PRC	People's Republic of China
PRI	Political risk insurance
PRS	Political risk services
PSU	Pennsylvania State University
PV	Political violence
REM	Rare earth mineral
RMB	Chinese renminbi (yuan)
SOE	State-owned enterprise
TDI	Trade disruption insurance
UK	United Kingdom
UNCITRAL	UN Conference on International Trade Law
UNCLOS	UN Convention on the Law of the Seas
UNCTAD	UN Conference on Trade and Development
US	United States
USD	US dollar
USPA	US power authority
WTO	World Trade Organization

Chapter **1**

Country Risk in Perspective

When you consider what a mystery the East Side of New York is to the West Side, the business of arranging the world to the satisfaction of the people in it may be seen in something like its true proportions.

Walter Lippmann, 1915[1]

Introduction

It became fashionable for political and economic pundits to declare in 2011 that as a result of the arrival of the Arab Spring, the world had become a more dangerous place, and that the risks associated with conducting cross-border business had risen. One could perhaps legitimately make such an argument in the countries directly affected by the Spring, but was cross-border risk in 2011 really more generally perilous than it was in, say, 1988 or 2001, when global shock waves resulted from the collapse of the Soviet Union and the beginning of the War on Terror? Not in my view—yet the chorus of analysts' voices made it sound as if the Arab Spring had an equally profound impact on global trade and investment.

If, as noted by Lippmann, the world was considered mysterious in 1915, the Arab Spring was indicative of how political change in the second decade of the twenty-first century could be characterized as evolutionary and in a seemingly constant state of metamorphosis. It is no longer so easy to define one's allegiance or to identify with a single country or strain of political thought. Globalization, interconnectedness, social media, and the age of instant communication have greatly changed the political and economic landscape, as well as the nature of structural change in countries throughout the world.

In 1988 and even as recently as 2001, trade and investment decisions were by definition based on less available information and less sophisticated means of assessing and managing risk. Today, cross-border traders and investors benefit from a more level playing field with respect to access to information, more open markets, and a more competitive landscape. More countries want to attract foreign direct investment (FDI), enhance international trade, and be members of the global "club" than ever before. To do so, they must maintain a competitive footing and constantly reinforce their comparative attractiveness as trade and investment destinations. That makes the global trade and investment climate *less* risky than in recent history, but it also makes the need to understand the true nature of cross-border risk more acute than ever before.

Insight into the Foundation of the Arab Spring[2]

Understanding why the Arab Spring erupted is important not only because so many dynamics were at play, but also because no one accurately predicted how or when such upheaval would occur, and its impact was dramatic. Businesses have naturally become more risk averse as a result of the changes that have taken place throughout the Middle East and North Africa (MENA) since Muhammad Bouazizi, a food cart vendor, lit himself on fire in Sidi Bouzid, Tunisia, in January 2011. He did so out of utter frustration and hopelessness, and his story resonated throughout the country and region. But the aspirations of the region's people as manifest by what came to be known as the Arab Spring must be considered in the context of an underlying unease about the scope and impact of political and economic change. While the region's businesses quickly adapted to the many changes that resulted from the onset of the Arab Spring, many of them also came to recognize that the likely result would be an extended period of uncertainty and some degree of doubt about whether all the change would in the end result in meaningful long-term benefits.

Let us examine why the Tunisian spark ignited a wildfire that spread throughout the Middle East, as it will provide insight into how politics are inextricably linked with economics and how some political change that is decades in the making can occur in an instant. A corollary to one of the best known theories of human development—basic needs theory—is that as long as governments deliver the basic services their citizens require, there is little inherent incentive for them to rise up in opposition. Even if there were an incentive for them to do so, it is reasonable to ask whether they are willing to risk what they have for the hope of achieving something better in the long term.

It can certainly be argued that citizenries that have only known one-party or one-person rule, as is so common in MENA, will be hesitant to embrace change. Even if they were given an opportunity to participate in a genuinely democratic vote, the fact that it would be for the first time in many countries in MENA raises doubt about whether voters would truly vote their consciences. As the recent democratic experiment in Iraq has demonstrated, the process can be highly politicized, and remnants of long-established political forces can clash with new political forces for many years before the dust settles and the benefits of change become apparent. Political change implies uncertainty and the average person is less likely to risk stability for an uncertain future.

The Middle East's remaining governments have considered what they must do to prolong their time in power. Their ability to be perceived to be providing meaningful basic services may in large part determine how long they can remain in power; this was certainly the case with Saudi Arabia in the months following Ben Ali's overthrow in Tunisia. Given that oil production costs in the region are generally below $15 per barrel, hefty short- and medium-term revenues gave the governments of oil-producing nations options they may not otherwise have had to help ensure that basic needs were met (see Figure 1).

If the Tunisian example is any guide, they have a lot of work to do. Ben Ali was ultimately driven out of power by a chain of events originating in Sidi Bouzid, in the country's western center. According to the World Bank, this part of Tunisia consistently had the highest rate of poverty in the country between 1980 and 2000—more than twice the national average in 2000. The people in Sidi Bouzid had little to lose by promoting political change once an opportunity was created. But the reason that the suicide of food cart vendor Muhammad Bouazizi triggered the riots and Ben Ali's subsequent departure is that opposition groups, trade unions, and much wealthier parts of the country became galvanized: They were collectively tired of being oppressed, too many of them were unemployed, and Ben Ali's family had enriched itself too grotesquely for too long.

Tunisia had been neither the worst nor the best at providing basic services to its people. As noted in the charts that follow, the country was either at or above average for lower middle-income countries in the region with respect to total spending on education between 1980 and 1995. But its spending on education actually declined or remained stagnant during the 1980s and 1990s. Tunisia was again an average performer in terms of health expenditures as a percent of gross domestic product (GDP) and one of the better regional performers in terms of health expenditures per capita. The

Tunisian government provided free or subsidized health care to its lowest income groups, but the percentage of GDP the government devoted to food subsidies declined by more than half between 1989 and 1999, in the first decade of Ben Ali's reign (see Figures 2 and 3 and Table 1).

So, Tunisia had done neither particularly well nor particularly badly in looking after the basic needs of its people in recent history. Tunisia's GDP per capita has risen notably over the past 50 years, reaching US$3,800 by 2009—at the top of the World Bank's classification for lower middle-income countries, albeit well below the global average. That the country is well integrated with Europe both from a business and tourism perspective has meant that the financial crisis hit Tunisia harder than other, less well integrated countries in the region. This undoubtedly raised the level of common dissatisfaction with the Ben Ali regime (see Figures 4 and 5 and Table 2).

Had the Tunisian masses been given greater freedoms and had the state not held such a vise-like grip on power, the spark that occurred in Sidi Bouzid may not have turned into a bonfire. Tunisia under Ben Ali had been

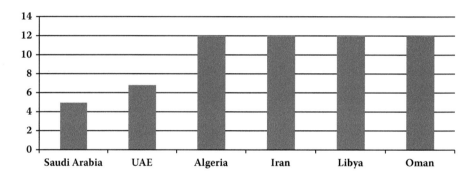

FIGURE 1 Estimated break-even oil production costs for selected MENA countries (US$). (From: http://www.reuters.com/article/2009/07/28/oil-cost-factbox-idUSLS12407420090728)

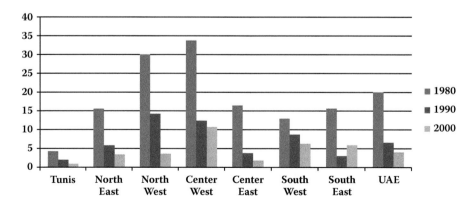

FIGURE 2 Percentage of population living in poverty in Tunisia by region (1980, 1990, and 2000). (From: http://siteresources.worldbank.org/INTPGI/Resources/342674-1115051237044/oppgtunisia11.pdf)

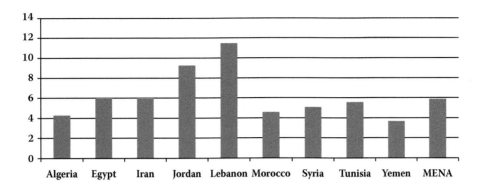

FIGURE 3   Health expenditures in 2002 as a percentage of GDP. (From World Bank, World Development Indicators, 2003.)

TABLE 1 Percentage of Total Government Spending on Education[a]

Country	1980	1985	1990	1995
Egypt	—	—	31.09	32.6
Iran	6.23	9.47	11.21	19.01
Jordan	15.22	24.28	24.83	24.44
Morocco	14.79	13.54	14.74	—
Syria	26.29	27.98	21.34	—
Tunisia	17.91	16.41	16.21	16.36
Lower middle-income average	14.55	16.42	15.85	16.34

Source: www.worldbank.org/education/edstats.
Note: "—" means not available.
[a] Selected countries in MENA (1980–1995).

a police state virtually since he assumed power in 1987; its security apparatus came to be larger than that of France, which has six times its population. With unacceptably high unemployment rates throughout the Middle East and millions of young people yearning for a greater voice, the potential for a similar backlash certainly exists in a variety of other countries, such as Algeria and Saudi Arabia.

While many of the region's governments made a more visible effort to appeal to the common citizen through enhanced public services, food and gas subsidies, and more funding for education, none of them released their own vise-like grips on power. They attempted to walk a fine line between enhanced reforms and an enhanced security apparatus, or they simply restricted freedoms even further. What would have been much smarter is for these governments to release their grip on power gradually while making genuine overtures to demonstrate that they were open to changing their tune. If the masses saw the door open a crack, their temptation to force it open may have been reduced. But the fact that this did not happen implies

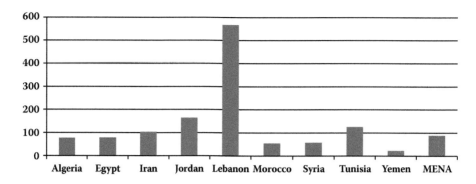

FIGURE 4 Health expenditures in 2002 per capita (USD). (From World Bank, World Development Indicators, 2003.)

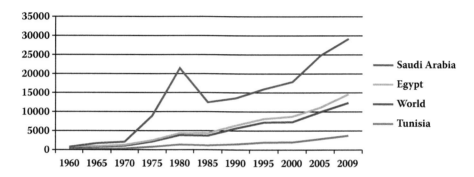

FIGURE 5 Tunisia versus selected countries and the world: GDP per capita at current prices (not adjusted for inflation; converted to USD at market exchange rates). (From World Bank, World Development Indicators, 2010.)

TABLE 2 Food Subsidies as a Percent of GDP (1989–1999)

Country	1989	1992	1995	1999
Algeria	2.9	3.3	0.9	0
Egypt	3.7	5.1	1.3	1.7
Iran	—	1.5	2.9	2.7
Jordan	3.1	1.5	2.9	2.7
Morocco	—	1.3	1.7	1.7
Tunisia	2.8	1.9	2.1	1.2
Yemen	—	3.7	2.6	0.3

Source: World Bank, World Bank Development Indicators, 2002.
Note: "—" means not available.

that entrenched governments throughout the world may be inclined to remain in power at any cost, which certainly has important implications for companies considering trading, investing, and lending abroad, as well as for the analysts trying to determine the true nature of the risks involved in doing so.

When the process of political change began in MENA in January 2011, there was much hope among its people and concern among its governments about the manner in which this change would evolve. For most of its people, there was tremendous hope that the decades of enduring repression under authoritarian governments would soon come to an end. For many of its governments, there was hope that the introduction of incremental reform would placate public sentiment and enable continuation of the status quo. The aspirations of neither have come true.

While citizens in Egypt and Tunisia had initial cause for celebration when Presidents Ben Ali and Mubarak were forced to abdicate their presidencies, it quickly became clear that their jubilation was premature. While the figurehead of the only government many of them had ever known was indeed removed, the infrastructure of the government and virtually all of its other members remained in place.

Historic Change, But Not "Revolutionary"

The reason why the political upheaval in MENA was historic is precisely because it involved establishing a new kind of relationship between governments and the people they govern: a fundamental overhaul of Arab state/society relations that have remained relatively unchanged for more than half a century. According to a study by Freedom House[3], in 67 countries where dictatorships have fallen since 1972, non-violent civic resistance was a strong influence more than 70% of the time. Change was made through civil society organizations that utilized non-violent action or other forms of civil resistance. It would be nice to believe that Egyptians, Libyans, and Tunisians have reasonable grounds to hope that the fruit of their labor will ultimately be democratically elected and functioning governments, yet the average citizen in these countries is unlikely to find that the governments they thought would replace the ancien regimes will be everything they had hoped for.

There will inevitably be immense pressure on whatever form of government ultimately succeeds the current regimes in all these countries. They must be seen to be bringing about meaningful change quickly, but this will be far more difficult to achieve than would ordinarily be the case and is likely to result in one of two scenarios. The first is that, frustrated by the slow pace of democratic change—something the populations of these countries are not familiar with—and frustrated at the lack of visible and rapid improvements in the economy, protestors are likely to continue to return to the streets, prolonging the economic chaos and adding pressure to the recovery process while at the same time increasing instability and insecurity. Secondly, wary of falling prey to the type of mass protests the new governments helped to foment, and falling into the trap of trying to be all things to all of their people, the new governments will rush through popular measures such as rises in the minimum wage and public sector wages—measures that they are not able to afford—sowing the seeds of even longer-term economic distress and postponing much needed genuine reform until some point in the future.

In no case can the political change that has occurred in Egypt and Tunisia be seen as 'revolutionary.' While the titular heads of government have been removed from power, the institutional underpinning of these governments, and many of the individuals responsible for implementing policies of repression for decades, remain in place. In their first year, the agents of change actually achieved very little. The majority of their original aspirations—greater democracy, an end to living in fear, and an easier life for the majority of the people—were, in fact, not met, and may not be met in the medium or even long-term. Rather, the introduction of instability and uncertainty into the average person's daily life has only increased frustration levels and decreased expectations for achieving their objectives, which in turn creates greater levels of frustration and sets the stage for ongoing uncertainty and instability.

In the first post-Spring polling of Egyptian opinion[4], there was great fear among moderates over the possible rise of Islamists and the possibility of greater sectarian violence. Egypt is a conservative country but evidence has mounted that the majority of people do not want the kind of Islamic rule prevalent in Iran, let alone in Saudi Arabia, but the Muslim Brotherhood was the best known and organized political force in the country and did well in elections. There is very little genuine confidence among policy makers or ordinary citizens that the transition to the Egyptian version of democracy will go smoothly, or proceed as originally envisioned. Economic hardship resulting from Mubarak's ouster has contributed to a climate of fear and uncertainty, and the military junta that took Mubarak's place has proven to be increasingly intolerant, having delayed the election until late 2012, and has not given any indication that it intends to abdicate power from behind the scenes.

Egypt's female activists expected the revolution to yield greater liberty, equality, and social justice for women. However, leading activists expressed their disappointment at the way women were being sidelined[5] by the military government in Egypt. Some fear an even worse outcome—that of a rise in Islamist political parties will force women back into a subservient role. Debate is flourishing in Egypt and no one can predict what sort of consensus or conclusions will emerge.

One consequence of the uprising and subsequent departure of Mubarak was a rise[6] in sectarian conflict, with several deadly clashes between Muslims and Coptic Christians erupting in Cairo in 2011. Supporters of the Mubarak regime point to this as evidence of the stabilizing role the Mubarak regime played in Egypt, where such clashes were rare. However, human rights groups[7] have blamed the Mubarak regime for long-standing failures in the protection of Egypt's Christian minority (approximately 10% of the population), impunity for perpetrators of religious-based violence, and its inability or unwillingness to promote religious freedom and tolerance among different groups.

In Tunisia, as elsewhere across the Arab world, Islamist movements were ruthlessly suppressed during the pre-Spring reign of the autocrats. Despite this, political repression went hand in hand with modernity in Tunisia and it boasts one of the most liberal societies in the Arab world, allowing divorce, scantily clad westerners on its beaches, alcohol, and women's rights. Fears[8] of an Islamist government have arisen in Tunisia as the previously banned Ennahda Party, many of whose leaders returned from exile, established themselves as one of the strongest[9] political movements in the country.

In Libya, Islamists quickly gained control of the post-Gaddafi government. The new Tripoli Municipal Governing Council was led by a member of the Muslim Brotherhood, the country's most influential politician was an Islamic scholar, and the country's most powerful military leader was the former leader of a group believed to be aligned with Al Qaeda. The democratic forces within Libya were quickly sidelined and crushed. The Muslim Brotherhood members of the interim government, who dominated the Governing Council immediately following Gaddafi's ouster, quickly declared their intention to impose fatwas, ban theater, prevent women from driving, and eliminate art that takes a human form. Article one of the "new" Libya's draft Constitution stated: "Islam is the Religion of the State, and the principal source of legislation is Islamic Jurisprudence (Sharia)." In other words, the law of Islam was the intended law of the "new" Libya. So there is every reason for democrats, liberals, and moderates throughout the region to be concerned.

The Rise of Unemployment and Poverty

In spite of these problems, polling[10] revealed that Egypt's citizens remained cautiously hopeful in the months following Mubarak's removal from power. Egyptians expressed high support for democracy and civil liberties, but were more concerned[11] with the immediate struggles of finding jobs, improving security and feeding their families. Unemployment predictably rose across the region as the unrest persisted, and has remained high. The problem of unemployment also disproportionately affects certain sectors as well as the young. In Yemen for example, one million workers[12] in the construction sector are thought to have lost their jobs since the uprising began.

The incidence of poverty in the region is also unlikely to change in anything but the medium-to-long term as cash-strapped transitional governments and embattled regimes suffer from rapidly deteriorating public finances. According to the UN Human Development Report 2009, approximately 19% of Egypt's population and 47% of Yemen's population lived on less than $2 per day.

Some inadvertent effects of the revolution hit the poorest the hardest. In Egypt for example, food prices quickly doubled[13] since the outbreak of unrest, and youth unemployment hovers around 30%. As intractable a problem in the Middle East as in many other regions of the world, poverty is likely to be a key factor in determining the agenda of newly elected governments in Egypt and Tunisia. Secular-minded parties are likely to be all too aware of this given the tendency toward Salafist extremism, particularly in Egypt, which tends to come more from impoverished rural areas. Indeed, the salafists did well in Egypt's first past-mubarak elections.

The Muslim Brotherhood also finds the majority of its support in the more rural, poor, and conservative towns and villages than in the major cities of Egypt, where the state security apparatus has a far greater presence. This is going to increase the risk of populist social spending should a secular party take control of the Egyptian government. However, given the strength and organization of the Muslim Brotherhood, it is more likely that some kind of fractious coalition government will emerge in Egypt and may well involve Islamists and secularists working side by side. Indeed, this scenario may actually work out to be worse for poor Egyptians because it is highly likely to delay decision making, and may make it more difficult for reform and change to take place as the different parties squabble over the means to an end.

The Impact on US Credibility in the Arab World

As is the case in other parts of the world, the US was waiting to see what type of regimes will emerge in post-Spring MENA. In the short term, US policy is likely to be a combination of hesitant, cautious, and outspoken, as on one hand it does not want to be seen as bullying or dictating, nor does it want potentially friendly new governments to be labelled as American stooges. However, America's influence in the region has clearly been weakened as a result of the Spring, having been criticized for cradling repressive, anti-democratic regimes for decades while spouting democratic rhetoric that many in the Arab street view as meaningless. America's inability or unwillingness to make a real difference in Syria and Yemen have similarly damaged its position as "the decider."

Egypt's military-led government has shown signs of independence from US foreign policy by acting as a mediator between Hamas and Fatah, resulting in the new cooperation agreement between the two Palestinian factions. The government also quickly re-opened the border crossing with the Gaza strip. Polling suggests that an independent foreign policy is popular among a broad swath of Egyptians.

All this has created particular unease for Israel, which finds itself once again surrounded by potentially hostile neighbors. Soon after the Spring erupted, President Obama told Israel's Netanyahu that it was in Israel's best interest to find a solution to the perennial Israel/Palestine issue as soon as possible for Israel's own sake. He rightly pointed out that if this issue continues to linger, Israel will find itself overwhelmed with the plethora of challenges it faces in the near term. What was left unsaid was that the US no longer has either the influence or stamina to be the driving force behind such a solution.

Paradoxically it may well suit the US to stand back from the regional tumult as it continues to unfold and evolve. US foreign policy appears to be of less interest to an American public that has become preoccupied with its own variety of home-grown concerns. Persistently high unemployment, a double dip in the housing crisis, political divisiveness, and the absence of a meaningful deficit-reduction strategy has caused the American government and public to turn increasingly inward. As has been the case with the foreign policy of other major nations, US policy in the Middle East has had to adapt to rapidly changing circumstances and will no doubt require further adaptation based on what occurs next in the region.

The average citizen in Tunisia, Egypt, Syria, and Yemen may well have been better off without the Spring, for they wouldn't have suffered the violent repression that ensued, economic chaos, and a less physically secure environment in which to live. The primary concerns of average citizens prior to the Spring have resurfaced and are now foremost in the minds of the majority of Arab citizens. There is little reason to believe these concerns will be addressed in any meaningful fashion in the near or medium term by governments that are finding their own footing and determining the right mix between reform and repression.

The sad fact is that every one of the MENA states that experienced dramatic political change in 2011 continues to stare at the edge of an abyss today. Their future is entirely unclear. No one really knows if what will ultimately replace the current governments will in fact be preferable to what they had to begin with. It is a huge leap of faith to presume that to be the case. Now that numerous forces from across the political spectrum have been introduced into the political process in Egypt and Tunisia, it is just as possible that what will emerge after the dust has settled are governments that are incapable of governing because of their attempt to placate and include all the various elements of the political process or that are radicalized by the participation of extreme forces in the process, ending up with the polar opposite of what existed before.

While it appears more likely that what will evolve in the end in most of these states is a Turkish approach to democracy, wherein the most important players in the political process have a seat at the table and the military has an important role to play under a veneer of democracy, it is certainly possible and even probable, perhaps, that in some states Muslim Brotherhood-esque political movements will gather steam and prevail. It is too soon to say which states may end up this way, but it would not be entirely surprising if extreme religious parties do well in the polls in Egypt, for example, where the Brotherhood won 20% of the votes in the presidential 2005 election before being banned.

What all this implies is that political change in MENA will continue to be a messy, imprecise, and painful affair wherein much blood will be spilled in the future and the aspirations of millions who simply wanted a better life for their children will probably find their dreams quashed by the power grab that has ensued. One would have hoped that in today's world of instant communication and high aspirations, the end game would look more promising.

How Political Change in MENA Is Impacting Country Risk Analysis[14]

Political change in MENA has had a profound impact on many countries in the region and beyond, pummeling some of the most established governments in the world. One of the unintended consequences of this change has been to prompt some country risk analysts to reevaluate how they analyze risk. In the rarified atmosphere of country risk analysis, this is a useful exercise, but for individuals and organizations that already think about the world in an esoteric fashion, the challenges are unique.

Country risk analysis probably sounds to a layperson as if it is the domain of number crunchers, political scientists, and intelligence agencies. In fact, it is, but how numbers and theories are used to arrive at a meaningful conclusion varies widely, depending on the individual or organization doing the analysis. For example, many banks tend to be skewed heavily toward plugging numbers into algorithms or spread sheets, political scientists often apply political theory to the behavior of nation-states, and intelligence officers use information to draw conclusions about the likely behavior of leaders, political parties, the military, and other state and nonstate actors.

The job of a country risk analyst can be overwhelming, given the amounts of information that must be absorbed and synthesized into easily digestible text. When one considers that country risk analysis is not only about politics, but also about economics, sociocultural dynamics, and history, there is a lot for an analyst to contemplate in drawing conclusions. This must, of course, all be applied to each country at a given point in time. Due consideration must be given to scenarios, unexpected events, and short- and long-term trends.

Given this, there are numerous risk management lessons a country risk analyst may learn from the recent upheaval in MENA. First, even though political change may be expected in any country at some point in time as a result of fundamental socioeconomic disparities, high levels of corruption, rumblings in the military, or the actions of a neighboring government, the ability to anticipate when and how such change may occur presents a daunting task. In the case of Tunisia, the fact that so many people were disenfranchised within society and that President Ben Ali had been in power and abusing that power for so long prompted large segments of society to coalesce to promote rapid political change. In the absence of the poor, middle class, business community, and elements of the military coalescing at the same time, the spark would in all likelihood not have created a flame. So one lesson here is that social, political, and economic disenfranchisement can reach a boiling point in an instant, given the right circumstances.

Second, although an analyst may expect that political change is likely to erupt from a larger, more important country in a given region, the fact that a country is larger and more important may prevent it from embracing political change. Very few would have predicted that Tunisia was to become the venue for the spark that turned into the flame in North Africa. Egypt was a likelier candidate, but Egypt's geopolitical importance, its prominence with respect to US foreign policy and military aid, and the size and strength of its military made it a less likely candidate for radical political change. The regional implications for radical political change in Egypt made it harder to achieve as a catalyst, but once change had begun elsewhere in the region, it was certainly ripe to participate.

Third, what may appear to be fundamental change is not really change at all, or change for the worse. In reality, not much changed in 2011 in either Tunisia or Egypt. Rather, figureheads were merely removed and the fundamental elements and people in charge of the governing system that was in place prior to the change remained in place. In addition, the aspirations of the Egyptian and Tunisian people were thwarted, even though some among them may want to believe something had really changed. Quite the contrary: Frustration levels were higher toward the end of 2011 than they were before Ben Ali and Mubarak departed the scene because so little had changed and so little appeared likely to change in the near term. In the case of Egypt, that frustration level quickly reached a boiling point as many citizens appeared to realize that what may have resulted from their efforts was either a military-led government protecting the status quo or a radical government represented by the Muslim Brotherhood or other political force—not an end game most people had anticipated or wanted.

Fourth, in today's linked-in, globalized world, political change that may have been limited in regional impact has great potential to explode in scope. This is not to say that profound political change cannot happen in remote corners of the world that are less linked in or globalized—of course, it can and does—but what might have been limited to the departure of former President Ben Ali became a tour de force for the entire region. A corollary here is that it will become more difficult for country risk analysts to predict accurately what happens next in the short and long term. While few analysts would have believed that one dictator after another would fall in succession in MENA, few also would have imagined that a military stalemate would have persisted for months in Libya. We are in uncharted territory, and the truth is that no one can really know with any certainty what will come next.

The job of country risk analysts has therefore just become more complicated. Many previously accepted assumptions about the way the world works have been shattered as a result of what has happened thus far in MENA. In the years to come, many unexpected events will no doubt continue to occur, impacting the foreign policies of most of the world's major governments. In order for country risk analysts to stay ahead of the game, they must excel in being able to use the past and present to try to predict the future. In that regard, their job is really no different than it was before—just a bit more complicated.

Perception versus Reality of Risk: Does Terrorism Negatively Impact Foreign Direct Investment?[15]

Risk perception is, of course, important and helps shape foreign investors' behavior. Such behavior is difficult to predict and depends on a number of factors, including conventional wisdom, prior experience, perception and tolerance of economic and political risk, and long-term objectives. For example, logic leads many foreign investors to believe that acts of terrorism have a negative impact on FDI flows. Yet, common sense dictates that the loss of foreign investor confidence following acts of terrorism would prompt large outflows of capital in affected countries and that, once a country is branded a terrorist target, it will attract reduced levels of FDI. Some academic studies have demonstrated that sometimes this is, in fact, the case; however, foreign investor sentiment is often not dictated by common sense. The lure of profit and desire to establish trade partnerships is often a stronger motivational force than perceived political risk is a disincentive to invest.

Although the growth of global terrorism is indeed on the minds of some corporate decision makers when contemplating whether or not to invest abroad, it did not prevent many of them from deciding to invest in the post-9/11 developing world. According to the United Nations Conference on Trade and Development (UNCTAD),[16] FDI flows to the developing world *surged* 200% between 2000 and 2004, up from 18% to 36% of global FDI. During the same period, FDI flows to developed countries *plunged* 27%, from 81% to 59% of global FDI. In every category of *developed* countries cited, the inward FDI trend was *down* significantly, while in every *developing* country category, the inward FDI trend was *sharply higher*. Although the vast majority of terrorist attacks take place in developing countries,[17] the FDI trend is clear.

Further to this point, the UN compiled a ranking of inward FDI immediately following 9/11—from 2001 to 2003[18]—that measured the amount of

FDI countries receive relative to their economic size (calculated as the ratio of a country's share of global FDI inflows to its share of global GDP), with some surprising results. Third, fifth, and seventh on the list were Azerbaijan, Angola, and The Gambia, respectively. Investment in oil and gas exploration and development accounted for much of the investor interest in these countries for the period. Interestingly, of the top 20 performers, only 3 were developed countries. Germany was ranked 102, the United States 112, and Japan 132, out of 140 total.

Does this mean that perceived terrorism risk negatively affects FDI decision making? That undoubtedly depends on where one intends to invest. Clearly, a company considering investing in Iraq would have far greater concerns about terrorism than one investing in Canada. Interviews and surveys of executives in multinational corporations in the 1960s and 1970s[19] found political events to be one of the most important factors influencing foreign investment decisions. This was no doubt due in large part to the Cold War and the perception that regime change could have stark implications for foreign operations.

Times have changed, however. Consulting firm A. T. Kearney produces an annual publication, *The FDI Confidence Index,* in which it polls top decision makers in the world's largest 1,000 companies and asks their opinions on a range of FDI-related issues. The conclusions are surprising. In 2003, just 2 years after 9/11, corporate leaders' top pick for global event most likely to influence their investment decision was recovery of the US economy. Terrorism and security concerns were tied with the Middle East conflict for number 7 on the list of 11 concerns.[20]

In 2004, with the US economy on the rebound, its recovery was still the top pick, but down from 84% to 60% of respondents' concerns. The list of decision-maker concerns had grown from 11 to 15, with terrorism and security staying stationary at number 7, this time tied with concerns about rising interest rates.[21] Although the A. T. Kearney studies do not focus on specific countries, it is worth noting that in each instance, economic concerns outweighed political concerns by a large margin. In addition to recovery of the US economy, the other top concerns in 2004 were the impact of global or regional trade initiatives, the threat of global deflation, and the depreciation of the US dollar. On this basis, it does not appear that terrorism per se had a heavy influence on FDI decision making.

Empirical Studies Can Yield Contradictory Results

Empirical studies examining the link between perceived political risk, terrorism, and FDI flows have yielded contradictory results. Some have found linkages, while others have not. The former have tended to be older studies; some of the newer studies challenge the previous results.

Some empirical studies have tended to put more emphasis on macroeconomic variables as explanatory factors in FDI flows, while others stress the importance of political variables. In practice and in theory, it appears difficult to make a clear-cut distinction between political and economic variables as definitive sources of influence, and it is reasonable to conclude that FDI decisions in developing countries are determined by both political and economic factors.[22]

A Harvard study[23] states that higher levels of terrorism risk are associated with lower levels of net FDI. In an integrated world economy, where investors are able to diversify their investments, terrorism may induce large movements of capital across countries. Another academic study[24] takes this a step further and examines the impact of terrorist attacks on capital markets. The authors researched the US capital markets' response to 14 terrorist/military attacks from 1915 to 2001 and concluded that they recover faster from such events now than they did a century ago. This is largely attributed to a stable banking/financial sector that provides adequate liquidity in times of crisis and thereby promotes market stability.

In their largest decline, the US markets dropped 21% over an 11-day period when Germany invaded France in 1940 and took 795 days to recover to their pre-event level. After 9/11, the markets dropped just 8% over an 11-day period and took just 40 days to recover. Other financial markets were not as resilient. For example, over the 11-day period following 9/11, Norway's stock market dropped 25% and took 107 days to recover. One possible reason for the favorable US performance is that the Federal Reserve took steps to provide liquidity throughout the banking and financial sector. This serves to emphasize that, to a limited degree, post-event investor perceptions can be managed by effective government response.

In a study done at Pennsylvania State University[25] (PSU), the effect of economic globalization on transnational terrorist incidents was examined statistically using a sample of 112 countries during the period 1975–1997. The strong results showed that FDI, trade, and portfolio investment have no directly positive effect on the number of transnational terrorist incidents among countries, and that the economic development of a given country and its trading partners reduces the number of terrorist incidents in a given country. To the extent that FDI and trade promote economic development, they have an indirectly negative effect on transnational terrorism. Perhaps the decision makers polled in the A. T. Kearney studies knew intuitively what the PSU study proved statistically: that economic development is a deterrent to terrorism.

A related study done at PSU[26] tested whether democratic forms of government reduce the number of terrorist attacks. In this case, 119 countries were examined between 1975 and 1997. Contrary to some earlier academic studies on this subject, which promoted the idea that terrorist groups are more often found in countries with democratic forms of government than authoritarian forms of government, the author found that some aspects of democracy—such as higher electoral participation, which produces a high degree of satisfaction among a general population—tend to reduce the number of transnational terrorist incidents, while other aspects of democracy—such as a system of strong checks and balances and the ability to restrict press freedoms—often serve to increase the number of such incidents.

The conclusions reached in both PSU studies make sense and are backed up by statistics, yet they do not address the fact that many countries with vastly different histories and forms of government have experienced long-term terrorism[27] on their soil (for example, Colombia, Israel, Turkey, Nepal, India, Pakistan, the Philippines, Spain, the United Kingdom, Saudi Arabia, and Algeria). The same is true of countries with "new" terrorism problems (such as the United States and Thailand). More often than not, it appears that countries with significant terrorist acts tend to have democratic forms of government. Terrorism does not appear to occur with great frequency in countries with authoritarian or communist forms of government, which lends credence to the earlier academic studies. In the complicated world of terrorism, undoubtedly, both arguments are true and neither is true.

The same PSU author produced another compelling study examining the impact of political violence (PV) on FDI.[28] The study posits that terrorist incidents do not produce any statistically significant effect on the likelihood that a country will be chosen as an investment destination or on the amount of FDI it receives. Further, it states that unanticipated acts of terrorism do not generate any changes in investor behavior in terms of investment location choice or the amount of investment.

However, a study done on the impact of terrorism and FDI in Spain and Greece[29] arrived at a completely different conclusion: that acts of terrorism had a significant and persistent negative impact on net FDI. The study's authors concluded that 1 year's worth of terrorism discouraged net FDI by 13.5% annually in Spain and 11.9% annually in Greece. On this basis, it was concluded that smaller countries that face a persistent threat of terrorism may incur economic costs in the form of reduced investment and economic growth.

Related to this, the same coauthors of the previously cited Harvard study produced a case study on the economic costs of the Basque conflict[30] and concluded that there is evidence of negative economic impact associated with terrorism in the Basque portion of Spain. On average, the conflict resulted in a 10% gap between per-capita GDP of a comparable region without terrorism over a two-decade period. Moreover, changes in per-capita GDP were shown to be associated with the level of terrorist activity. The coauthors also demonstrated that once a cease-fire came into effect in 1998–1999, Basque stocks outperformed non-Basque stocks. When the cease-fire ended, non-Basque stocks outperformed Basque stocks.

An interesting corollary is the research done by the Asian Development Bank (ADB) when it created a terrorism insurance facility for investors in Pakistan. ADB learned that in nearly every instance, acts of terrorism in Pakistan were directed at government and/or military targets; commercial loss (if any) was nearly always the result of collateral damage. A survey of local insurance companies in Pakistan revealed that the incidence of commercial loss due to acts of terrorism was almost zero. This is in sharp contrast to the image of Pakistan that prevails in the global media, where it is portrayed as a poor place to invest because of perceived terrorism risk. *Yet, 9/11 produced more than $50 billion in commercial losses in the United States, which remains one of the top FDI destinations.* This demonstrates just how flawed common perceptions of risk can be.

The Impact of Perception on Investment Decisions

Perceptions of terrorism risk have a great deal of influence on some investment decisions, but very little on others. Among the factors that influence decision makers are:

- Economic health of the investment destination
- Difficulty associated with doing business in a given country
- Existence of rule of law and good corporate governance
- Existence of corporate and government connections
- Level of public discord
- Media attention
- Cost of production

Investors may also distinguish between "perceptions" of the existence of a terrorism threat in a given FDI destination and "acts" of terrorism, or between "domestic" acts of terrorism and "international" acts of terrorism. However, one factor often not considered when contemplating making a cross-border investment is consumer behavior and its linkage to the political process. Perceptions are important here, as well. Predicting consumer behavior correctly can be as important in determining the success of an investment as predicting whether terrorism will have an impact on operational capability.

For example, one would think that the rise in hostility toward the US by a variety of Europeans in response to the Iraq War would result in fewer European sales of goods by American companies. Interestingly, one of the first detailed empirical studies on consumer behavior after 2003[31] noted that although up to 20% of European consumers did consciously avoid purchasing American-made products, sales by American companies in 2000–2001 and 2003–2004 grew at least as quickly as those of their European rivals in

Europe. In the case of Coca-Cola, McDonald's, and Nike, European sales grew 85%, 40%, and 53%, respectively, for the period. Apparently, Europeans make a distinction between the actions of the US government and the products of American companies.

Short-term corporate costs directly or indirectly linked to acts of terrorism can be substantial, but the potential long-term costs of terrorist threats to national economies can be devastating. A study by Australia's Department of Foreign Affairs and Trade[32] found that developing countries stood to lose the most because of their dependence on FDI and export-led growth. The developing economies of East and Southeast Asia were deemed to be the most vulnerable. The study estimated that economic growth in the region could decline by 3% after 5 years of ongoing terror threats and by 6% over 10 years.[33] The attacks of 9/11 were estimated to have cost the US some $660 billion through 2005 and significantly reduced global investment levels.[34] The International Monetary Fund (IMF) estimated at the time that the loss of US output from terrorism-related costs could be as high as 0.75% of GDP, or $75 billion per year in the future.[35]

So does perceived terrorism risk negatively affect FDI decisions? There is no single answer to this question because it is dependent on numerous variables. The empirical evidence answers the question in both the affirmative and the negative, and persuasive arguments have been made on both sides. Similarly, some theorists maintain that democratic political systems are a breeding ground for terrorism, while others claim just the opposite. And some earlier studies concluded that corporate executives consider political and terrorism risks to be among the most important factors influencing the decision-making process, while later studies minimize their importance.

It can probably be said with some certainty that all of the studies are correct and all of them are incorrect because it does not make much sense to generalize about what motivates foreign investment decisions. Existing theories and arguments fail to explain the rationale behind what motivates many foreign investment decisions. One is left to speculate about such motivations, although the A. T. Kearney surveys lead one to conclude that economic motivations are stronger than political deterrents in influencing foreign investment decisions. Perhaps, in the future, a brave academic will tackle this question.

Also yet to be addressed in the literature is the question of whether certain sectors or industries of an economy are more sensitive to the negative effects of terrorist attacks than others. Or why do some countries experience protracted terrorism over time, and what is its impact on FDI decision making? A lengthy history of terrorism has not prevented foreign oil companies from making, and continuing to make, long-term investments in Colombia or Algeria. Angola continued to receive huge foreign investments in its energy industry at the height of its civil conflict. Of course, investment in all these countries would presumably have been much higher in the absence of recurring terrorism or civil conflict. The US continues to be one of the world's top foreign investment destinations, even though it remains Al Qaeda's number one target. Although the level of FDI is down significantly in the US after 9/11, it is hard to say for certain whether this is due primarily to a changed perception of the US as a "safe haven" destination or whether the prevalence of low interest rates in the US prompted capital investors to seek more lucrative alternatives.

Risk Management versus Profit Maximization

Some companies are concerned primarily with profit maximization, while others are more concerned with risk management and loss minimization. The impact of government-to-government relations on the FDI equation can be an important factor motivating FDI flows, as can the desire to establish and maintain international trade links. Experienced foreign investors may discount terrorism risk automatically because they will have had good experience or strong corporate and government relationships locally. Inexperienced foreign investors may never pursue cross-border investment opportunities because of the absence of prior experience or meaningful corporate and governmental relationships.

The question of what would happen in the event of a truly catastrophic terrorist event must also be considered. Would new construction-related investment flow in, as is the case when natural disasters occur? Would the explosion of a dirty bomb make a city so dangerous that the replacement of damaged buildings would not be possible? It is questions like these that serve to reemphasize the limited value of generalizing about terrorism's impact on FDI. Theorists can speculate all they want about what "may" happen if such an event were to occur, but theories and complicated forecasting models have been proven wrong many times in the past.

Depending on the investment destination, terrorism either already is or has the potential to become a primary consideration in formulating investment decisions. Much will depend on the motivations, experience, and resources of a given foreign investor. As the Pakistan example noted earlier demonstrates, it is vitally important not to rely solely on widely held perceptions about the nature of terrorism risk in a particular country. A wise foreign investor will separate fact from fiction to arrive at an investment decision based on reality on the ground that is consistent with investment objectives.

Be Wary of Statistics

Many of us were taught the importance of utilizing numbers in order to measure and understand the nature of cross-border risk. Clearly, quantitative risk analysis is quite useful in that regard, but a common mistake that is made by practitioners is to over-rely on statistics and numbers, at the expense of qualitative means of assessing risk. Take, for example, the idea of measuring the likelihood that business operations may be interrupted by frequent strikes. Would one be more likely to imagine that strikes would occur with greater frequency in developed or developing countries, in democratic countries or those run by military dictatorships, in established democracies, or newly established democracies? According to Figure 6, strikes are actually more common in developed democracies.

In this case, labor strikes are generally undertaken to fight for higher wages or better working conditions. Given that all of the top 10 countries listed are democracies, the frequency of the strikes is higher than they may be expected to be under a military dictatorship, but what is their impact? Do they often shut the country down? Do they last for days or weeks? More than likely, they last for a single day and, depending on the industry in which they occur, they may not occur at all. For example, it may be deemed illegal for air traffic controllers or policemen to strike in a country where the rule of law prevails.

Contrast this with the possible length and impact of a strike in a country undergoing dramatic political change. When demonstrators were putting pressure on former Egyptian President Mubarak to step down, it emboldened workers to press for long-standing demands that they felt unable to pursue while he remained at the height of his powers. The strikes went on for weeks and impacted numerous types of public and private sector businesses, such as power generation, railways, bus transport, telecommunications, and food production. The country was virtually shut down while protests gathered momentum. Would this have happened in Denmark? Even in strike-prone France, has there ever been a time when workers from throughout society struck repeatedly at the same time? No. If one were to have relied solely on the statistics in Figure 6, one would believe that strikes are mostly a problem in well-developed democracies, where people have a voice and the rule of law is strong.

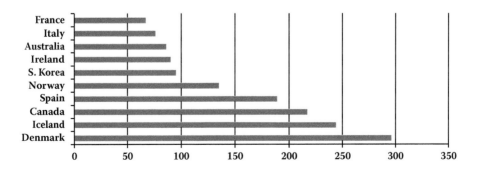

FIGURE 6 Number of strikes by country (top 10 countries: 1996–2000). (From www.nationmaster.com/graph/lab_str-labor-strikes)

Consider the widely accepted belief that infant mortality rates say something fundamental about the relative development of an economy or society. People generally believe that developed countries have lower rates of infant mortality and developing countries have higher rates. Based on the data in Figure 7, that may or may not be the case.

According to these data, Cuba—a very poor country—has a lower infant mortality rate than wealthy Canada. The rate for China—a BRIC (Brazil, Russia, India, China) country and soon to be the world's largest economy— is only slightly lower than that of desperately poor Nicaragua. Iraq—even with all its problems—is lower than the world average. That of India—also a BRIC country, with one of the world's highest rates of economic growth—is the highest of them all. Clearly, a single indicator cannot tell a country's story.

In Figure 8, it is evident that Indonesia under Suharto (in blue) had a much stronger sustained economic growth rate than staunchly democratic Italy. Only during one year (1977) in this 25-year example did their growth rates intersect. Otherwise, Indonesia exhibited a much stronger performance for the period.

Table 3 notes that Indonesia had only one recorded strike, no recorded assassinations, and no changes of government between 1970 and 1995; however, Italy had a multitude of each. Yet, Indonesia's 32 years of stability under Suharto did not prevent the dramatic change of government and end of Suharto rule in 1998.

Italy did much better in terms of attracting FDI, however. Although the two countries were not far apart until 1995, FDI in Italy has dramatically increased since then, while FDI in Indonesia has proved to be sensitive to global economic trends, experiencing wide swings during the Asia Crisis

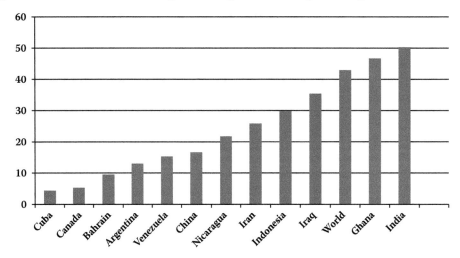

FIGURE 7 Infant mortality rates for selected countries (2009: rates of death per 1,000 people). (From www.google.com/publicdata)

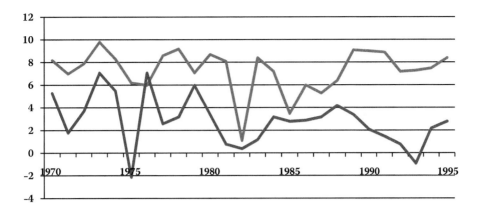

FIGURE 8 GDP growth rates: 1970–1995, Indonesia versus Italy (percent change from the previous year, adjusted for inflation). (From World Bank, World Bank Development Indicators, 2010.)

TABLE 3 Incidences of Political Instability (1970–1995)

	Indonesia	Italy
Strikes	1	26
Assassinations	0	41
Number of governments	0	29

Source: www.cosmopolis.ch/english/cosmo6/italy.htm; Sam Wilkin.

and the Great Recession. Based on this, Italy's tendency toward political instability mattered less with time vis-à-vis FDI, while Indonesia's post-1998 political instability proved to matter more (see Figure 9).

One of the cardinal rules of country risk management, therefore, is to consider statistical information in the context of the history of a country, how its existing political structure influences its economic performance, and how a given country influences and may be influenced by the region and world around it.

What Statistics Say about the Global Recovery since 2009[36]

Statistics compiled by the World Bank[26] show that net FDI flows contracted by approximately 40% in 2009—at the height of the Great Recession—representing the sharpest decline in 20 years, but this was much less than the net decline in private bank lending, which plummeted 134% that year. FDI began to improve in the second quarter of 2009 among both developed and developing countries. As noted later, FDI into developed countries fell further than into developing countries from 2008 through 2009, but proportionately, developing countries made up more ground after Q1 2009

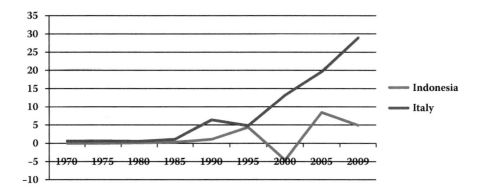

FIGURE 9 FDI growth rates: 1970–2009, Indonesia versus Italy (net inflows of investment, billions of USD). (From World Bank, World Bank Development Indicators, 2010.)

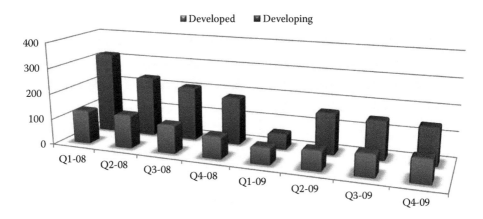

FIGURE 10 Global net FDI flows: 2008–2009, billions of US dollars. (From World Bank and country statistics.)

than did developed countries. If the collective view of foreign investors was that country risk was rising during the period, the FDI statistics would not have demonstrated such strength following the peak of the crisis among either developed or developing countries (see Figure 10).

According to the World Trade Organization (WTO) and World Bank,[37] unlike during the Great Depression, overt acts of trade protectionism were largely absent from the global trade arena during the Great Recession, but the number of restrictive trade actions taken on the part of governments exceeded those of liberalized trade actions by 10 to 1. This is not surprising, as countries naturally seek to protect domestic industries in times of crisis. As noted later, the top five countries restricting trade transactions were (in order) India, Argentina, China, the United States (see Figure 11).

In spite of this, global trade volumes rose by 21% year-on-year in January 2010, in terms of both volume and value. Interestingly, during the period October 2008 to February 2010, the number of antidumping investigations

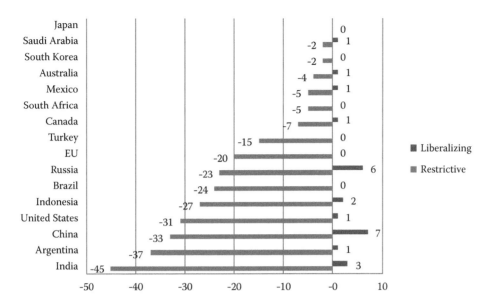

FIGURE 11   Trade measures taken by the G20: October 2008–February 2010. (From World Bank and WTO Secretariat.)

initiated by G20 governments fell by 21%. Given the number of restrictive actions taken by governments during the period, new antidumping investigations should have risen considerably, but did not. So, does this point to rising country risk? Again, the answer appears to be no. Having avoided tit-for-tat protectionist measures among the world's major economies, and having seen an impressive rebound in trade during the height of the crisis, country risk remained stable.

What all this means is that our perceptions of risk must change. Simple categorization of countries into good or bad, rich or poor, and risky or not risky no longer captures the scope of risk companies face when trading or investing in today's evolving mosaic of trade and investment climates. Greece was clearly perceived as riskier than India in 2011, but that was not the case in 2008. Rather than saying the world is a riskier place, it is more accurate to say that depending on where a company invests and in what sector, a developed country can easily be riskier than a developing country. For example, the country that was the boldest in taxing mining company profits in 2010 was not a corrupt, poor, developing country, but Australia. As a result of the Australian government's actions, other mineral-rich countries in the developed and developing world were likelier to follow suit.

Gone are the days when the West called the shots and the rest of the world snapped to attention. Gone also is the time when so many of the good ideas, best risk management practices, and acceptable standards of behavior were automatically derived from the developed world. Countries such as Brazil, China, and India are showing dramatic progress in establishing improved governance, business practices, and advances in technological prowess. If the global economy is akin to a business cycle, then the developed countries are mature markets in the process of gradual decline, while the most dynamic economies of the emerging world have yet to hit their prime.

Country risk management is a function of where one invests, in what sectors, and in what manner. Country risk may indeed be rising at a given point in time, but in the developed world—as the Great Recession of 2008/2009 has taught us—the price paid for years of living on credit and lax regulatory oversight finally exacted a price. Country risk is largely perceived to be falling in many parts of the emerging world, where opportunity abounds, governments continue to liberalize foreign investment regimes, and trade and investment volumes continue to outpace those of the developed world.

Managing Country Risk in the "New Normal"[38]

Since the global economy stabilized, trade and investment flows are returning to more conventional patterns, which means that cross-border transactions are set to continue to rise in the current decade. Among the many challenges facing risk managers now that the economic convulsions have stopped is to manage cross-border risk effectively. This is more important today than in recent memory for a simple reason: The rules of engagement for conducting international business have changed—the risks associated with cross-border transactions are high, risk aversion is high, but the margin for errors is low.

It is only natural after recovering from global economic trauma that international businesses would think more carefully about assuming and managing cross-border risk, but doing so has become more difficult. One of the things that has changed since 2008 is that the "new normal" includes a paradigm shift. Just as the rule book changed after the collapse of the Soviet Union, it has changed again as a result of a combination of a decade of globalization and a decoupling in growth patterns between the developed and developing worlds, which implies a change in risk profile between the two.

There was plenty of debate when the financial crisis began about whether industrialized and emerging countries would move in tandem downward. Indeed, they did, by and large, but what has become clear over the past several years is that many developing countries are galloping ahead of the developed countries. They are projected to have sustained average growth rates between 6% and 8% per year in the medium to long-term, while North America and Europe may experience growth rates of 1% to 3% for the foreseeable future. The temptation among many international companies will be to trade and invest in developing countries as a result of the disparity in growth rates without, perhaps, fully considering the implications of doing so from a political risk perspective. The need to do so has always been present, but the way many businesses traded or invested internationally before the Great Recession did not require the same degree of due diligence that is required today.

You have heard the story before. It all sounds good on paper: Country X is growing rapidly, it has a democratic government, demand for your product there is high, and the country or buyer appears to have the money to pay for it. But in an era when economic volatility is high and many financial professionals have little more than a quarterly orientation to the future, it is important to consider what may happen 5 or 10 years from now, after your long-term investment has been made, the government changes, and the country can no longer pay its bills. What tools, if any, does your company have to assess and manage such risks?

To the extent that international companies devote any resources at all to understanding cross-border trade and investment climates (in my experience, most do not), they tend to over-rely on internal sources of information or on externally generated country risk analyses, which are more often than not produced generically and are not necessarily appropriate for specific transactions. This is perhaps the most common mistake risk managers make. They believe that because they have information about the general political and economic profile of a country, they have a true handle on the nature of the risks associated with doing business there.

What about gauging legal and regulatory risk, the country's friendliness toward foreign trade and investment, and other companies' experience there? Too often, companies get caught in an "investment trap": They commit long-term resources to a country only to find that the bill of goods they were sold—or thought they understood—turned out to be something completely different. There are plenty of stories about companies whose investments turned into disaster because the regulatory environment changed, a legal issue arose, international sanctions impacted their ability to operate, or they selected the wrong joint venture partner. After the investment has been made, it is often too late to pull out without incurring large losses and experiencing reputational risk once the story hits the press.

Another common issue is that the lines of communication between risk management personnel, risk management and decision makers, or decision makers is bypassed, convoluted, or just plain wrong. I have seen instances where

- Risk management is given only cursory participation in the transaction approval process.

- Sales teams bypass risk management entirely or ignore risk management's recommendation because they fear a transaction will be canceled as a result of unacceptably high levels of risk.
- A CEO delivers a presentation to a board of directors that is false, but he believes it to be true because the risk manager's staff said it was.
- A board of directors has no idea what questions they should be asking of corporate decision makers.

A risk manager may have the right information, based on a short-term assessment of the risks. The long-term view may be completely different, but in the absence of knowing what questions to ask and having clear lines of communication, the right information may not be taken into consideration.

The simple way to limit the possibility that unforeseen adverse events will occur is to establish clear reporting lines and do your homework—I mean really do your homework—and hire one or more individuals in your company to focus full time on managing these risks and/or hire an external firm to create a customized risk profile for each and every investment your company plans to make. The expense involved pays for itself many times over when a problem is uncovered and avoided, yet many companies are happy to invest millions of dollars to make cross-border investments without doing their homework.

Notes

1. Kosovo's dark meaning. *Newsweek,* March 15, 2008 (www.newsweek.com/2008/03/15/kosovo-s-dark-meaning.html).
2. Tunisia and implications for political change in the Middle East. Institute for Near East & Gulf Military Analysis (INEGMA), January 24, 2011. Reprinted with permission from INEGMA. Also, The Arabs' perpetual spring, *The Journal of International Security Affairs,* No. 21 (Fall/Winter 2011). Reprinted with permission from *JISA.*
3. Freedom House, *How Freedom Is Won: From Civic Resistance to Durable Democracy,* 2005.
4. http://www.mcclatchydc.com/2011/06/25/116485/us-fares-poorly-in-first-modern.html.
5. *BBC News,* Egypt's Defiant Women Fear Being Cast Aside, June 19, 2011 (http://www.bbc.co.uk/news/world-middle-east-13796966).
6. *Human Rights First,* Sectarian Violence in Egypt, June 11, 2011.
7. Ibid.
8. *The Telegraph,* Tunisia: Birthplace of the Arab Spring Fears Islamist Resurgence, October 13, 2011 www.telegraph.co.uk/news/worldnews/africaandindianocean/tunisia/8543674/Tunisia-Birthplace-of-the-Arab-Spring-Fears-Islamist-Insurgence.html.
9. *New York Times,* Tunisia is Uneasy over Party of Islamists, May 15, 2011 (www.nytimes.com/2011/05/16/world/africa/16tunis.html?_r=2).
10. McClatchy U.S. Fares Poorly in First Modern Polling of Egyptian Views, June 25, 2011 (http://www.mcclatchydc.com/2011/06/25/116485/us-fares-poorly-in-first-modern.html).
11. McClatchy (Ibid).

12. *Al Arabiya News*, Yemen Unemployment Rates Hike and Yemen Unrest Continues, March 30, 2011 (www.alarabiya.net/articles/2011/03/30/143616.html).

13. *BBC News*, Egypt Suffers Post-Revolution Blues, May 12, 2011 (www.bbc.co.uk/news/world-middle-east-13371974).

14. How political change in the Middle East and North Africa is affecting country risk analysis. International Risk Management Institute, April 21, 2011. Reprinted with permission from IRMI.

15. The impact of terrorism on foreign direct investment. International Risk Management Institute website, February 2006. Reprinted with permission from IRMI.

16. Compiled from the UNCTAD website and UNCTAD's World Investment Report, 2005.

17. In 2003, for example, 28% of terrorist attacks took place in developed countries (US State Department, Patterns of Global Terrorism, 2004).

18. World Investment Report 2004. United Nations Conference on Trade and Development, 2004, p. 14.

19. Such as Aharoni (1966), Basi (1963), Bass et al. (1977), and Schollhammer (1974).

20. *FDI confidence index*. A. T. Kearney, September 2003, Vol. 6, p. 7.

21. *FDI confidence index*. A. T. Kearney, September 2004, Vol. 7, p. 7.

22. Political risk and foreign direct investment. Guy Leopold Kamga Wafo, Faculty of Economics and Statistics, University of Konstanz, 1998.

23. Terrorism and the world economy. Alberto Abadie and Javier Gardeazabal, Harvard University/NBER and the University of the Basque Country, October 2005.

24. The effects of terrorism on global capital markets. Andrew Chen and Thomas Siems, Cox School of Business and the Federal Reserve Bank of Dallas, August 2003.

25. Economic globalization and transnational terrorism. Quan Li and Drew Schaub (Department of Political Science, Pennsylvania State University), *Journal of Conflict Resolution* 48 (2), April 2004, pp. 230–258.

26. Does democracy promote or reduce transnational terrorist incidents? Quan Li (Department of Political Science, Pennsylvania State University), *Journal of Conflict Resolution* 49 (2), April 2005, pp. 278–297.

27. The "academic consensus" definition of terrorism as noted by the UN is "Terrorism is an anxiety-inspiring method of repeated violent action, employed by a (semi-) clandestine individual, group or state actors, for idiosyncratic, criminal or political reasons, whereby the direct targets of violence are not the main targets. The immediate human victims of violence are generally chosen randomly (targets of opportunity) or selectively (representative or symbolic targets) from a target population, and serve as message generators. Threat- and violence-based communication processes between terrorist (organization), (imperiled) victims, and main targets are used to manipulate the main target (audience(s)), turning it into a target of terror, a target of demands, or a target of attention, depending on whether intimidation, coercion, or propaganda is primarily sought" (Schmid, 1988). (www.unodc.org/unodc/terrorism_definitions.html).

28. Political violence and foreign direct investment. Quan Li (Department of Political Science, Pennsylvania State University). In *Regional economic integration*, ed. M. Fratianni and A. M. Rugman. Burlington, MA: Elsevier Publishing.

29. Terrorism and foreign direct investment in Spain and Greece. Walter Enders and Todd Sandler, *Kyklos* (Blackwell Publishing) 49 (3), 1996, pp. 331–352.

30. The economic costs of conflict: A case study of the Basque country. Alberto Abadie and Javier Gardeazabal, Harvard University/NBER and the University of the Basque Country, July 2002.

31. *Anti-Americanisms in world politics,* ed. Peter Katzenstein and Robert Keohane. Ithaca, NY: Cornell University Press, 2006.

32. Combating terrorism in the transport sector—Economic costs and benefits. Australia Department of Foreign Affairs and Trade, 2004.

33. *The Business Times,* June 22, 2004.

34. Indiamonitor.com, November 16, 2005.

35. *The Business Times,* June 22, 2004.

36. Country risk really rising? International Risk Management Institute, July 30, 2010. Reprinted with permission from IRMI.

37. http://blogs.worldbank.org/prospects/prospects-weekly-protectionism-muted-fdi-plummets-in-2009-global-oil-demand-now-rising

38. Managing political risk in the new normal. International Risk Management Institute website, January 21, 2011. Reprinted with permission from IRMI.

Chapter **2**

Foundations of Country Risk Management

If you jump off the top of an 80-story building, for 79 floors you may think you're flying. It's that sudden stop at the end that tells you you're not.

Thomas Friedman[1]

Introduction

Governments often take a short-sighted, opportunistic approach to adopting policies and laws governing foreign investment. They tend to want their investment climates to be sufficiently appealing to lure prospective investors into their countries, but not so appealing that having foreign investment would be disadvantageous in the long term by virtue of putting too much pressure on local competitors. The competitive global economy requires that governments roll out the red carpet. However, investment landscapes can and do change quickly, often depending on a country's balance of payments, a change in government, or the outbreak of war, thus forcing foreign investors to operate in dramatically altered environments after having become established.

The following examples of natural resource extraction in Bolivia, Pakistan, and Papua New Guinea demonstrate that it does not necessarily matter in which sector a business may be operating, how large the business may be, or with what local entity the business may be allied: Any foreign investor is at risk of becoming embroiled in conflicts or changes in operating environments that it did not anticipate and cannot control.

Economic Nationalism in Pakistan[2]

A prospective investor may think that a country experiencing one of the worst political and economic crises in its history would choose not to pick a fight with one of its most important foreign investors; however, times of crises often prompt governments to do desperate things, with negative consequences for foreign investors. In January 2010, the government of Pakistan threatened to cancel the $3 billion Reko Diq copper and gold project led by Canadian investor Barrick Gold and Chilean mining company Antofagasta in the country's resource-rich Baluchistan province. Pakistan cited the need to protect its strategic national interests. With an economic life of 25–30 years, the project was expected to earn $40–$50 billion from the extraction of raw copper and gold, making it one of the largest mines of its kind in the world. It is therefore not a surprise that the government was interested in maximizing its potential long-term monetary benefits from the project.

Given that the mine is located near the Afghan border, in a province that has been at odds with the central government over revenue sharing from natural resource projects and the base of a nationalist insurgency for decades, the original investors were given some incentives to proceed with exploration and feasibility studies and, in return, given a lucrative deal. The government subsequently appeared to think the deal was too lucrative and that some of the terms agreed upon were unfavorable to Baluchistan and the central government. Baluchistan was required to provide 25% of the project funding in order to get a 25% return—a tall order for a province with limited financial resources. Baluchistan decided it wanted 80% of the proceeds.

The project was controversial. Proponents claimed it would generate much needed jobs and, if successful, act as a magnet for future investment in the province and mining sector. Proceeds from the project would help fund infrastructure development in the area. Opponents cited concerns about by-product pollution from mining, security issues, whether revenues would actually lead to infrastructural development, and whether corruption among local government officials would actually be exacerbated as a result of the project.

These are all legitimate issues, but the bottom line is that Baluchistan stood to gain from Reko Diq, as did the central government. Without the seed capital to fund exploration and produce a feasibility study from private investors, the project would never have gotten off the ground. Having accomplished that, Pakistan jeopardized the 15 years it had spent to get to that stage by playing the nationalism card, at a time when FDI had fallen 57% in Pakistan since July 2009.

Extractive Enterprises Are Particularly Vulnerable

Extractive industries (involving prospecting for and extracting natural resources) are generally more vulnerable to adverse action on the part of host governments for several reasons:

- They tend to be large and high profile.
- They employ thousands of people and have significant economic impact on local communities.
- They are strategically important to host countries.
- They are subject to a wide range of legal regimes and laws, which frequently change.
- They involve the production of waste products, which makes them more highly scrutinized for environmental compliance than other forms of investment.

Mining projects, in particular, have been the object of numerous instances of expropriatory types of actions on the part of host governments since the 1970s. Interference by local or national authorities and revocation of mining or export licenses are the most common ways in which governments indirectly expropriate mining investments. Although rare, outright acts of expropriation on the part of host governments do still happen, as has been demonstrated in recent years in Bolivia, Ecuador, and Venezuela.

In addition, mining projects are prone to development-related operational complications, largely due to the impact they have on local environments and populations. Many mining companies have made great progress in taking the initiative to avoid conflict with nongovernmental organizations (NGOs) and indigenous peoples by taking care to be inclusive in the planning, construction, and operation of mines. Many recent investors in the sector have taken care to establish strong relationships with tribal leaders and negotiate agreements that give all participants a sense of fair play.

Among the most famous cases involving local population backlash for agreements that were not perceived to be fair is Bougainville in Papua New Guinea (PNG), beginning in 1989 (discussed in more detail below). Disputes over environmental impact, financial benefits, and social change brought by the mine renewed a secessionist movement that had been dormant since the 1970s and forced the mine to close permanently. The conflict led to a war that lasted 8 years, claimed an estimated 20,000 lives, and resulted in the island becoming politically independent. While an extreme example, Bougainville serves as a reminder of how quickly events can spin out of control and of the lasting impact of failing to take indigenous interests seriously.

The Danger of Focusing Too Much on Net Income

That Pakistan made such a bold move with Reko Diq when facing one of the worst political and economic crises in its history implies that governments can take action that is contrary to investors' interests at any time. Pakistan had demonstrated that it would not hesitate to look after its own interests, for its own benefit. International investment law states that governments have a right to seize foreign investments in the national interest, to the extent that investors are given fair, equitable, and timely reimbursement. Even if a government does not have the financial means to provide such reimbursement, it can still take unilateral action, leaving investors to seek legal recourse through arbitration or other means. This is indeed one of the risks of engaging in cross-border investment.

One of the biggest mistakes international investors and cross-border partnerships make is to focus on their own future net income generation rather than on what makes sense from all parties' perspectives. Experienced investors in natural resource projects know that when they agree to tariff, tax, or revenue sharing arrangements that give local participants and host governments a real sense of fairness, their projects generally proceed with minimal conflict. This minimizes operational complications and usually ends up contributing handsomely to the bottom line. Yet, in the negotiation process, too many companies make the mistake of being too focused on their own well-being and not enough on what benefits local communities and the long-term health of provincial and host governments.

The message in the Reko Diq case is that a cash-strapped government with limited sources of revenue will naturally seek to protect its long-term interests by either seizing high-profile foreign exchange generating projects or renegotiating them. Barrick and Antofagasta would have been wise to consider the possibility of a change in Baluchistan's posture over the long term and negotiate a deal that gave the province a better sense of genuine benefit and fair play. Many other mining companies have learned the same lesson.

Bolivia's Mass Nationalizations[3]

In 2006, Bolivian President Evo Morales decided to seize the assets of foreign-owned oil and gas operations and to nationalize large, privately held property holdings. Bolivia first expropriated foreign-owned assets in 1937 (Standard Oil of New Jersey, which is ExxonMobil's corporate ancestor) and has seized control of oil and gas assets on numerous occasions since that time. As noted above, international law permits such actions, as long as investors are given fair, adequate, and prompt compensation. Contrary to international law, Morales initially ruled out compensation to foreign investors, claiming companies such as British Gas, Petrobras of Brazil, Repsol of

Spain, and Total of France had recovered their initial investment and made a handsome profit for many years while operating in the country.

At the time President Morales said he intended to nationalize land holdings of wealthy farmers who held large unutilized tracts of land that were, in some cases, acquired by force or illegal means. His plan sought to reclaim illegally obtained parcels and redistribute them to Bolivia's poor. Private investors who owned the land legally were not targeted by the action. But since the 1990s, hundreds of Brazilian farmers have invested more than $1 billion to purchase land in Santa Cruz, an eastern region of Bolivia that borders Brazil and has some of the most fertile land in South America. Those farmers today grow more than a third of Bolivia's soybeans, which account for almost 7% of the national economy.

President Morales's actions are particularly noteworthy because they came at a time when many in global business thought nationalizations were passé—a legacy of the Cold War. But they also came at a time when economic nationalism was on the rise and the state had demonstrated a growing propensity to become more engaged in business. This was a global phenomenon and evidence of the value placed on securing long-term energy and natural resources at a time of sky-high commodity prices, dwindling energy resources, and seemingly insatiable demand. Can it therefore be any surprise that the interests of business were taking a back seat to national interests?

The Importance of History

History is at the heart of this issue. Since the nineteenth century, Bolivia has fought with its neighbors over land and what lies beneath it. Approximately half of the land Bolivia once held, which at one time extended to the Pacific coastline, is gone:

- In 1884 a Chilean attack on Bolivia's Litoral Province cost Bolivia its coastline (the war was ultimately fought over the ability to export dried bird dung, prized at the time for making fertilizer and saltpeter).
- In 1903 Brazil persuaded the large state of Acre to secede. Brazil thus gained a highly productive rubber-growing state, at Bolivia's expense.
- A 3-year war with Paraguay ending in 1935 was motivated by Bolivia's desire to secure a disputed border in which it hoped to find oil (it wound up losing a region the size of Utah to Paraguay in the process).
- Argentina and Peru secured additional portions of Bolivia through diplomatic demarcations later in the twentieth century.

The cumulative history of land loss, the resulting national humiliation, and Bolivia's desire to secure and control its natural resources were ultimately behind President Morales's actions. Resentment over the war with Chile stopped plans for a gas pipeline to the Chilean coast, even though financial backing and export markets were already in place.

Bolivia was one of the first Latin American countries to adopt 1980s IMF policies, which tied loans to privatization, debt reduction, and a relaxation of labor standards. State-owned companies were sold, government spending and regulation were reduced, and foreign capital was courted with the promise of a new beginning. But 20 years later, the average Bolivian was worse off than before, exports had declined, incomes were stagnant, and half the population lived on less than $2 per day. Bolivia's experience is similar to that of other Latin American countries (Brazil, Chile, Uruguay, and Venezuela), whose cumulative disillusionment such as had led to the revival of leftist/populist governments.

It would be easy to dismiss President Morales's action as simply the result of his friendship with Hugo Chavez and Fidel Castro. Chavez had, after all, made similar noises with respect to foreign-owned energy businesses and routinely rattled his saber against the United States, as Fidel Castro has done for decades. But Morales was responding to the long-simmering desire among Bolivians for more control over their natural resources. This desire was as strong in Bolivia as it is in Venezuela and many other countries that opened their doors to foreign investment, even though they may owe the current strength of their natural resource industries to these investors.

From a diplomatic perspective, Bolivia paid a price for Morales's actions. Spain initially stated that its bilateral relationship with Bolivia might be affected by the decree of nationalization—one implication being that financial assistance would be withheld in the future. Brazil, which derived 51% of its natural gas supplies from Bolivia, expressed concern, but took comfort from President Morales's guarantee that Bolivia would continue to honor its gas supply contracts. Brazil was concerned that it would also pay a political and economic price in the longer term for having become so closely aligned to Bolivia and Venezuela.

In the end, although Bolivia's neighbors were shaken, bilateral relations remained virtually unchanged over the next 5 years. Bolivia's neighbors needed its gas and had few viable alternatives. President Morales continued to nationalize businesses, but at the same time tried to attract foreign investment. Of course, it became much more difficult to do so, but businesses continue to invest in Bolivia.

Ramifications

While nationalization is a short-term "fix" for national economic aspirations, its longer term consequences are usually damaging since foreign businesses will hesitate to invest in countries that demonstrate a propensity to nationalize foreign-owned assets. Brazil, Chile, and Uruguay had achieved what

Morales had failed to achieve, having managed to combine fiscal prudence with open trade and investment policies and preserving their options with respect to foreign traders and investors, while addressing broader national social needs. Morales was unlikely to be as successful by closing the door to foreign investors and violating international law in the process. Five years later, foreign investors, lenders, and insurers needed to be convinced that a transaction in Bolivia was worth supporting.

Another reason why Morales's actions were important is that they came after nearly all of Latin America had embraced democracy. Latin American democracy produced Morales and Chavez; the populist "backlash" subsequently experienced in Bolivia and Venezuela was the people's will. Democracy does not always produce the results other countries or investors would like.

The larger lesson to be derived from Morales's actions is that despite the era of globalization, in which all countries are presumed to play by the same rules and national economies are inextricably linked with the global economy, human behavior and aspirations remain unchanged. Citizens of every country want to be able to say they have control over their own destiny and natural resources. The rise of democracy in Latin America accentuated this desire, for it raised pressure on leaders to ensure that national economic aspirations were achieved. Businesses that embrace globalization by investing abroad would be wise to remember this. A democratic election is no guarantee of friendly foreign investment policies and may in fact work against it.

Papua New Guinea's Natural Resource Curse[4]

PNG has long been recognized as a treasure trove of natural resources, home to some of the most significant mines and oil and gas ventures in the world. In December 2009, a consortium led by ExxonMobil approved a massive and logistically challenging liquefied natural gas (LNG) project in PNG. The project (PNG LNG) represented a significant vote of confidence in the suitability of PNG's business environment for FDI, and a variety of governments backed the project with export credits. Given its size, scope, and foreign government support, the project was bound to become a litmus test for future investment in the country.

PNG LNG's $15 billion initial phase investment was greater than any other single foreign investment in the country by a wide margin. In 2008, total FDI stock was approximately $2.3 billion. The project is set to produce an estimated $35 billion in revenue over its economic life and may double the country's gross domestic product ($8.6 billion in 2009) and triple its export earnings. On completion in 2014, PNG LNG's production capacity is expected to reach 6.6 million tons of liquid fuel per year, generating more than $100 billion in sales over 20 years. By comparison, the Ok Tedi mine, the country's largest by export earnings, earned approximately $1.5 billion in 2007, representing 32% of total exports and 22.9% of GDP. Exxon concluded sales agreements with China, Japan, and Taiwan and believes PNG LNG will help meet increased demand, estimated to triple globally by 2030.

Many potential natural resource investors in the country have wondered whether a project of this scale and visibility would help PNG transform itself into a more developed country with a more responsible government, or whether it would simply encourage more of the same type of behavior investors have come to expect of PNG over the past several decades. Unfortunately, the latter seems more likely.

It Takes Two to Tango

While PNG LNG had the potential to create a windfall for the country, it was also a test. PNG's economy has long been heavily dependent on the proceeds from resource extraction. The government will likely realize a total $5.6–$7.5 billion revenue stream from PNG LNG—more than from any existing single revenue source. However, the country has a long history of government interference with FDI and of squandering the gains. The government has not always competently implemented or managed natural resource projects in the past. Such mismanagement has led to significant downside risks for investors.

The primary risk facing investors is not outright expropriation of foreign investments, but rather blowback from local stakeholders regarding the manner in which resources are developed and how proceeds are allocated, causing significant operational disruption. By nature, large-scale extractive projects impact the environment and result in hearty revenue streams whose distribution tends to be politicized. Environmental degradation and a perception that proceeds have been distributed inequitably have led to violence and investor loss numerous times in the past.

The most infamous episode of political violence by indigenous groups against FDI in decades is Bougainville. The Panguna copper mine, operated by a subsidiary of Rio Tinto, opened on the island in 1969. Bougainville's leaders claimed mining activity was causing environmental degradation, while the local population received neither compensation nor a share of the mine's revenue. The local populace perceived the government's policy as promoting colonial exploitation. In 1989, guerillas began a campaign of sabotage against the Panguna mine and civil war erupted. More than 20,000 people were subsequently killed. The mine never reopened, though there was talk of doing so in 2011. Although Bougainville eventually became autonomous in a 2001 settlement, it has become the best known and most commonly referred to example of what not to do as a natural resource sponsor and responsible host government.

More recent projects have faced similar problems. The Ok Tedi copper mine and Porgera gold mine—two of the largest mines in the country—have faced disruption from local stakeholders and international groups due to land rights disputes or environmental issues. Ok Tedi is widely believed to have created an environmental disaster by releasing mine tailings into the Fly River system. BHP Billiton, the mine's operator, transferred its 52% equity share in the mine to an offshore trust for PNG's people in 2002 and paid a $26.8 million settlement to local groups. Barrick Gold's operation of the Porgera mine has attracted international attention: The Norwegian government disinvested $230 million from the company due to "irreversible environmental damage" related to mining operations. In January 2010, Amnesty International criticized Barrick for complicity in the government's illegal destruction of homes and forced eviction of villagers near the mine.

In response, a number of foreign investors adopted internationally recognized best practices to minimize adverse environmental impacts and foster a spirit of cooperation with indigenous communities. Chevron and Oil Search's management of the Kutubu oil field—the largest in the country—provides a good example: A World Wildlife Fund observer described the operation as "by far the largest and most rigorously controlled national park in Papua New Guinea." Newcrest Mining's Lihir gold mine was created with heightened sensitivity to local customs and a desire to create the perception of legitimacy and fair play among the indigenous population. Other firms have tried to address the concerns of all stakeholders from the planning stage forward. By building relationships with local leaders outside government, such project sponsors have gained an understanding of local concerns, built trust, and provided a conduit through which concerns can be negotiated and addressed before they can erupt into violence.

Instead of relying on the government to ensure local economic development, many companies now commonly include the construction of schools, roads, and hospitals in project budgets. One example is Harmony and Newcrest's Hidden Valley mine. After consultation with landowners, the group facilitated the creation of a dedicated business development vehicle owned by local landowner communities (NKW Holdings). NKW supplies a range of goods and services to the Hidden Valley mine, thereby providing immediate local economic benefits. In addition, Harmony is assisting NKW to establish long-term sustainable businesses beyond the life of the mine, including agriculture, tourism, and food processing. Such efforts are laudable from a moral standpoint, and they also benefit the bottom line by minimizing conflict and disruption.

Systemic Corruption Creates Risk

Following a boom in investment in the 1990s from the Porgera and Kutubu operations, the government borrowed heavily and spent inefficiently. The resulting economic calamity ultimately caused severed ties with international donors until 1999 and erased all of the country's growth in per-capita income since its independence in 1975. At a regional level, the southern and western highlands—the two richest provinces and the location of the Kutubu fields—witnessed gross corruption and fiscal mismanagement. While revenue from the project flowed, previously sound service provision collapsed, and violence increased as politicians treated the revenues as personal slush funds.

Corruption is strongly correlated with unsound governance. In 2009, Transparency International's Corruption Perceptions Index—a measure of corruption—ranked PNG 154 of 180 countries surveyed, placing it below the rankings of Zimbabwe, Belarus, and Pakistan, among others. Despite a modern constitution, range of laws, and institutions designed to attract FDI, much of the government continues to perform poorly due to years of cronyism, underinvestment in basic services, and graft.

The national government transfers revenue to landowners in a variety of ways, including direct payments, the allocation of funds earmarked for infrastructure to provincial governments, and partial local landownership of a given project. Each is vulnerable to the diversion of funds at the national, provincial, and local levels, and such diversion is common. In January 2010, the minister for labor and industrial relations, Mark Maipakai, claimed to have uncovered $81.4 million in fraud related to development projects in the Gulf Province. When landowners feel exploited, there is a real potential for project-disrupting violence, and they have done so numerous times in the past.

Lessons Unlearned

In the last decade, the government managed to improve its performance at the national level, investing much of its windfall revenue from the 2005–2008 commodity price boom in trust funds with the support and encouragement of multilateral development banks (MDBs). However, that did not prevent the government from raiding the windfall funds for social and infrastructure spending in 2009 and 2010. The 2010 spending program (the District Services Improvement Program) was criticized for the same problems that plagued regional spending in the 1990s: a lack of transparency and oversight. Oversight of the government's investment in PNG LNG has been concentrated in the hands of Public Enterprises Minister Arthur Somare, the prime minister's son—a move the opposition at the time called immoral and irresponsible. At provincial and local levels, government corruption and mismanagement continued to run rampant.

As scrupulous and thoughtful as ExxonMobil had publicly claimed to be with respect to engaging the indigenous population and adhering to internationally accepted environmental guidelines, PNG LNG encountered the same old problems. Landowners as a group have sought a larger equity share in the project. Others claimed to have been unfairly frozen out of benefits or not to have seen those that were promised. Unhappy landowners were blamed for disrupting construction of an international airport at Komo to service the project site. Among other incidents, tribal disputes related to PNG LNG contracts or funds resulted in multiple fatalities in the Hides district and Central province, areas where extraction and processing are planned.

PNG LNG is recent evidence that improved performance by the PNG government vis-à-vis implementing and maintaining meaningful FDI will require changes to existing laws, stronger oversight mechanisms, and a change in administration. The latter is likely a precondition for the former. The existing system of revenue sharing from FDI needs reform. A radical attempt at reform gathered steam at the provincial and national levels. During the summer of 2009, Julius Chan, a former prime minister, introduced a motion with the unanimous backing of provincial governors (who concomitantly serve as ministers of parliament) to review the 1992 Mining Act, which largely governs the current revenue distribution structure. Chan proposed to transfer revenue from FDI directly to an investment vehicle owned by landowners. Landowners would then release a portion to the national government for discretionary spending, essentially reversing the current arrangement. However, as the administration at the time was opposed to the change, passage of any real reform had to await a change in national government.

Politics in PNG has remained status quo—dominated by despots with similar thinking and practices since its independence. The odds of PNG LNG ushering in a new era of government accountability and sustainable economic development are therefore slim in the near or even medium term. The onus is on the government to transform itself; outsiders are neither capable of nor responsible for doing so. Most likely, PNG LNG will have a neutral or somewhat negative effect on the political environment if its revenue is used to entrench corrupt politicians, as can be expected. If that is the case, then the same "natural resource" curse that bedeviled previously poor/newly rich developing countries will continue to do so with PNG.

Given PNG's natural bounty of gas and mineral resources, it remains a lucrative investment opportunity despite downside risk from the political environment. Gas and minerals will continue to find their way to market. The ExxonMobil consortium and future investors will apply a range of best practices to minimize risk, working around the government as much as through it. Fortunately, most natural resource sponsors have received and understood the message repeatedly delivered to them by PNG's people and have the ability to deliver what the PNG government cannot and will not: economic development.

Defining Country Risk[5]

All three of the preceding cases demonstrate how the exercise of political power can be the root cause of country risk in international business. In the case of Pakistan, its desperate political and economic situation prompted the government to take a bold action that it would not otherwise have been prepared to take in order to generate future revenue. In the case of Bolivia, the desire to impress his electoral base and be perceived as a champion of the people led President Morales to seize foreign-owned oil and gas assets. And in the case of PNG, the failure of the government to deliver economic benefits to its people created an environment that made it more difficult for foreign investors to operate successfully.

How political power is exercised often determines whether government action—or inaction—threatens a firm's value. For example, a dramatic political event may pose little risk to a multinational enterprise, while subtle policy changes can greatly impact a firm's performance. A student-led protest for political change may not change the investment climate at all, while a change in local tax law can erode a firm's profits very quickly. It is usually the task of the local manager, the corporate risk manager, treasurer, or chief financial officer to identify whether a government action poses a threat to a firm's financial well-being and then to act upon it.

However, before being able to make the right decisions, risk managers and decision makers must first be able to identify and measure what country risk is. The first distinction that must be made is between *firm-specific political risks* and *country-specific political risks*. Firm-specific political risks are directed at a particular company and are, by nature, discriminatory—for instance, the risk that a government will nullify its contract with a given firm or that a terrorist group will target the firm's physical operations. By contrast, country-specific political risks are not directed at a firm, but rather are countrywide and may affect firm performance. Examples include a government's decision to forbid currency transfers or the outbreak of a civil war within the host country.

Firms may be able to reduce both the likelihood and impact of firm-specific risks by incorporating strong arbitration language into a contract or by enhancing on-site security to protect against terrorist attacks. By contrast, firms usually have little control over the impact of country-level political risks on their operations. The only sure way to avoid country-level political risks is to stop operating in the country in question.

There is a second key distinction to be made between types of political risk: *government risks* and *instability risks.* Government risks are those that arise from the actions of a governmental authority, whether that authority is used legally or not. A legitimately enacted tax hike or an extortion ring that is allowed to operate and is led by a local police chief may both be considered government risks. Indeed, many government risks, particularly those that are firm specific, contain an ambiguous mixture of legal and illegal elements. Instability risks, on the other hand, arise from political power struggles. These conflicts could be between members of a government fighting over succession or mass riots in response to deteriorating social conditions (see Table 4).

Country versus Sovereign versus Political versus Transactional Risk

It is important to distinguish between some commonly used and often misunderstood terminology in the country risk arena. Too often, risk practitioners tend to use the terms "country risk," "sovereign risk," and "political risk" interchangeably, when in fact, they mean different things. Although the term country risk is widely and generically used to refer to the risks assumed by operating in another country, country risk is really a misnomer in this context. Even the term political risk does not fully encompass the scope of risks a company encounters when operating in a foreign country. The following common definitions are useful in considering the differences between the three:

- *Country risk* broadly refers to the likelihood that a sovereign state may be unable or unwilling to fulfill its obligations toward one or more lenders.[6] It involves an assessment of economic performance in the context of a country's demand for external financing and judgments about the prospect for changes in financial returns.
- *Sovereign risk* is the risk that a foreign central bank will alter its foreign-exchange regulations, thereby significantly reducing or

TABLE 4 Firm-Specific versus Country-Level Risks

	Government risks	Instability risk
Firm-specific risks	Discriminatory regulations; "Creeping" expropriation; Breach of contract	Sabotage; Kidnappings; Firm-specific boycotts
Country-level risks	Mass nationalizations; Regulatory changes; Currency inconvertibility	Mass labor strikes; Urban rioting; Civil wars

Source: Daniel Wagner, Defining Political Risk, International Risk Management Institute, October 2000.

completely nullifying the value of foreign-exchange contracts.[7] It also refers to the risk of government default on a loan made to it or guaranteed by it.

- *Political risk* concerns those political and social developments that can have an impact upon the value or repatriation of foreign investment or on the repayment of cross-border lending, which may originate within a host country, the home country, or the international arena.[8] This includes arbitrary or discriminatory actions taken by governments, political groups, or individuals that have an adverse impact on trade or investment transactions.

Based on these definitions, country and sovereign risks are more related to payment risk, while political risk is more related to trade and investment risk. However, for purposes of this book, I will define country risk as: *changes in a business environment that may adversely affect operating profits or the value of assets in a specific country.*[9]

To help distinguish among country, sovereign, and political risk, and to emphasize the point that each transaction has a unique risk profile, I have coined the term **transactional risk**, which I define as *the country, sovereign, political, economic, financial, technical, environmental, developmental, and sociocultural risk that an organization assumes in every international transaction in which it engages.* The idea here is that every trade and investment transaction is unique, given the time, the place, and the nature of the transaction. By definition, each such transaction will have some characteristic or set of characteristics that distinguishes it from every other transaction.

How Banks Approach Transactional Risk Management[10]

Much can be learned from the experience of international banks in how they manage transactional risk. In spite of the absence of a "super" regulator that can effectively monitor and control global systemic banking risk—or perhaps in reaction to the absence—most large banks have created their own methods of managing cross-border risk. Nearly all banks have developed formal programs to address transactional risk, and most of these are centralized so as to establish and maintain control over an entire network of operations. More often than not, a board of directors will approve the risk management policy, but the nature of a risk management reporting system will vary by organization. Transactional risk management is usually integrated with the credit risk management function; larger banks tend to integrate transactional risk management into their overall risk management process.

Responsibility for transactional risk management generally resides with a high-level risk management committee at headquarters or the senior country officer (in the case of foreign operations). Although there is general inconsistency about who within an organization actually takes responsibility for determining transactional risk, common approaches include a formal country risk committee, a credit department, or country managers.

No bank relies entirely on external sources of information, but smaller banks are more inclined to rely more heavily on such sources due to lack of internal resources. A number of regional and multinational banks have established procedures to deal with risk tolerances and deteriorating conditions in a country. The most common approach simply relies on informal lines of communication among experienced managers in times of crisis.

Almost all banks assign formal country ratings, most of which cover a broad definition of risk. Ratings are typically assigned to all types of credit and investment risk, including local currency lending. Transactional risk ratings establish a ceiling that also applies to credit risk ratings. Most banks do not generally have formal regional limits, but some banks monitor exposures for a given region informally and most have specific country limits.

Most banks take a comprehensive view of risk, but tend to differ in terms of how specific risks affect their risk rating system. Many banks apply a single country rating to all types of exposure, while distinguishing between foreign and local currency funding. Formal exposure limits tend to be set annually and managed through the use of aggregate country exposures. Risk tolerances are recommended primarily by line management and approved by a high-level committee. The maximum level of exposure for a given country is generally determined by the assigned risk rating.

The Lessons of the Asia Crisis[11]

Although most banks indicate that existing macroeconomic data needed to assess country risk are generally adequate, there are gaps in the data necessary to evaluate country vulnerability to payment shocks. Most banks use a system of country risk ratings that relies on monitoring of real and financial macroeconomic indicators. This has, at times, failed to give them adequate warning to arrange to exit a market in a timely fashion. Better information on foreign currency reserves and short-term debt would have been useful in that regard.

The Asia Crisis taught banks some important lessons about transactional risk management—among them, the need to incorporate several additional sources of information more effectively in risk analyses to include the credit risk associated with private sector counterparties, the potential loss of liquidity, and contagion effects. *An over-reliance on historical volatility to measure risk contributed to an underestimation of risk.*

One of the lessons learned from the Asia Crisis was the relevance of measuring available official foreign exchange resources and short-term public sector obligations denominated in foreign currencies that constitute a drain on resources. There is a need for timely and transparent reporting of official foreign exchange reserves and other information needed to assess the short-term liquidity positions of the official sector. Another area of generally insufficient data is the outstanding short-term foreign currency exposures of nonfinancial corporations in emerging markets. Means must be found to address these shortfalls, which serve to highlight the importance of obtaining a variety of types of data to measure the same variable.

Elements of an Effective Risk Management Process

A sound transactional risk management process will include certain basic elements that result in the creation of an environment conducive to managing risk effectively[12]:

- Effective oversight by a board of directors
- Adequate risk management policies and procedures
- An accurate system for reporting country exposures
- An effective process for analyzing country risk
- A country risk rating system
- Established country exposure limits
- Regular monitoring of country conditions
- Periodic stress testing of foreign exposures
- Adequate internal controls and an audit function

Within this context, it is important to establish clear tolerance limits, delineate clear lines of responsibility and accountability for decisions made, and identify in advance desirable and undesirable types of business. Policies, standards, and practices should be clearly communicated and enforced with affected staff and offices. Quarterly reporting should be imposed—more frequently if foreign exchange exposure impacts a given investment.

It is naturally also important that analyses be adequately documented and conclusions communicated in a way that gives decision makers an accurate basis on which to gauge exposure levels, and that sufficient resources be devoted to the task of assessing risk. Communication methods should clearly convey the level of risk and urgency (e.g., through use of a color-coded system). Since the crisis, some banks have centralized the analytical process and engage in periodic assessments of risk on a more regionalized basis (as opposed to strictly on a country-specific basis).

Best practices dictate that a number of actions should be taken to create a transactional risk management program. Among them are the following:

- The transactional risk management function should be centralized.
- Transactional risk guidelines should be established and widely disseminated.
- Country/sector limits should be established.
- A system to delineate the severity of perceived risks better should be established.
- Quarterly transactional risk reporting should be implemented.
- A company should make maximal use of internal information capabilities while incorporating a wide array of external information sources into analyses.

Much can be learned at a corporate level by the approach and experience of international banks in addressing transactional risk. Nearly all banks have developed formal programs to manage transactional risk, and most of these are centralized so as to establish and maintain control over an entire network of operations. Almost all banks assign formal country ratings, most of which cover a broad definition of risk. Ratings are typically assigned to all types of credit and investment risk, including local currency lending.

Transactional risk ratings establish a ceiling that also applies to credit risk ratings. Most banks do not generally have formal regional limits to lending, but some banks monitor exposures for a given region informally and most have specific country limits. Many banks apply a single country rating to all types of exposure, while distinguishing between foreign and local currency funding. Formal exposure limits tend to be set annually and managed through the use of aggregate country exposures.

The ability to obtain primary knowledge through inputs from local offices, as well as by regular visits on the part of country risk officers, cannot be overemphasized. Best practice should encourage in-house assessments before relying on external sources of information in order to build internal rating applications. This should not come at the expense of utilizing external sources of information, however. Too often, organizations over-rely on internal sources of information and in the end self-impose "blinders" on country risk management processes.

In most organizations, the country risk function operates autonomously, as there tend to be diverging interests between the operating side of the business and risk management. It is therefore important for senior management to oversee interaction between the two sides effectively. The risk assessment decision chain should be transparent and independent of compromise by business unit practices.

Even if there is a rating guide at one's disposal, it is best to utilize information from a variety of sources, identify the central themes that keep reappearing, and make a judgment about the nature of the risk. This should not be done in a vacuum, however. The underwriting and pricing process should be viewed as collaborative, seeking the affirmation of others in the decision-making chain who have the ability to contribute meaningfully to the risk management process. This is often not the case, however.

The Boardroom Vacuum[13]

At a board meeting of a top 20 multinational corporation, the question of whether to invest $50 million in a project in a Middle Eastern country was discussed. The president of the company's subsidiary, who was seeking the board's approval, insisted that the country was a safe place to invest because of its recent history of economic and political stability. Satisfied with the president's assurances and facts, the board approved the investment—a decision the board members came to regret.

As it turns out, the country in question was not as stable as it was portrayed and the company's investment became tied up in costly legal limbo, which had far-reaching and potentially damaging implications for the company's brand and reputation. To make matters worse, the interests of some of the corporate actors involved were not directly aligned with those of the company. The corporate sales team and underwriters promoting the transaction were incentivized to sell the deal internally so that they could meet their production targets and receive their annual bonuses. While the underwriters sought the views of the country risk manager charged with vetting the transaction, as they were supposed to do, a large portion of that analysis was deleted by the underwriters from the final version. Because of the absence of checks and balances in the risk management system, neither the country risk manager nor the corporate risk manager had any way of knowing that the underwriters had manipulated the risk analysis. The corporate risk manager sent it to the division president for approval before sending it on to the board of directors. Everyone up the chain of command believed all necessary approvals had been obtained in the manner previously mandated by the board and senior management.

This is just one example where the due diligence process in place failed to alert decision makers to the risks associated with their international business operations. As is illustrated by this real example, companies often rely exclusively on their own managers and risk management processes, which they believe are bulletproof, but which may in fact be riddled with holes, inconsistencies, and contradictions. Clearly, the company's risk management function and the final version of the country risk analysis were faulty. Without more comprehensive data or insight of its own, the company's senior management and board were too reliant on the deal team's version of the risk assessment to make an informed decision and fulfill their duty to protect the interests of the company and shareholders.

If the board had been better educated about the economic, social, media, and political situation in that country, it might have been able to detect and respond to the errors in the assessment it received. The board might then have forced the company to conduct more thorough due diligence before requesting a vote, rejected the request outright, or made the approval conditional on receipt of the company's plans to mitigate and address the potential risks. This example is far from extraordinary. In the last several years, a number of high-profile international investments have faced serious unanticipated obstacles; for example, a Middle Eastern port operator's management of US ports was derailed by political opposition and an Australian mining company's executives were accused of engaging in industrial espionage and jailed in China.

As company operations and holdings continue to expand into all corners of the globe, decision makers too often pay too little attention to specific country risks and other matters of crucial importance. Boards of directors are particularly vulnerable to this glaring oversight due mainly to a lack of direct insight into a particular country—which leads to an inability to discern fact from fiction—and not knowing the right questions to ask of corporate management.

How can boards make better decisions with respect to country risks? One place to start is in the composition of the board itself. Too often, board members are selected from a small group of high-profile, well-connected, and prestigious individuals who may not have relevant experience in foreign investments or operations and may not want to appear ignorant about a subject matter being discussed; thus, they may fail to contribute meaningfully (or at all) to board discussions. A case in point is the former board of directors of Lehman Brothers. Lehman's board consisted of 10 high-profile individuals, many of whom had served for more than 10 years before the firm's collapse. Nine of the board members were retired, four were more than 75 years old, and only two had financial services experience. Dina Merrill, the 83-year-old daughter of E. F. Hutton and a former actress, served on Lehman's board for 18 years, until 2006 (2 years before Lehman's collapse). It is hard to imagine what value she added to the board; she was presumably a net negative.[14]

Company management clearly needs to emphasize experience and knowledge when selecting board members. That said, it is difficult, if not impossible, to find individuals who have direct and timely experience in every country that may be an investment target for a large corporation.

Another solution is for boards of directors to press companies to update their own risk management procedures regularly and insist on implementing appropriate checks and balances. Given the competing interests that may influence an internal risk management team, a better solution is to look outside the company's country risk management function and insist that the company hire an independent third-party assessor or, ideally, do so themselves. A qualified third party can conduct regular risk management audits that test and stress the system; provide insights into the target country that incorporate political, economic, and social risk; and thus provide board members with unbiased information, empowering them to ask the right questions.

Ultimately, a company's and board's ability to address risk successfully rests with the establishment of a sound risk management process that creates an environment conducive to managing risk effectively. An essential place to start is to establish an effective in-house process to analyze country risk. This should include:

- Country exposure limits and an accurate system for reporting country exposures,
- A country risk rating system, and
- Regular monitoring of country conditions.

Adequate internal controls and an audit function can give management the ability to stress test foreign exposures and engage in scenario planning. It is important to establish clear tolerance limits, delineate clear lines of responsibility and accountability for decisions made, and identify in advance desirable and undesirable types of business in which to be engaged. Policies, standards, and practices should be clearly communicated to and enforced with affected staff and offices. Unfortunately, even when a problem is identified, boards are sometimes reluctant to confront management. Candor often gets lost in the politeness of board proceedings, and, too often, boards are focused on building consensus, which inhibits due diligence and proper risk management. By remaining polite and silent, boards can do more than contribute to monetary losses and they may unwittingly cause risk to reputation, often with long-lasting and severe consequences.

When gathering and managing information, it is best to utilize information from a variety of sources, identify the central themes that keep reappearing, and make a judgment about the nature of the risk. This should not be done in a vacuum, however. Therefore, board members must exercise their responsibilities with renewed vigor and with a solid base of knowledge and insight. If that had been the case with the company described earlier, the outcome would have been much different.

The Impact on Firm Performance

The risk manager or decision maker's ultimate challenge when assessing transactional risk is to determine whether a political event poses a current or future threat to a firm's financial performance. A mass demonstration in a stable developing country may be less significant to a firm's performance than one occurring in an unstable developed country. Similarly, as noted before, a worker strike for higher wages is very different from a nationwide strike to overthrow an incumbent government.

The nature of transactional risk varies most fundamentally by the category of investor (direct or portfolio) because the exposures to country risk differ. In general, portfolio investors are more likely to be affected by country-level risks, such as a sudden hike in interest rates or unanticipated currency devaluation, while direct investors tend to be affected more by firm-specific risks. It is therefore necessary to focus on those political dynamics that affect the overall business environment in a host country.

When assessing political stability, the focus should be on the legitimacy of state authority, the ability of that authority to impose and enforce decrees, the level of corruption that pervades the system of authority, and the degree of political fractionalization that is present. Where economic policy is concerned, the focus would be more along the lines of the degree of government participation in an economy, the government's external debt burden, and the degree to which interest groups can successfully obstruct the decision-making process. *Effective country risk management requires distinguishing between emerging events and trends that pose true risks, such as a well-defined threat to corporate performance, from political events that are merely dramatic.*

Although there are a number of ways to protect a firm against country risks, *proper planning* and *due diligence* are most important. Too many businesses begin operations in an unfamiliar country without having taken the time and devoted the resources necessary to ensure a better than average chance of success. Developing solid relations with relevant governing authorities is the preferred approach, but this may not always be possible or even desirable.

Another important component of creating a country risk-friendly investment environment is to establish a good relationship with the local workforce. Too often, foreign businesses are perceived as having uncaring managers who do not appreciate their workers, which can have dire consequences. One of the best ways to protect a firm's assets is to generate a loyal workforce. Management can be replaced much more easily than can a workforce, and it is becoming more common for host governments to remove foreign managers and replace them with local managers that will operate in accordance with government objectives.

It is easy to lose track of the bigger political picture once an operation is established. After an operating environment has changed, it is often too late to do anything about it. It is therefore important to remain engaged with one's local embassy, chambers of commerce, and other support networks and information collection sources. A collective voice is more powerful than that of an individual firm, even if a firm has a solid relationship with governing authorities.

Separating Fact from Fiction[15]

Let us go back to Indonesia in 1998. At that time, a lot of people thought that country was about to fall off the end of the earth. President Suharto had just been overthrown, ending more than 30 years of his rule, and the country seemed to be teetering on the edge of an abyss. Widespread rioting and anarchy had left the global investment community under the impression that the end was near. But pandemonium did not break out, Indonesia remained intact, and the country eventually returned to stability. That political drama was a perfect example of how a *perceived* level of political risk, based on media reports or outside opinions, may differ from the *actual* degree of political risk, based on the reality on the ground.

Although Indonesia did have a rough ride in 1998 and 1999, its economic performance began to improve in 2000. The country exported $62 billion worth of goods that year, which included 23% growth in non-oil/gas exports, and the economy grew 4.8%. So, while countries like Taiwan and Malaysia suffered as a result of the slowdown in electronics purchases in the United States, Europe, and Japan during the Asia Crisis, Indonesia's economy turned in a respectable performance. However, since the bulk of media reports about Indonesia were overwhelmingly negative, the business community did not focus on some of the more positive news, and the perceived level of country risk was as a result higher than the actual degree of country risk at the time. This impacted investment levels, and it took years for the government to turn around the mistaken impression that Indonesia was imploding for years after Suharto's overthrow.

Unlike those outside the region who relied on media reports of Asia's various political, economic, and social woes, businesspeople in Asia knew the difference between fact and fiction when discussing political risk in Asia during the crisis. Unfortunately, as a result of a tendency to rely on media reports and an absence of on-the-ground fact-finding, many decision makers outside the region were more inclined to believe the media reports.

For years the media had much of the world believing that any business-person who set foot in the Philippines would be kidnapped. The truth is that while kidnapping is indeed an issue among a small groups of high-level businesspeople (mostly from indigenous Chinese families), the number of cases is very small and tends to occur in only a few of the more than 7,000 islands in the country. Wealthy local Chinese businessmen are far more likely to be kidnapped in the Philippines than are foreign businesspeople or tourists. And yet the media continue to create a negative impression about the business climate in the Philippines.

Another example is how the media have completely exaggerated the risk of armed conflict between Taiwan and the People's Republic of China (PRC), prompting some foreign businesses to question the wisdom of doing business in Taiwan. While the risk of armed conflict is possible, it appears to be more remote than ever, as more than 50 years of history has demonstrated. Both sides know that Taiwan and the PRC gain much more by engaging in cross-border trade and investment than by rattling sabers, and the two countries have taken significant steps to embrace each other economically. The truth is that the two countries have far more in common culturally, linguistically, and historically than they have issues that separate them. This demonstrates the importance of separating fact from fiction when investing abroad.

Notes

1. http://www.nytimes.com/2010/11/14/opinion/14friedman.html
2. Expropriation: Pakistan's message to foreign investors. International Risk Management Institute, February 12, 2010. Reprinted with permission from IRMI.
3. Bolivia's larger message, International Risk Management Institute website, May 2006. Reprinted with permission from IRMI.
4. New era for PNG. *Project Finance International*, May 19, 2010. Reprinted with permission from *PFI*.
5. Defining political risk. International Risk Management Institute website, October 2000. Reprinted with permission from IRMI.
6. Krayenbuehl, T. *Country risk: Assessment and monitoring.* Cambridge, England: Woodhead-Faulkner, 1985.
7. TheFreeDictionary.com
8. Simon, J. D. Political risk analysis for international banks and multinational enterprises. In *Country risk analysis: A handbook*, ed. R. L. Solberg, 118. London: Routledge, 1992.
9. http://en.wikipedia.org/wiki/Country_risk
10. Effective transactional risk management. International Risk Management Institute website, November 2007. Reprinted with permission from IRMI.
11. Bank of International Settlements. On the use of information and risk management by international banks. Basle, Switzerland, 1998.

12. Comptroller of the Currency. Country risk management, comptroller handbook, October 2001, p. 3.
13. The boardroom vacuum. *Risk Management Magazine*, December 2009. Reprinted with permission from *RMM*.
14. Williams, M. T. *Uncontrolled risk*, 189. New York: McGraw–Hill, 2010.
15. Political risk in Asia: Fact or fiction? International Risk Management Institute website, November 2001. Reprinted with permission IRMI.

Chapter 3

Assessing Country Risk

Five states of risk management:

> You know what you know.
> You don't know what you know.
> You know what you don't know.
> You don't know what you don't know.
> You know but you don't want to know.

Professor Walter Ingo, New York University

Introduction

As has been noted in the previous chapters, politics and economics are inextricably linked. They do not exist in a vacuum and their impact on each other cannot be separated. Similarly, the link between probability and consequences also cannot be separated. Risk may simply be defined as *risk = probability × consequences*.[1] In other words, the higher the probability that an event may occur, the greater its likely consequences. The word *risk* comes from the ancient Greek word *rhiza*, which means "that which comes from a root."[2] The Greeks used the term to refer to the *fear* of sailing a ship around a cliff. The ability to manage risk is what drives our economic system forward, and defining a rational process of risk taking is at the core of our modern market economy. The goal should be to make *reward* commensurate with *risk;* the challenge is to understand and manage risk. The best way to make rational risk-taking decisions is by being armed with the best intelligence possible.

The definition of risk can be further defined as that based either on *randomness of events* or a *lack of knowledge*. **Aleotoric risk** is derived from a contingent event, based on the intrinsic randomness of nature.[3] This type of risk can be managed through insurance and other risk mitigation measures. **Epistemic risk** is a function of lack of information about risk, is controllable, and can be minimized by being armed with knowledge in order to ensure that one is making the best decisions.

Having the right risk management tools at your disposal—whether it is an insurance product or knowledge—is the best means of managing risk. Yet, assessing country risk involves much more than simply collecting data. Getting good data is relatively easy, given the wealth of information at our disposal. *Interpreting* data is the real challenge. To do so well, risk analyses should be:

- *Consistent* and made using rigorous frameworks that allow for valid cross-country comparisons
- *Concise,* with the conclusion easy to understand, but with sufficient detail to make it meaningful
- *Informative,* giving the end user the rationale behind any assessment without any "black boxes" that are difficult to understand
- *Decisive,* with a clearly defined position on prevailing country conditions and future implications

As noted earlier, *perception* (or fear) of a risk may often be very different from the *reality* of a risk. A good risk analyst must be able to tell the difference. But data can only tell you so much. *Gut instinct* is often as important as all the risk indicators one can identify—sometimes even more so. Including *intuition* and *experience* in the risk analysis process is extremely important in the country risk analysis process. Relying too much on numbers and methodologies can lead to trouble, as they may prevent an analyst from thinking in broad terms. Ultimately, each risk must pass our own "smell" test, based on our own inherent experience, knowledge, and biases because country risk analysis cannot be a purely objective undertaking.

In considering the approach to country risk management that may be best for your organization, bear in mind the following basic guidelines:

- *Politics can defy logic.* The political process is generally not logical, so applying logic to the creation of a country risk management tool does not make much sense.
- *Know your data sources.* Data may be obtained from any number of sources, but it is important to be able to trust the information sources being used. Where did the source you may select obtain its

information? Too often, external information providers or consultants may not reveal where they got their information, which may raise questions about its *validity* and *accuracy*.

- *Question official statistics.* Analysts tend to rely too much on statistics generated by governments or multilateral organizations. While these are important sources of information to include in the analytical process, it should be remembered that governments often manipulate statistics for political purposes and that international organizations often rely on such information to produce their own analysis and projections.
- *Benefit from the power of observation.* There is no better way to arrive at a conclusion about the nature of country risk than to see it for yourself. If you have the opportunity to visit the country and/ or project site, it is often the best means of arriving at a conclusion about the nature of the risks associated with a given transaction. One's own experience and interpretive abilities add a lot of legitimacy to the analytical process.
- *Qualitative risk assessment can ultimately undo all quantitative approaches.* Relying too much on quantitative measures can be dangerous. Adding texture to analyses by refusing to categorize them as either black or white, or good or bad, can be the single most effective addition to the analytical process. Human behavior (an unpredictable variable) can only be assessed through the incorporation of qualitative measurement.

Country risk management is all about casting aside long-held assumptions and applying insight and foresight to imagine what a country and the world will look like in the future. In our debt- and conflict-ridden world, without an obvious leader and yearning for democracy, country risk can only continue to rise in the near and medium term, so the ability to look at history and the present with an open mind is essential.

Information Sources

Of course, a plethora of information is available to country risk analysts, much of it public and free of charge. Information gathering is much easier today than it was 20 years ago because of the Internet, but finding the right information can still be a challenging task. The following is a noncomprehensive list of some of the publicly available options:

- *Central bank websites*
- *General publications* such as websites of newspapers, magazines, and newsletters

- *Government sources* such as embassies, commerce and state departments, and export–import (EXIM) banks
- *International financial organizations* such as the Bank for International Settlements (BIS) and the International Monetary Fund (IMF)
- *Internet search engines* such as Bing, Google, and Yahoo

MDBs such as the African Development Bank (AfDB), Asian Development Bank (ADB), European Bank for Reconstruction and Development (EBRD), Inter-American Development Bank (IADB), Islamic Development Bank (IDB), World Bank Group (which includes the International Bank for Reconstruction and Development (IBRD), International Finance Corporation (IFC), and MIGA).

- *Newswires* such as Bloomberg, Dow Jones, and ThomsonReuters

Some of the best and most useful information is generated by a handful of information providers who specialize in publishing daily, weekly, monthly, quarterly, or annual data, including

- *Alternative sources* such as the Institute of International Finance (IIF), think tanks, and private research
- *Consulting firms* such as Country Risk Solutions
- *Ratings agencies* such as Fitch, Moody's, and Standard & Poors
- *Specialist publications* such as Business Monitor International (BMI), The Economist Intelligence Unit (EIU), Eurasia Group, IHS Global Insight, and Political Risk Services (PRS)

Examples of specific websites include:

- Asian Development Bank: www.adb.org
- African Development Bank: www.afdb.org
- Central Intelligence Agency: www.cia.gov
- Country Risk Solutions: www.countryrisksolutions.com
- European Bank for Reconstruction and Development: www.ebrd.com
- FDI.net: www.fdi.net
- Freedom House: http://www.freedomhouse.org
- Inter-American Development Bank: www.iadb.org
- International Energy Agency: www.iea.org
- International Finance Corporation: www.ifc.org
- International Monetary Fund: www.imf.org
- Islamic Development Bank: www.isdb.org
- Oanda (Foreign Exchange): www.oanda.com
- US State Department: www.state.gov
- Transparency International: www.transparency.org
- World Bank: www.worldbank.org
- World Development Indicators: http://data.worldbank.org/indicator

- United National Conference on Trade and Development: www.unctad. org

Nothing beats on-site data collection, however. As noted before, the ability to see for yourself what is happening in a country or at a project site and ask your own questions of knowledgeable people can make all the difference between making an accurate or inaccurate risk assessment.

Are Rating Agencies' Ratings Worth Using?

The reputation of the rating agencies suffered a lot as a result of the Great Recession. They were rightly blamed for awarding high ratings to financial institutions and corporations that should have received a failing grade based on the composition of their balance sheets prior to the Recession. Although the agencies did give passing grades to organizations that should not have received them, an equally significant problem was that they tended to be reactive rather than proactive and continue to be so today. Even after all that has happened, rating agencies will often downgrade a country *after* it has become a problem. Standard & Poors' downgrade of the US from AAA to an AA+ rating in August 2011 is a good example.

Remember that rating agencies give "opinions" on a country's ability and willingness to pay their bills. They generally offer a medium-term (18- to 24-month) view of corporate and sovereign risk. Although rating agencies assess political, economic, and social risk; regime legitimacy; international security; and dispersion of power, they may differ widely in their assessments or be surprisingly similar. Rating agencies often end up with the same views; some just take longer to get there than others. As is noted in Figure 12, two rating agencies rate a sampling of 10 countries identically for the four quarters between third quarter 2007 and second quarter 2008 (one full calendar year). Ratings can be wrong and should be absorbed along with other sources of information.

The similarity of ratings is even more surprising when you consider that the agencies include a range of quantitative and qualitative inputs to arrive at their ratings, which makes you wonder how they could possibly be so similar. The three major agencies did the same thing in response to the Greek debt crisis, beginning in 2008. All three rated Greece A or A+ through the summer of 2008, when S&P dropped it one notch from A to A–. Fitch followed in the early part of 2009 with a one-notch downgrade. Moody's followed by mid-2009. Remember that Greece's GDP growth had already fallen from 4.3% in 2007 to 1.0% in 2008; its government deficit had been negative the entire decade, was –6.4% of GDP in 2007 and grew to –9.8% in 2008. Greece's national debt had been running well above the EU average since it

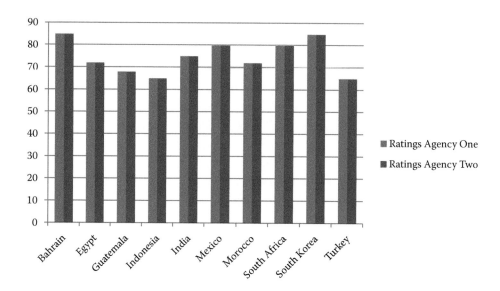

FIGURE 12 **Two ratings agency ratings for 10 countries: Q3, 2007 to Q2, 2008. (From author's research.)**

joined the European Union in 2000. The alarm bells were ringing loudly, but the rating agencies reacted late in the game (see Table 5).

The three rating agencies continued to downgrade Greece on an ongoing basis in 2009 and through the middle of 2011. What started as either A or A+ ratings in 2008, when Greece was already in big trouble, ended up being downgraded to either B+, CCC+, or CCC (selective default) by July 2011.

The following indicators are frequently used by the rating agencies to generate ratings with respect to a country's debt and political risk:

- *Macroeconomic performance:* for example, growth prospects and inflation record
- *Public/external debt sustainability:* Is a country on a sustainable path? What is its vulnerability to shocks and can it stand external shocks?
- *External financing needs:* Foreign exchange liquidity, current account balance, capacity to borrow domestically, and capital flight
- *Structural features:* for example, openness to trade and investment
- *Social pressures:* demographics, civil liberties, income growth, religious/ethnic pressures, and domestic conflict
- *Regime legitimacy:* political rights, political freedoms, and the nature of corruption
- *International security:* cross-border conflict and relations with a country's neighbors

Standard and Poors includes the following in its sovereign ratings methodology[6]:

TABLE 5 Greece's GDP Growth Rate and Deficit: 2000–2010

	2000	2001	2002	2003	2004	2005	2006	2007	2008	2009	2010	2011 (Predictions)
GDP growth[4]	4.5	4.2	3.4	5.9	4.4	2.3	5.2	4.3	1.0	–2.0	–4.5	–3.5
Deficit[5]	–3.7	–4.5	–4.8	–5.6	–7.5	–5.2	–5.7	–6.4	–9.8	–15.4	–10.5	–9.5

Source: http://epp.eurostat.ec.europa.eu/portal/page/portal/statistics/themes

- Political risk
  - Stability and legitimacy of political institutions
  - Popular participation in political processes
  - Orderliness of leadership succession
  - Transparency in economic policy decisions and objectives
  - Public security
  - Geopolitical risk

- Economic structure
  - Prosperity, diversity, and degree to which economy is market oriented
  - Income disparities
  - Effectiveness of financial sector in intermediating funds; availability of credit
  - Competitiveness and profitability of nonfinancial private sector
  - Efficiency of public sector
  - Protectionism and other nonmarket influences
  - Labor flexibility

- Economic growth prospects
  - Size and composition of savings and investment
  - Rate and pattern of economic growth

- Fiscal flexibility
  - General government revenue, expenditure, and surplus/deficit trends
  - Compatibility of fiscal stance with monetary and external factors
  - Revenue-raising flexibility and efficiency
  - Expenditure effectiveness and pressures
  - Timeliness, coverage, and transparency in reporting
  - Pension obligations

- General government debt burden
  - General government gross and net (of liquid assets) debt
  - Share of revenue devoted to interest
  - Currency composition and maturity profile
  - Depth and breadth of local capital markets

- Offshore and contingent liabilities
  - Size and health of nonfinancial public sector enterprises
  - Robustness of financial sector

- Monetary flexibility
  - Price behavior in economic cycles
  - Money and credit expansion
  - Compatibility of exchange-rate regime and monetary goals

- Institutional factors, such as central bank independence
- Range and efficiency of monetary policy tools, particularly in light of fiscal stance and capital market characteristics
- Indexation and dollarization

- External liquidity
  - Impact of fiscal and monetary policies on external accounts
  - Structure of the current account
  - Composition of capital flows
  - Reserve adequacy

- External debt burden
  - Gross and net external debt, including nonresident deposits and structured debt
  - Maturity profile, currency composition, and sensitivity to interest rate changes
  - Access to concessional funding
  - Debt service burden

Rating agencies' analytical methodology and the amount of data taken into account may be quite comprehensive, but in the end, the actual rating may be largely based on a subjective interpretation of the data. In that regard, a rating agency's interpretive process may not be all that different from that utilized in a corporation. Best practice calls for reference to external ratings without too much reliance on them. External ratings are often used to benchmark or compare against internal ratings an organization may produce.

Any glaring discrepancies can be a useful basis of discussion. Some organizations use them primarily for determining the nature of default potential (on a corporate or sovereign basis), but ratings are sometimes considered too far behind the curve, particularly in a fast paced and dynamic business environment. They can be politically influenced or of limited perceived value by assessing the risk of default in 5 or 10 years, which is difficult to do accurately. Ratings can be important as they can influence a country's access to and cost of capital markets on a short-term basis, but can ultimately become self-fulfilling prophecies because of their impact on liquidity.

Measuring Political Stability

Many of the problems that arise in the course of trading, investing, or lending abroad are the result of either acute or chronic political instability, so the ability to measure stability is an important component of country risk management. Naturally, it is not an easy thing to assess accurately. Sources of potential political instability include changes in leadership and government, economic distress, social upheaval, and unforeseen events, and they do not lend themselves to easy quantification. The potential negative impact political instability has on business operations is what matters most from the perspective of country risk management.

Among the factors that can most influence political instability is popular discontent, which often translates into political demands and requires a response from a government. If a government responds in a manner that falls short of popular will, it will likely spur even greater demands, as was seen in Greece in 2010. This, in turn, can lead to a cycle of tit-for-tat responses between citizens and governments that may eventually result in either a heightened degree of protest or a demand for the overthrow of the existing leadership. Popular discontent usually ends only when a specific set of demands is satisfied.

Social change can also become a primary source of political discontent, which can include anything from frustration about urbanization and its cumulative impacts to gender or labor inequality. As time goes on, a consequence of such discontent can be a transformation in the cultural context in which people live or the appropriateness of the ways in which they think or behave. Cultures take time to adapt to the economic, social, and technological changes that occur in dynamic societies. Most countries experience significant social changes as their economies develop, but developing countries often experience proportionally greater transformation, with proportionally greater potential impacts.

Yet another source of popular discontent is the perception of economic failure relative to other countries. When citizens' expectations of economic growth or personal income fail to match those of other, wealthier countries, their frustration levels will rise and, eventually, they will rebel. This is often seen in countries that have never experienced rapid growth and the rising income levels that accompany it, or where rapid growth occurred and then stopped. Otherwise known as an "inverted J-curve," when this pattern of growth is compared against time in Figure 13; it slopes upward initially, then downward as time goes on. The level of economic growth declines as time progresses and the degree of frustration among a population grows.

In countries where this occurs, inequalities of wealth that may have been tolerated by a population when expectations of future wealth seemed achievable end up generating resentment. As these countries fall further and further behind their peers, frustration levels inevitably boil over. A government's skill or lack of skill in addressing frustration levels will ultimately determine whether it stays in power or not. That is the current dilemma in Saudi Arabia, which sees turmoil in virtually every neighboring country. Its government recognized early on during the Arab Spring that it could also be sucked into the regional political morass if it did not make an overt effort to appease the disenfranchised among its citizenry by greatly enhancing entitlements and benefits, so it did.

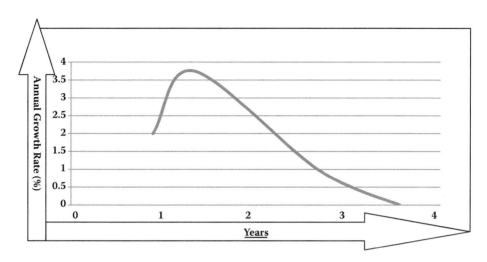

FIGURE 13 Inverted J-curve: growth rate versus time. (From http://en.wikipedia. org/wiki/J_curve)

Another way of representing the J-curve is to correlate stability and openness,[7] wherein the x-axis measures openness of the economy and the y-axis measures the stability of the same state. It suggests that those states that are "closed," undemocratic, or not free (such as Cuba and North Korea) are quite stable, but as the curve progresses to the right along the x-axis it becomes evident that stability (for a relatively short period of time in the lengthy life of nations) decreases, creating a dip in the graph until it begins to pick up again as the openness of a state increases. At the other end of the graph are the open states of the West, such as the United Kingdom and United States, forming a J-shaped curve (see Figure 14).

Figure 15 illustrates the various paths a government may take toward development. A state may have:

- Poor state capacity and low levels of democracy, such as Somalia, in which case it may be a failed or failing state.
- A high degree of state capacity and a well developed democracy, such as the United Kingdom, in which case its longevity is likely.
- A moderate degree of capacity and democracy, such as Bolivia, in which case the government's longevity is not assured.

States can travel both forward (right) and backwards (left) along this J-curve, so stability and openness are rarely static. The curve is steeper on the left side, as it is easier for a leader in a failed state to create stability by closing the country than to build a civil society and establish accountable institutions. The curve is higher on the far right than left because states that succeed in opening their societies (such as Eastern Europe) ultimately become more stable than authoritarian regimes. The entire curve can shift up or down depending on economic resources available to a government. So, while an

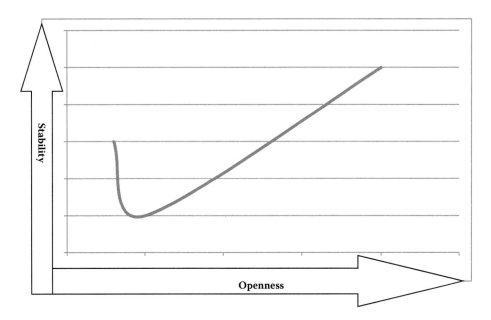

FIGURE 14 The J-curve: a liberalized market. (From http://en.wikipedia.org/wiki/J_curve)

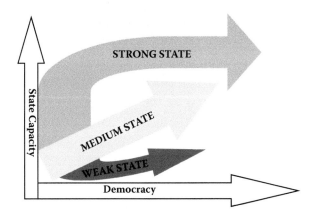

FIGURE 15 Paths toward state development. (From Tilley Charles, *Democracy*, Cambridge, England: Cambridge University Press, 2007.)

oil-producing state may have relative stability at every point along the curve, it may rise or fall based on the price of oil, while China's curve may depend more on economic growth levels.[8]

Depending on the type of government, it may have the ability to influence one element of a society or political system, but may be ineffective in doing the same with another element. Dictatorships, for example, are powerful in some respects but weak in others. For example, a dictator can order detentions and executions, but may be relatively powerless to stop corruption. By contrast, the Australian government could order the creation of a new central banking system or the construction of an interstate highway system and have complete confidence that it will be achieved. States with real organizational and coordinating power rarely experience large-scale instability and are generally able to quash threats to their power. Military coups usually occur in countries where the opposite is true.

A state that derives enormous income from the sale of natural resources (otherwise known as "rental income") can bribe its citizens into political complacency, which is what the government of Saudi Arabia has tried to do as a result of the Arab Spring. This ability to pay off those who are discontented enables such states to maintain political stability, but usually only delays the day of reckoning. Sooner or later, a time will come when the state no longer has the ability to bribe its population or money will no longer satisfy the aspirations of the population, as is noted in the example in Bolivia in Box 3.1.[9]

When one or two parties dominate a country's political system, the country tends to be stable. When a coalition of many small parties determines the composition of a ruling coalition, governments tend to rise and fall with far greater rapidity (e.g., Israel). Rapid or frequent political changes create uncertainty about government policy and often result in real economic damage to an economy, while infrequent changes in leadership experience less damaging forms of instability.

Wealthy states generally produce the most desirable economic policies, which generate wealth and contribute to their own legitimacy. The size of a country's external debt is a good indicator of past policy failures. The existence

---

BOX 3.1 BOLIVIA'S TRANSPORTISTAS

Bolivia's President Morales has a history of sending his political opponents packing; the country's transportistas—who own and drive buses and taxis—were victorious each time they clashed with Morales in late 2010 and early 2011 after the government announced a steep rise in the price of petrol and banned secondhand cars. Morales had earlier banned imports of the worst polluting cars in an effort to cut pollution and ease traffic congestion.

Following much opposition, the government declared a short amnesty wherein vehicle owners could register illegally imported vehicles and pay a fine for Bolivian cars, only to find them sold out. Some people began to steal Chilean cars, which prompted the Chilean Senate to protest Bolivia's "laundering" of stolen vehicles. Bolivia's taxi drivers, who feared competition from new imports, called a 1-day strike, prompting the government to issue a decree banning the use of vehicles more than 12 years old for public use. The transportistas objected, saying that included 95% of taxis and buses. Even though the decree did not take full effect for 7 years, the transportistas called a strike. Morales then apologized for his "mistake" and promised full consultation over the new law. He will think twice before challenging the transportistas a third time.

of large external debt casts doubt on a government's policy-making abilities and the need to service a large amount of debt makes it difficult for even the most competent regime to operate effectively. In such cases, the state must devote enormous economic resources to paying off its debt, which leads to large budget deficits and, ultimately, even larger debt. Yet, macroeconomic stability is critical to future growth because a stable economic environment encourages rational decision making. In unstable investment climates, long-term commitments are difficult to make since future expected returns cannot be meaningfully estimated. In other words, high levels of savings and investment cannot occur without macroeconomic stability.

Comparing Indonesia and Vietnam

To give you a better sense of the importance of the policy decisions a government chooses over the course of decades, its impact on stability, and how data may be used to compare and contrast country risk between two countries, what follows is a comparison between Indonesia and Vietnam. Table 6 compares some basic developmental indicators. Indonesia has a population more than two and half times larger than that of Vietnam and an economy three and half times the size of Vietnam's, but its gross national income (GNI) per capita is only 41% larger than Vietnam's. This implies that Vietnam is much better at utilizing and benefiting from its indigenous resources in an efficient manner.

By all accounts, the average person in Indonesia should be much wealthier than the average person in Vietnam. Life expectancy and access to clean water are roughly the same, but Indonesia's external debt ($159 billion)

TABLE 6 Comparative Developmental Indicators: 2010

	Indonesia	Vietnam
Population (millions)	226	85
GNI (PPP[a] in USD)	$855 billion	$244 billion
GNI per capita (PPP in USD)	$3,570	$2,530
Life expectancy at birth	71 years	74 years
Access to improved water	80%	92%
Total external debt	$158 billion	$29 billion
Total debt as a percent of exports	10.5%	2.3%
Internet users	5.8%	21%

Source: World Bank Development Indicators, 2011, World Bank website.

[a] PPP = purchasing power parity

as a percentage of exports is four and a half times higher than Vietnam's ($29 billion), reflective of the decades Suharto spent borrowing money to help fuel Indonesia's long-term growth. Figure 16 compares the external debt of both countries. Note how between 1970 and 1998, when Suharto was overthrown and Indonesia's external debt peaked (at $151.5 billion), the country's external debt rose by more than 3300%. Indonesia's export income was $158 billion in 2010 (its primary exports being oil, natural gas, crude palm oil, coal, appliances, textiles, and rubber)[10] compared to Vietnam's $72 billion (its primary exports being crude oil, textiles, footwear, seafood products, rice ([the world's second largest exporter], pepper [the world's largest exporter], wood products, coffee, rubber, and handicrafts).[11] Despite its geographic, population, and economic size, Indonesia is roughly only twice as capable of generating export income as Vietnam.

Interestingly, both countries have a similarly sized middle class. The Asian Development Bank (ADB) defines the middle class as individuals earning between $2 and $20 per day—a broad range in one sense, but noteworthy also for being the dividing line between those who can generally afford to eat on a daily basis and those who cannot. According to the ADB, approximately 35% of both countries' populations earn just $2 to $4 per day (just above the poverty line), while 10% of Indonesia's population earns $4 to $10 per day, compared with nearly 15% in Vietnam. Between 1% and 2% of both countries' populations earn $10 to $20 per day. In short, there is not that much difference in the percentage of the population belonging to the middle class in either country, but what is important to recognize is that the middle class in both countries cannot really afford to purchase appliances, cars, or other higher end goods. Businesses considering investing in either country should modify their expectations with respect to how likely it is that they may be successful selling particular products there, since it may be assumed that very few individuals will be considered wealthy and the majority of the population may be considered poor (see Figure 17).

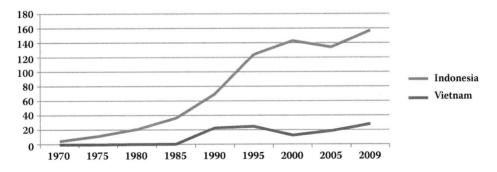

FIGURE 16 Indonesia and Vietnam's external debt. (From World Bank, World Bank Development Indicators, 2011.)

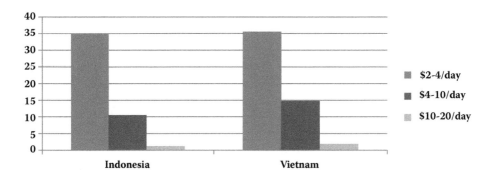

FIGURE 17 **Percent of the population in the middle class (based on purchasing power parity, 2005). (From Asian Development Bank.)**

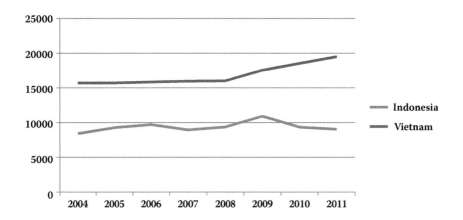

FIGURE 18 **Comparative exchange rates: Indonesia and Vietnam (2004–2011). (From www.oanda.com)**

An examination of both countries' historical foreign exchange rate also provides useful insight into the relative health of their economies. As noted in Figure 18, Indonesia's foreign exchange rate hovered between 9,000 and 10,000 rupiah (IDR) per dollar between 2004 and 2011, indicating relative stability. By contrast, Vietnam's currency, the dong, depreciated by about a third between 2008 and 2011, indicating relative economic weakness. Further investigation reveals that although the economy grew well during the period (averaging about 7% per annum), it did not perform up to its potential (perhaps 10% annually), and the Vietnamese economy has had difficulty being competitive with its neighbors more generally. Also, being a centrally planned economy has stifled innovation and growth potential. Yet, as noted in Figure 19, Vietnam had consistently higher annual GDP growth than Indonesia since the early 1990s and was only mildly affected by the Asia Crisis, while Indonesia's GDP growth rate has been inconsistent and gyrated wildly during the Asia Crisis. So, economic statistics should be viewed in context, and longer term data can yield surprising results.

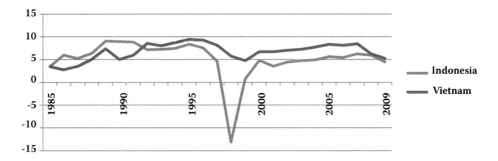

FIGURE 19 Indonesia and Vietnam's GDP growth: 1986–2009. (From World Bank Development Indicators, 2011.)

TABLE 7 Doing Business in Indonesia versus in Vietnam

	2011 Ranking		2010 Ranking		Change in ranking	
	Indonesia	Vietnam	Indonesia	Vietnam	Indonesia	Vietnam
Starting a business	155	100	159	114	+4	+14
Dealing with construction permits	60	62	60	70	0	+8
Registering property	98	43	94	39	–4	–4
Getting credit	116	15	109	30	–7	+15
Protecting investors	44	173	41	172	–3	–1
Paying taxes	130	124	125	126	–5	+2
Trading across borders	47	63	49	59	+2	–4
Enforcing contracts	154	31	153	31	+1	0
Closing a business	142	124	141	125	–1	+1
Overall ranking	121	78	115	88	–6	+10

Source: www.doingbusiness.org; World Bank Group.

Finally, let us consider a variety of factors involved in doing business in both countries. The World Bank Group publishes a fascinating and very useful annual series entitled "Doing Business" (www.doingbusiness.org), which provides objective measures of a variety of types of business regulations in 183 countries. As noted in Table 7, comparing Indonesia and Vietnam as destinations for doing business is instructive in better understanding just what is really involved in setting up a business and operating successfully in both countries. The rankings are out of 183 countries and the *lower* the score is, the better.

The two countries have vastly different ratings on a variety of levels. The only areas where they are roughly similar are in obtaining construction permits and paying taxes. In terms of simply starting a business, Vietnam is a much more desirable destination according to the ranking, but not in every category. In terms of protecting investors and trading across borders, Vietnam ranks much worse than Indonesia. This has to do with the lack of progress in developing an internationally acceptable legal regime and some of the restrictions on free trade that remain in place. Vietnam comes out on top in a variety of other categories, however, such as registering property, obtaining credit, and enforcing contracts. Vietnam is still evolving from a strictly centrally controlled economy to one that is more market oriented, and its regulatory environment reflects this. Vietnam's overall ranking is much better than Indonesia's, and its 2011 score improved dramatically over the 2010 score, while Indonesia's fell further behind. Vietnam's overall ranking is comparable to that of China and the Bahamas, while Indonesia's ranking is similar to that of Russia and Uganda.

Indonesia and Vietnam are, of course, very different investment destinations, but they share a surprising amount in common from a general perspective. Both countries have tremendous potential, endemic corruption, a tainted judicial system, and an inconsistent regulatory structure. Indonesia has long been the home of powerful vested interests, but it has a vibrant press and growing social freedoms. Its private sector is thriving even though bureaucracy, inefficiency, and corruption are pervasive. Change is rapid, and one gets the sense that it is moving forward—so much so that many businesspeople in Jakarta expect that Indonesia will reach investment grade status by 2013 (which may be wishful thinking).

In Vietnam, an inflexible one-party state makes decisions based on compromise and consensus, although the Communist Party is encouraging a broader range of participants, much as the Chinese Communist Party (CCP) has done over the years (mostly to ensure the perpetuation of its existence and power). Vietnam's powerful vested interests have created tension between the socialist system and the market. The economy is dominated by state-owned enterprises—what the government calls "market forces with a socialist orientation." Like Indonesia, the bureaucracy is inefficient and corruption is pervasive. But unlike Indonesia, change is slow and incremental, and there are limited press and social freedoms.

Indonesia has been much more successful at attracting FDI because it threw open its doors to the global economy decades ago, recognizing that in order to grow and meet its developmental needs, it needed the assistance that only foreign investors can provide. Vietnam has been less successful in attracting FDI, in part because it has failed to embrace the benefits of FDI fully, but also because there is growing uncertainty about the shape and pace of change. Investors do not like uncertainty. It has been a decade since a major foreign infrastructure investment reached the finish line in Vietnam. Even though in many respects Indonesia is just a 14-year-old country (given that the "new," post-Suharto Indonesia was born in 1998), it has done a much better job of removing that uncertainty in the minds of foreign investors. Although its position in the "doing business" ranking is much less desirable, many foreign investors continue to choose Indonesia over Vietnam for that reason.

Notes

1. http://www.slac.stanford.edu/cgi-wrap/getdoc/slac-wp-049-ch14-Kenny.pdf
2. http://strongsnumbers.com/greek/4491.htm
3. http://dictionary.reference.com/browse/aleatory
4. Real GDP growth rate: Growth rate of GDP volume—Percentage change on previous year. Brussels: Eurostat. http://epp.eurostat.ec.europa.eu/tgm/graph.do?tab=graph& plugin=1&pcode=tsieb020&language=en&toolbox=data (retrieved June 25, 2011).
5. General government deficit (–) and surplus (+). Brussels: Eurostat. http://epp.euro-stat.ec.europa.eu/tgm/graph.do?tab=graph&plugin=1&pcode=teina200&language=en&toolbox=data (retrieved June 25, 2011).
6. Standard and Poors. Sovereign credit ratings: A primer, May 28, 2009.
7. Bremmer, Ian. *The J curve.* New York: Simon & Schuster.
8. http://en.wikipedia.org/wiki/J_curve
9. Car crash. *The Economist,* June 25, 2011.
10. http://www.state.gov/r/pa/ei/bgn/2748.htm
11. http://www.state.gov

Chapter 4

Country Risk Assessment in Practice

Not everything that can be counted counts, and not everything that counts can be counted.

Albert Einstein[1]

Creating a Risk Management Framework

One of the challenges corporate management and country risk analysts face in crafting a methodology that will gain wide acceptance in an organization is a tendency for existing risk management practices and biases to inhibit development of a tool that does not reproduce the defects inherent in the system. Among the most common impediments are:

- A breakdown in communication between analysts, risk management, and senior management
- Unresolved conflicts between staff and management
- A tendency to overlook or ignore defects or problems
- Killing the messenger instead of rewarding the messenger
- Covering up mistakes
- Screening information, then denying there is a problem
- A lack of incentives to find and correct a problem

- A tendency to accept the most popular or favorable point of view—one that will not rock the boat
- Lack of flexibility and innovation
- Loss of institutional memory

Any tools that are adopted or systems that are put in place must be simple and easy to use, so as to encourage their broad acceptance and avoid encouraging or exacerbating these common pitfalls.

There is an inherent trade-off between the relative breadth of an analytical tool and the amount of detail it can provide. Analytical tools are used to make judgments, but they are not omnipotent, nor should they be used as an alternative to other forms of due diligence. Most tools fail to capture subtleties that can be important in the country risk analysis process, such as the economic impact of political change, the political impact of economic change, if or how governments may be held to account, or how the discretionary powers of political leaders may be constrained. Broad indicators are more likely to produce greater variance and error, while more narrowly focused indicators may be more accurate, but for a limited context of problems. So the objective in crafting any such tool is to include enough variables so as to be able to read between the lines and derive sufficient nuance to be able to arrive at a meaningful conclusion. It is also important to be clear about underlying assumptions, rationale, and purpose of creating and using analytical tools, which can introduce bias into the analytical process.

Two basic sets of steps are involved in deciding, from a risk management perspective, whether to proceed with a trade or investment transaction. As noted in Figure 20, the first involves devising a general *risk* management framework to determine whether the risks associated with a proposed transaction can be properly managed and then doing a cost/benefit analysis to make a decision about whether to proceed. The second, shown in Figure 21, is a *country risk* management process that involves six steps in a constantly evolving process of identifying exposures, evaluating options, and monitoring results. The first two steps involve identifying and analyzing the nature of an organization's or transaction's exposures, followed by devising a technique to manage risks. After selecting and implementing an appropriate technique, results must be monitored and revised on an ongoing basis.

Considering whether or not to proceed with a trade or investment transaction need not be a particularly complicated or time-consuming process in the first instance. It may be simply accomplished by identifying perhaps half a dozen areas of primary potential concern and then deciding whether, at a 38,000 foot level, these issues are acceptable or not. In considering whether to do business in China or India, for example, one method of very simply identifying the primary issues is to put them in concentric circles and see where the two intersect, as noted in Figure 22. Or simply examine the

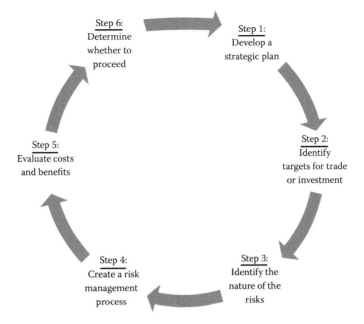

FIGURE 20   The risk management process.

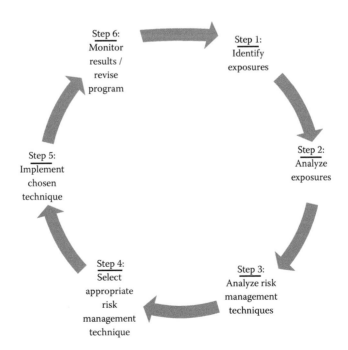

FIGURE 21   The country risk management process.

country's history in attracting FDI, as noted in Figure 23, which shows that China has been much more successful at it.

There are, of course, an enormous number of indicators one can use to make a determination about whether a country is a desirable place in which to trade or invest; not surprisingly, most of the more commonly used indicators are quantitative in nature. Depending on which indicators one chooses to use, the results may be quite different. For example, looking at the projected working-age population of China and India, as shown in Figure 24, one could conclude that China's workforce has peaked, workers are becoming scarcer, and labor costs will rise. This will probably only exacerbate one of the biggest problems employers in China face today: an inability to keep

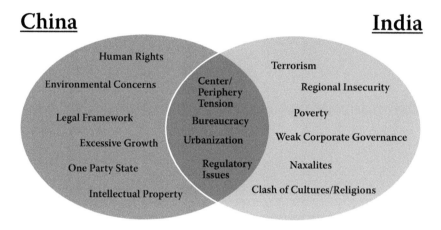

FIGURE 22 Comparing China and India's investment climates.

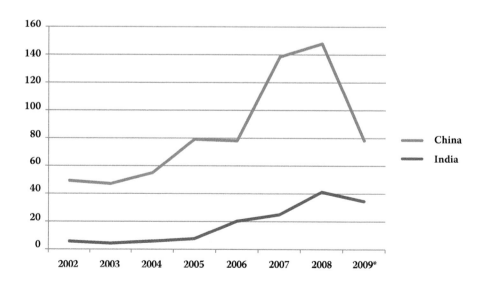

FIGURE 23 FDI in China and India (2002–2009). (From http://www.miga.org/documents/WIPR10ebook.pdf; 2009: estimate.)

talented workers because they are lured away by higher wages at other firms. India's labor force may not peak until 30 years after China's does, but a host of problems may arise in the interim, such as increasing competition for workers and what may become increased regulation in the labor market, resulting in more onerous terms of employment for employers. Any number of other interpretations could be added to interpreting the graph.

India has a long way to go to reach the stage of economic development China has achieved on a per-capita income basis. As noted in Figure 25, India is about where China was 10 years ago. This implies a lot of growing

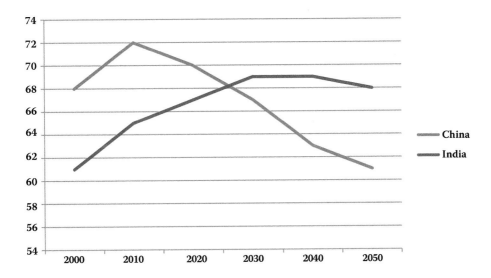

FIGURE 24 **Projected working-age populations: 2000–2050 (ages 15–64). (From http://iussp2005.princeton.edu/download.aspx?submissionId=50865, p. 39.)**

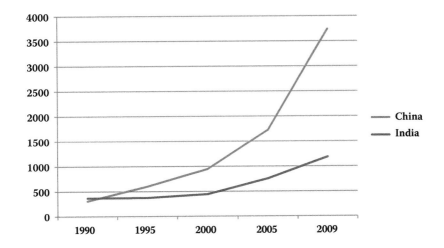

FIGURE 25 **Real GDP per capita during takeoff (1990–2009). (From http://www. google.com/publicdata?ds=wb-wdi&met_y=ny_gdp_pcap_cd&idim=country:CAN &dl=en&hl=en&q=gdp+per+capita)**

pains for India along the way, which any business will want to bear in mind when considering investing in India. Clearly, as was the case with China, India holds great promise as an investment destination, but also teething pains for some time to come.

Any organization attempting to make sense of the vast amount of information available to it regarding potential risk and reward when trading and investing abroad will introduce its own biases and preferences in the course of producing a country ranking or when making a decision. This includes the country risk information providers and ratings agencies. Figure 26 compares the ratings of 20 countries from a country risk information provider with that of a rating agency, with the lowest rankings being the highest country risk (the ratings agency risk scores are multiplied by a factor of 10 to allow for similar comparison).

What is striking is not only the disparity in country risk ratings between the two, but also the relative uniformity of the information provider's rankings: 16 of the 20 rankings fall in the 60–80 range. The information provider's rating does not appear to have the same depth as that of the rating agency and appears to have utilized fewer factors to arrive at its ratings.

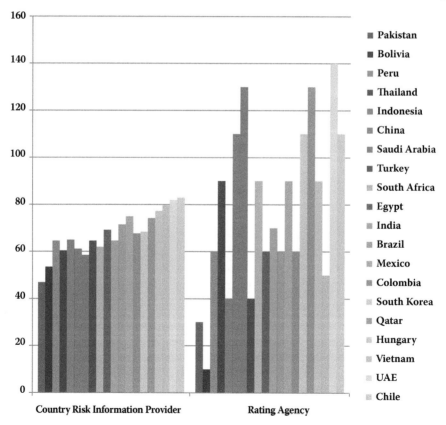

FIGURE 26   Selected country ratings of a country risk information provider and rating agency (rating agency on a weighted scale to allow for comparison).

It also does not appear to punish countries with lower ratings by dropping them very low on the rating scale; the lowest rated country, Pakistan, achieves a rating of 44 (high risk). This provider's rating scale ranges from 44 to 84, or a 40-point spread out of 100. By comparison, the rating agency ratings range from 10 for Bolivia to 150 for the United Arab Emirates—a 140-point spread. This demonstrates just how different the risk scale and result can be depending on the methodology used.

Figure 27 compares the rankings of the same country risk information provider used in the previous example (provider "A") with that of another country risk information provider (provider "B"). This comparison also reveals some surprising differences. Provider A again rates in a relatively narrow range, given the spread of countries, with a low of 46 for Vietnam and a high of 75 for Chile. Provider B rates in a slightly higher range, with Pakistan as the low point on its scale at 44 and Chile as the high point at 84, but has much greater variation among other countries. Among the biggest variations between the two providers are Vietnam (46 vs. 79), Hungary (47 vs. 79), and Turkey (51 vs. 69). Provider A presumably overweights some factors and underweights others, which would account for the absence of low lows and high highs.

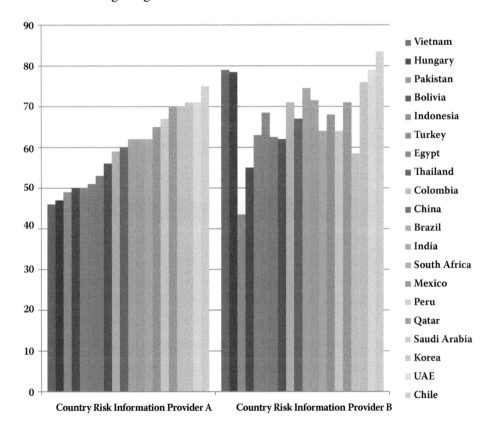

FIGURE 27 Selected country ratings of two country risk information providers.

Selecting Country Risk Management Tools

So, how is one supposed to make sense of it all? Some of the best analysts in the country risk management business clearly disagree about relative risks, weights, and measures; if they all agreed, there would presumably be little reason to use any of them. Yet, this also means most of them will be wrong much of the time. The key is to craft a country risk management program that meets your organization's specific needs while utilizing information in which you have confidence. One of the best ways to achieve that is to use information from a plethora of sources, toss out the "fringe" viewpoints, and concentrate on what they all seem to be saying.

A good place to start is to create a common platform for classifying all the countries where you may be doing business, and an easy way to do that is simply to categorize them by number and color, based on a composite of information sources. You may wish to subscribe to several information providers, create a weight for their rankings (which allows for comparison), and assign a number corresponding to a color for them, per Figure 28, which uses green/higher numbers to identify countries of lower risk and red/lower numbers to show higher risk. Using a color-coded system also helps communicate the level of risk in a universally understood manner.

To determine whether a country may need to be listed as "red," consider the following parameters:

- Is the country known to be fully compliant with international law?
- Are there any outstanding embargoes imposed by the United Nations or individual states? Is there a history of embargoes?
- Is the country labeled as or has it ever been labeled as a state sponsor of terrorism?

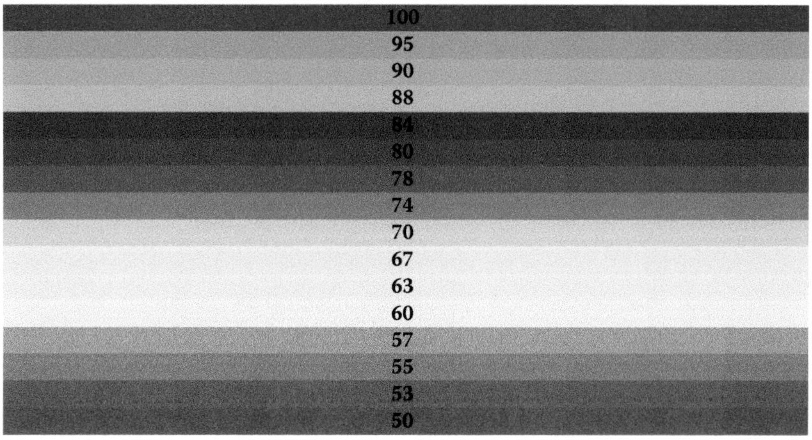

FIGURE 28   Country classification by number and color.

- Does it produce chemical, biological, or nuclear weapons?
- Does it produce military- or defense-related items; if so, does it sell such items to any country that could result in its being labeled either an illegal arms shipper or a transit point for illegal arms?
- Have any financial restrictions been placed on the country?
- Is travel prohibited to or from that country; if so, by whom and why?

You may wish to establish cut-off points for country approvals, wherein, for example, any country ranked above 90 would gain automatic managerial approval and any country below 50 would automatically fall into the "forbidden zone." Countries could also simply be assigned a color or a number, instead of both. Some examples of how countries might be categorized by color are:

- *Green*: Australia, Canada, United Kingdom
- *Blue*: Chile, Malaysia, South Africa
- *Yellow*: Costa Rica, Jordan, Mauritius
- *Orange*: Bangladesh, Ecuador, Ivory Coast
- *Red*: Iran, North Korea, Venezuela

Three other simple qualitative approaches are:

- Two options for a simple, grade-based rating scheme (Table 8, which depicts lower risk in the "A" category and higher risk in the "C" category),
- Listing risks and mitigants for a specific transaction and considering their comparative costs and benefits (Table 9), and
- Measuring event probability (Table 10).

Three additional types of approaches using color coding may be based strictly on qualitative measures. In the example in Table 11, five colors are used to rate the relative risk to project operations, physical assets, and financial impact, while in Table 12, letter ratings correspond to general definitions of country risk. Table 13 rates risk by number, potential impact, and color.

TABLE 8 Two Grade-Based Rating Options

Letter option A	Letter option B
Aaa	AAA
Aa	AA
A	A
Baa	BBB
Ba	BB
B	B
Caa	CCC
Ca	CC
C	C

TABLE 9 Risks versus Mitigants for Turkey

Risks	Mitigants
• Domestic: pro- versus anti-Islamic political parties/population and a lengthy secessionist movement from the PKK (Kurdish Worker's Party).	• A radical change of government is not expected for the foreseeable future.
• International: lengthy battle for accession to the EU; its engagement of the PKK/Iraqi Kurdish movement puts it on a collision course with EU/US foreign policy.	• All ratings agencies consider Turkey to be stable.
• It is likely that the ruling AK Party will remain a majority political force for some time to come. A future coalition government could result in weakened fiscal discipline, reduced incentive to promote economic and political reform, and enhanced political instability.	• Turkey is a growing force in regional politics.
	• The treasury extended the average life of foreign debt maturities, easing pressure on the budget and ensuring smooth debt repayment going forward.
• There is an increased risk of nationalism as the driver of foreign policy. If Iraq implodes, Turkey intervenes to address the Kurdish issue across its border.	• FDI flows are growing at a rapid pace.
• Turkey has an alarmingly high current account deficit, which, along with a recent decline in economic growth, makes the lira vulnerable to shifts in investor sentiment.	• Recent economic performance has made the country less vulnerable to adverse economic impacts. The current government is expected to continue with economic reforms, generating large budget surpluses, assisted by higher revenue generation.
• Rising interest rates are choking private consumption and investment. Increased political and/or social turmoil could drive interest rates even higher.	• Turkey weathered the financial crisis well and is similarly well positioned to continue on a path of economic growth, peace, and stability.
• Turkey remains vulnerable to capital flight.	
• Instability could provoke a strong lira depreciation and a sharp correction in domestic and external asset prices.	
• If the Assad government in Syria implodes, Turkey may be negatively impacted as a result of an inflow of refugees and possible strengthening of Turkish Kurds.	

TABLE 10 Measuring Event Probability

Grade	Probability	Description
E	Certain	Event always occurs.
D	Likely	Event will occur in most circumstances.
C	Possible	Event could occur at some point in the future.
B	Unlikely	Event is less likely to occur.
A	Rare	Event would only occur under exceptional circumstances.

Economic Measures

TABLE 11 Qualitative Assessment by Color Coding and Impact

Risk rating	Level of risk	Operational impact	Physical asset impact	Financial impact
1	Negligible	Little likelihood of interruption	No meaningful likelihood of loss or damage to property	Low chance of any impact
2	Minor	Interruption, but little impact	May or may not require an insurance claim	Impact will not affect financial performance
3	Moderate	Partial shutdown	Requires an insurance claim to repair damage	Financial performance impacted
4	Significant	Long-term shutdown	Damage may or may not be repairable	Severe impact on the bottom line
5	Extreme	Permanent cessation of operations	Damage not repairable; asset must be abandoned.	Could result in significant impact on corporate performance

The range of quantitative measures available to assess economic risk seems

TABLE 12 Letter Ratings with General Definitions of Country Risk

Letter rating	Level of risk
A	Industrialized economy with negligible risk of political instability or liquidity crisis; a strong ability to withstand economic crisis
B	A developed economy with low political or economic risk
C	A country with structural weakness and moderate risk of either political or economic distress
D	A developing economy with a range of structural weaknesses and a high risk of political or economic distress
E	A failed or failing state prone to political and economic instability; no ability to withstand economic distress

endless and, indeed, there are hundreds or even thousands of ratios, comparisons, and indices that could be used. Table 14 lists some of the most commonly used among them.

There are numerous quantitative variations on a theme that can add depth to an analytical framework. Naturally, the objective will determine which variable is being measured, and how. Here are some examples of different variables and how they can be used:

- Economic growth
  - Gross domestic product (GDP) growth versus oil demand growth
  - Growth in industrial production
  - Foreign capital as a share of total investment
  - Household and corporate liquidity
  - Urban versus rural population growth
  - Population growth by age
  - Projected labor force growth

- Economic health
  - Gross domestic savings as a percentage of GDP
  - Expenditure on health and education as a percentage of GDP
  - Military expenditures as a percentage of GDP
  - Labor force as a percentage of the total population
  - Government/provincial/municipality fiscal deficit

TABLE 13 Impact Matrix Using Number, Impact, and Color Ratings

Type of risk	Letter rating	Impact rating	Color rating
Payment default	D	5	
Coup d'état	C	3	
Terrorism	B	2	
Civil disturbance	B	2	
Natural disaster	C	3	

TABLE 14 Commonly Used Quantitative Economic Measures

Nominal GDP	Real GDP growth	GDP per capita	GDP by sector
GDP by expenditure	Debt service/GDP	Stock of M1	Stock of M2
Foreign exchange rate	Months of import cover	Medium- and long-term payments due	Short-term debt due
Inward FDI levels	Inflation rate	Consumer price index	Current account balance
Foreign exchange reserves	Interest rates	Budget balance	FDI by industry

- Government expenditure by municipality, province, or state
- Source and allocation of funds by financial industry
- A country's share of global projection for a given commodity or product
- Destination of and dependence on exports

- Power sector
  - Sources of demand for power (by economic sector)
  - Amounts of energy used to generate GDP growth
  - Power generation capacity growth and utilization hours
  - Power demand forecast and generation mix
  - Variation in energy prices by province or city

Mapping Out a Country Risk Analysis Methodology

In developing a methodology best suited for your organization or purpose, it is useful first to determine the risk attributes/indicators that should be included. An easy way to do this is to identify which indicators are likely to apply to the majority of countries to be included in the framework. This can be as general or specific as necessary. The example in Figure 29 includes both broad and narrow topics.

Let us examine some of the subtopics that might be included. These are meant to be suggestive rather than comprehensive in nature. The topics that a specific firm may wish to include will be dependent on the scope and nature of its international operations; however, much of what is listed here will apply to many types of trade transactions and investments:

- Economic environment
  - Degree of economic openness

FIGURE 29 Examples of risk attributes/indicators for inclusion in an analytical methodology.

- Monetary stability
- External financing needs
- Fiscal imbalance

- Trade and investment climate
  - Import/export restrictions
  - Capital controls
  - Protectionism
  - Embargoes
  - Shifting regulatory climate

- Financial considerations
  - Availability of consumer credit
  - Excessive growth in national debt
  - Ability to convert/transfer currency freely

- Local environment
  - Prone to natural disasters
  - Endemic corruption
  - Labor unrest
  - Existence of civil society

- Developmental issues
  - Adequacy of infrastructure
  - Degree of poverty
  - Sufficiency of income levels
  - Progress toward middle income or developed country status

- Cultural issues
  - Orientation toward Western values
  - Work ethic
  - History of ethnic conflict
  - Degree of homogeneousness of population

- Geostrategic considerations
  - Position/perceived value on the global political stage
  - Relationship/centrality to existing or future regional conflicts
  - Perceived military value in a regional conflict

- Social environment
  - Friendliness toward people from other cultures
  - International orientation
  - Active civil society influence

- Political stability
  - Degree of political competition

- Regularity of elections
- Political legitimacy
- Frequency of changes in government

- Personnel risks
  - Mobility of labor force
  - Employment regulations
  - Staffing regulations
  - Labor relations
  - Legal environment (enforceability of contracts, rule of law)

- Currency risks
  - Nature of conversion/transfer regime
  - Existence of wide fluctuations in currency value
  - Vulnerability to exogenous shocks

- Legal/regulatory risks
  - Rule of law
  - Sanctity of contracts
  - Central bank independence
  - Judiciary independence
  - Presence of nepotism/corruption

- Asset risks
  - Local ownership requirements
  - Control issues (designated board seats)
  - Joint venture partner
  - Intellectual property protection

- Supply/delivery risks
  - Vulnerability of critical raw materials
  - History of supply interruption
  - Reliability of transportation into and out of the country

- Operational risks
  - Domestic participation requirements
  - Denial of permits or licenses
  - Production quotas

- Security risks
  - Existence of civil war, insurrection, protracted conflict
  - History of cross-border conflict
  - Vulnerability of location of specific project/transaction
  - High-profile nature of project/transaction
  - Security protocol/procedures at project site

Alternative Measures of Country Risk

A variety of other measures can be used to gain insight into the relative risk level of an economy or society. However, it is often the case that more widely used means of measuring such risk lack texture or fail to take into account important considerations in the assessment of risk. Thus, the following alternative measures of country risk can be a crucial subcomponent of arriving at a thorough analysis.

Corruption Perceptions Index

The best known indicator for perceived corruption is the Corruption Perceptions Index of Transparency International (TI), which is based on 13 independent surveys and measures public sector corruption in 178 countries. Unstable governments with a history of conflict score the worst. The top three and bottom three countries are listed in Table 15.

No country is immune from corruption and the level of corruption is an indication also of the level of good governance in a country. Many highly developed countries are affected by corruption, based primarily upon private sector corruption in business. Yet it is among the poorest and most fragile countries where corruption takes its largest toll in the form of violence and poverty enhancement.

Democracy Index

The Democracy Index is compiled by the Economist Intelligence Unit and measures the state of democracy in 167 countries based on 60 indicators from five categories: civil liberties, the electoral process/pluralism, the functioning of government, political culture, and political participation. On a 10-point scale (10 being the greatest democracy and 0 being the least), Norway ranked highest and North Korea the lowest. As noted in Map 1, the

TABLE 15 Top and Bottom Three Countries in TI's 2010 Rankings

Country	Ranking
Denmark	9.3
New Zealand	9.3
Singapore	9.3
Afghanistan	1.4
Myanmar	1.4
Somalia	1.1

Note: 10 = highly clean; 0 = highly corrupt.

countries included in the index are categorized either as full democracies, flawed democracies, hybrid regimes, or authoritarian regimes.

Freedom in the World

Freedom House is an independent watchdog organization supporting the expansion of freedom around the world that monitors freedom and advocates for democracy and human rights globally. Freedom House publishes the results of an annual survey of global political rights and civil liberties, which were in decline for the fifth consecutive year in 2010—the longest period of consecutive declines in relative freedom in the almost 40-year history of the report. This is a sign that although democracy may be on the march in the Middle East and North Africa, overall, it has been on the decline. Freedom House ranks political rights and civil liberties on a seven-point scale, with one being the most free and seven being the least free, as illustrated in Table 16.

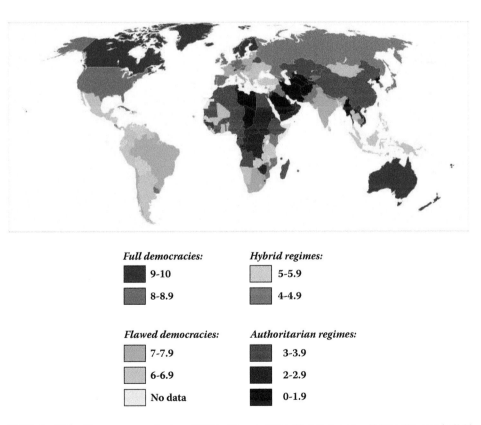

Full democracies:
- 9-10
- 8-8.9

Hybrid regimes:
- 5-5.9
- 4-4.9

Flawed democracies:
- 7-7.9
- 6-6.9
- No data

Authoritarian regimes:
- 3-3.9
- 2-2.9
- 0-1.9

MAP 1   The Democracy Index 2010. (From http://commons.wikimedia.org/wiki/ File:Democracy_Index_2010_green_and_red.png)

TABLE 16 Freedom in the World 2011: The Examples of France and Turkmenistan

Country	Freedom status	Political rights[a]	Civil liberties[a]
France	Free	1	1
Turkmenistan	Not Free	7	7

Source: http://www.freedomhouse.org/images/File/fiw/ FIW_2011_Booklet.pdf

[a] On a seven-point scale.

Gini Coefficient[2]

The Gini coefficient is used to measure social inequality on a scale of zero to one, with zero being total equality and one being total inequality. It is commonly used to measure income or wealth and can say a lot about underlying tension in a society. If inequality is perceived to be high, there is a good chance of underlying social tension, which can manifest itself in a variety of possible ways, such as through violent crime or civil strife. Map 2 is a Gini coefficient heat map compiled by the CIA in 2009.

It is interesting to note that the countries with highest perceived inequality are not necessarily the poorest (South Africa, for example), that Brazil is in the next tier down (i.e., the next highest perceived inequality), and that the United States and China are in the third tier from the top. On this basis,

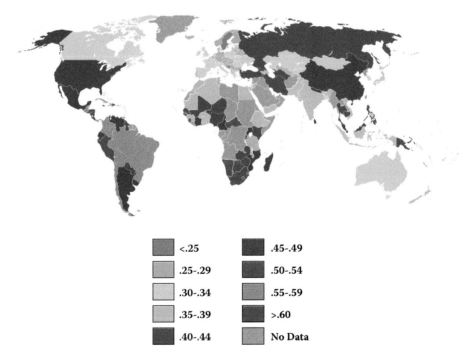

<.25		.45-.49	
.25-.29		.50-.54	
.30-.34		.55-.59	
.35-.39		>.60	
.40-.44		No Data	

MAP 2 The Gini coefficient. (From http://en.wikipedia.org/wiki/File:Gini_Coefficient_World_CIA_Report_2009.png)

it would appear that the Chinese government's fear of social instability is only partly well founded.

Global Peace Index

The Global Peace Index is produced by the Institute for Economics and Peace and measures the relative peacefulness of nations. It is developed in consultation with a panel of international experts from think tanks with data collected and collated by the Economist Intelligence Unit. It is the first index to rank countries globally on this basis. The index includes 153 countries and addresses such factors as a country's external conflicts, military expenditures, and levels of crime and violence, as noted in Map 3. The most peaceful countries score below 1600; the least peaceful countries (implying higher risk) score above 3,100.

Human Development Index

Based on the human development reports of the United Nations Human Development Program, the Human Development Index (HDI) ranks countries based on a combination of education levels, literacy rate, years of schooling, income, life expectancy, and standards of living—or their perceived level of "human development"—from low to high. In essence, it measures overall well-being and is used to classify countries as underdeveloped, developing, or developed (see Maps 4 and 5). The index rates countries on a one-point scale, with higher numbers meaning more developed and lower numbers meaning less developed. The least developed countries using this index tend to be in Africa. The HDI can also be used to classify states or

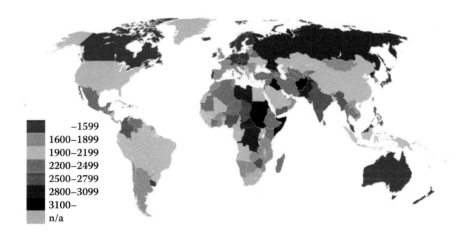

MAP 3 The Global Peace Index 2011. (From http://en.wikipedia.org/wiki/File: Global_Peace_Index_2011.svg)

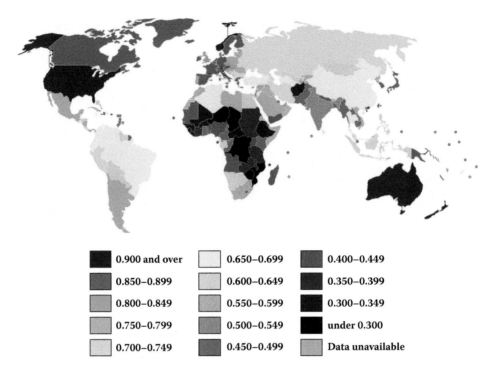

■ 0.900 and over	□ 0.650–0.699	■ 0.400–0.449
■ 0.850–0.899	■ 0.600–0.649	■ 0.350–0.399
■ 0.800–0.849	■ 0.550–0.599	■ 0.300–0.349
■ 0.750–0.799	■ 0.500–0.549	■ under 0.300
■ 0.700–0.749	■ 0.450–0.499	■ Data unavailable

MAP 4 The Human Development Index. (Based on 2010 data, published November 4, 2010.) (From http://en.wikipedia.org/wiki/File:UN_Human_Development_Report_2010_1.PNG)

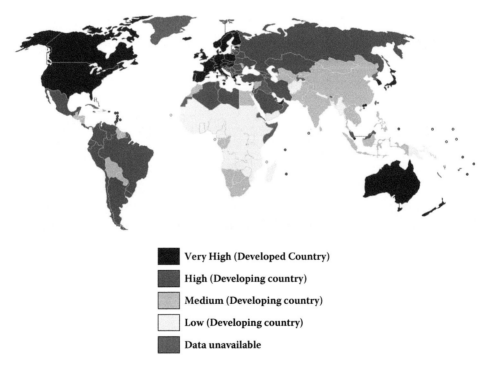

■ Very High (Developed Country)

■ High (Developing country)

■ Medium (Developing country)

□ Low (Developing country)

■ Data unavailable

MAP 5 The Human Development Index, category by country (2010 data). (From 10_UN_Human_Development_Report_Quartiles_.png)

provinces and cities. The methodology may be found at: http://en.wikipedia.org/wiki/Human_Development_Index.

Youth Unemployment

Measuring the level of unemployment among a country's youth is a leading risk indicator and can provide insight into where there may be trouble down the road. A good sample population is 18 to 30 year olds, representing high school and college graduates through young people in their 20s. A useful example here is the case of Iraq. For all the progress Iraq has made since 2003, it has many lingering problems, of course. One of the biggest is that of youth unemployment, which translates into disaffection.

A 2010 study[3] in Iraq warned of the dangers of high unemployment among new graduates and the lack of new investment in the country to offset new entrants in the labor force. The study noted that approximately 78% of those who were unemployed were between the ages of 18 and 30. If 78% of new graduates in the UK or Canada were unemployed, there would be serious visible social impacts and a means for the government to do something about it. But when such a problem occurs in a country like Iraq, it goes largely unnoticed by the rest of the world and the government is ill equipped to do much about it. It can only do so much to try to attract new investment, battle insurgents, and manage its oil revenue. The very fact that unemployment among 18 to 30 year olds is so high in an oil-producing country such as Iraq is a statement in itself of how improperly oil revenues are managed and the level of corruption in the society. New graduates' prospects are extremely poor in Iraq, which means the opportunity for social upheaval is high.

Conclusion

The variety of quantitative and qualitative tools within any country risk analyst's reach can be daunting. Each of them contains biases and subjectivity. The challenge is first to identify the issues to be addressed and the tools that are best suited to enable one to do so. If possible, it is best to have a healthy mix of quantitative and qualitative measures for almost any inquiry, as it adds depth and texture to the process. Numbers alone cannot provide that. In the end, the interpretive process can be only as good as the person who creates the analysis. Be prepared to think outside the box, ask probing questions, and go to the right sources to get the right answers. Chances are that the right answer will be obtained through creative thinking. As with any analytical process, experience is ultimately the best teacher.

Notes

1. http://www.quotationspage.com/quote/26950.html
2. A coefficient is a multiplier or factor that measures a property – in this case, inequality.
3. http://currencynewshound.wordpress.com/2011/05/08/economists-warn-of-unemployment-in-iraq/

Chapter 5

Political Risk Insurance[1]

In crises, the most daring course is often the safest.

Henry Kissinger[2]

What Is Political Risk Insurance?

Political risk insurance (PRI) is a specialized line of insurance that protects traders, investors, and lenders against noncommercial risks that interfere in the successful completion of trade contracts, the ability to own or operate investments successfully, or to service debt under the terms of a loan agreement. In the context of PRI, political risks are arbitrary or discriminatory actions, taken by home or host governments, political groups, or individuals, that have an adverse impact on international trade or investment transactions. Although such actions may be commercially motivated, quite often they are politically inspired. Their result is often the same: At a minimum, they can disrupt business operations; at worst, they can cause a business to shut down permanently.

To give you a better idea of what I mean, let me share with you some of the transactions I was asked to underwrite while I worked as a PRI underwriter. I was once asked by a US company to insure a shipment of missile gyroscopes it intended to sell to the office of the prime minister of India. I was not too keen on insuring that shipment against the risk that it would not make it to the prime minister's office because I thought the risk that the US State Department would revoke the shipper's export license was too high. (It was amazing to me that the State Department ever issued an export license for the transaction in the first place, given the sensitivity of missile technology in the subcontinent.) The license was in fact revoked, and the shipment never occurred.

I was asked to insure a shipment of wheat headed for southern Sudan on behalf of a Christian charity. I did not like that one because I thought the risk that rebels in Sudan's south would attack the convoy delivering the wheat was too high. However, I did insure scores of cross-border trade and investment transactions that I believed were likely to succeed and get paid. Some examples include power plants, mines, and telecommunication projects that employed thousands of people, paid hundreds of millions of dollars in taxes to the host governments, and contributed significantly to the development process.

One of the most interesting trade transactions I was ever asked to insure was the sale of cigarette rolling papers to Iraq. The seller in this case was a large cigarette manufacturer, based in the United States, which saw an opportunity to make some money. It was 1988 and Iraq was at war with Iran. The war had been going on for many years and hundreds of thousands of soldiers on both sides had been killed. Saddam Hussein and Ayatollah Khomeini (Iran's leader at the time) were desperate to win the war, not only to put an end to the killing, but also to salvage their prestige and satisfy their territorial ambitions. One of the best ways to keep troop morale up (apart from winning battles) is to provide them with basic needs. In wartime, when a soldier has little else to rely on, cigarettes become a precious commodity. I therefore agreed to insure that transaction because I thought that there was an excellent chance Saddam would pay for those rolling papers. If he did not, the exporter in question would not sell to him again and word would quickly spread that he was not paying his bills for such items. I reasoned that the average man in the trenches would value a cigarette more than just about anything. I was right. I insured the exporter against nonpayment, and Saddam paid his bill.

For that insurance, the exporter could have paid a premium rate of as much as 25% per annum (i.e., 25% of the value of the shipment—the prevailing market rate for Iraqi payment risk during the war). The premium was paid without hesitation, even though it was very expensive, because that exporter knew that at the end of the day, he would get paid, either by Saddam or by the company I worked for. The markup on that rolling paper was tremendous—hundreds of percentage points—so the exporter still made a handsome profit.

The same was true for the pharmaceutical manufacturer desiring to export antibiotics to Saddam. Its markup was equally high (300%) so a 25% premium meant it would make 275% profit. By purchasing the insurance, it was in a no-lose situation. That is how many businesses justify purchasing PRI. There was no way either of these companies would have exported their products to Iraq in the absence of the insurance. With the insurance, there was no way they would not have shipped the product.

In the context of PRI, political risk can take many forms: the risk that an exporter cannot ship a product or does not get paid, the risk that a dissident political force blows up a foreign-owned asset, or the risk that a government does not have enough foreign exchange to permit a foreign investor to repatriate its dividends, profits, or share capital. What these scenarios all have in common is that noncommercial actions are the root of the problem. Indeed, PRI does not, by definition, cover commercial risks, which are the responsibility of the trader, investor, or financier.

Political actions are unpredictable. They lack consistency. Uncertainty about the future created by political risks affects more international business transactions than ever before, as more and more companies may decide not to invest in or trade with a country with which they are unfamiliar. Yet, there is more trade and investment going on around the world than ever before and the need for protection against the unknown is greater than ever before. This is why PRI has become an indispensable tool for so many international businesses: It allows them to operate abroad without fear of the unknown.

The preceding examples illustrate how varied international trade and investment transactions can be, as well as how risky. However, risk is in the eye of the beholder. Most companies purchase PRI for balance sheet protection. Simply put, by purchasing the insurance, they are protecting their company against losses that could negatively impact corporate fiscal performance. Whether a company purchases PRI very often depends on its risk management philosophy. Some companies believe that every transaction should be insured and view it as a cost of doing business. Some think that no transaction should be insured, rationalizing their decision by believing that, if a country is too risky to invest or trade in, they would not be doing business there in the first place. Still other companies insure against political risks on an "adverse selection" basis—that is, only in those countries they view as truly risky. There is no right or wrong way to view how to utilize PRI. What matters is what is consistent with a company's risk management philosophy.

The risk that an international business will encounter some form of loss due to political causes is high, particularly if it trades or invests in the developing world. That is not to say, of course, that there is no political risk implied when doing business in developed countries. There is no country on earth where political risks do not exist. For example, a US investor might think that Mozambique is a risky place to invest, but an investor from Syria might believe the United States is a risky place to invest. The US government has frozen the assets of numerous governments and individuals, passed laws that may make it more difficult to operate a business, and established an extremely onerous regulatory environment—particularly following the Great Recession.

Any country may be subject to arbitrary changes in law or actions taken by a government, particularly in difficult economic times or when elections occur. As an example, let us say you have invested in a mine in Canada and your operation has gone smoothly for several years. The Canadian economy then starts to go sour as an election year approaches. As the owner of the mine, you decide you need to lay off a substantial portion of your workforce in order to remain viable. Your mine just happens to be in an important province that the current ruling party believes it must win in order to win the national election. Learning of your plans, the government nationalizes your mine to prevent you from laying off the workers, removing the possibly negative impact such an action could have on its ability to carry the province in the election. This is an example of how a seemingly benign action on the part of an investor can lead to a politically risky scenario.

The risk that a bilateral diplomatic conflict could impact your business is also very real. There are numerous well known examples of mass expropriations of US investments—following the fall of South Vietnam, the ouster of Anastasio Somoza in Nicaragua, and the fall of the Shah in Iran. More recently, Bolivia nationalized many oil and gas investments in 2006 and the power sector in 2010, and the Ivory Coast nationalized cocoa production facilities in 2011.

If you are an individual investor or a multinational corporation, there is a reasonable chance that if you do business abroad with any regularity, you may get caught up in some form of diplomatic tiff or bureaucratic nightmare in your home country or in a host country, and it can cost you money. While some of the interplay between nations retains an emphasis on the exercise of military and political power, acquiring and utilizing economic power and competitive advantage has become more prominent. The rise of economic nationalism, ethnic turmoil, and a propensity toward separatism have certainly greatly complicated the landscape, while national economic battle lines are being drawn with greater frequency by nations formerly considered to be peripheral players.

As the twenty-first century's political and economic order continues to evolve, the risks inherent in trading, investing, and lending abroad will grow, as will economic nationalism, thus causing future trade disputes and prompting harsher retaliatory responses. With the creation of each new state or the election of each new government, a new set of foreign trade and investment regulations may be adopted, with the potential to impact existing contracts or investments or those being planned adversely.

Who Needs PRI?

Any organization whose balance sheet cannot readily absorb an unanticipated financial loss certainly could use PRI. This can be the largest corporation or the smallest exporter. Any entity that needs to secure financing also may benefit from PRI because it may find that it is much easier to obtain financing for a transaction. Many financial institutions will not provide project financing without it, and having PRI may reduce the cost of capital, as financial institutions may provide lending at a lower interest rate if PRI is in place. Obviously, if you are doing business in politically or economically unstable environments, PRI is a good thing to have, as it is if you are trading or investing with new partners, buyers, or sellers. The largest Fortune 500 companies, multinational corporations, defense contractors, and financial institutions purchase PRI, as do the smallest foreign investors, leasing companies, franchisers, importers, exporters, and credit-based sellers.

One of the by-products of this insurance is that, if all goes well, everyone wins. The exporter; importer; investor; lender; credit-based seller; the end-user receiving the export, import, or investment; and the host country all win. The developmental benefits associated with this insurance are significant. International business is a two-way street; PRI simply facilitates cross-border capital flow. If, at the end of the day, the use of PRI will help you to gain additional market share, achieve a long-sought business objective, or transform your corporate risk management philosophy, you will come to recognize the value of this highly specialized line of insurance.

An Overview of Investment Insurance

There are two broad types of PRI: *trade* coverages and *investment* coverages. For a trader, the objective of these coverages is to ensure that goods are successfully shipped to a destination and that payment is received. Trade coverages tend to have a short life span—anywhere from a few days to perhaps 2 years. Investment coverages, by contrast, have a much longer life span and take into account the long-term orientation of equity investments. The objective of the investment coverages is to ensure that a business may be operated as originally proposed under the terms of an investment agreement, a joint venture contract, or an agreement with the host government.

Although trade coverages encompass the lion's share of PRI by volume (since more trade transactions occur on a daily basis than investments), the increased flow of foreign capital into developing countries over the past 20 years has meant that cross-border investment is often a subject of PRI. Not only are more countries interested in receiving FDI, but also more companies are seeking enhanced profits and market share by investing abroad. The following description of investment coverages is by no means intended to be all inclusive. As PRI may be tailored to address almost any scenario, it would be beyond the scope of this chapter to review all of the conceivable forms and combinations of coverage. Rather, what follows is a broad-based description of the most commonly utilized investment coverages.

Expropriation

While less common today than in the 1970s, the impact of an expropriatory action can be devastating, causing a company to cease operations overnight. Governments expropriate foreign assets for a variety of reasons. It may be because of a deterioration in bilateral relations between two countries, in retaliation for unilateral actions taken by one country against another, in response to the imposition of sanctions by the international community, to protect an infant industry, or simply to divert a population's attention away from domestic affairs. The ability to expropriate is a powerful tool every government has in its arsenal of international weapons.

Often referred to among underwriters as confiscation, expropriation, nationalization, and deprivation (CEND) coverage, expropriation coverage (as it is commonly known) protects against partial or total loss of an investment as a result of actions taken by a host government that may reduce or eliminate a foreign investor's ownership of, control over, or rights over an insured investment. Under international law, governments have a right to seize a foreign-owned asset, but by law they must:

- not violate any contractual agreements between the government and the investor
- take the action in accordance with due process
- take only nondiscriminatory action
- take action only for a public purpose
- provide adequate, prompt, and fair compensation to the investor (expropriation insurance is designed to reimburse the investor if such compensation is not received)

If a government is inclined to expropriate a foreign-owned asset, it may not be inclined to compensate an investor following such action, or it may not have the money to do so. One notable example occurred with an oil exploration and production company in Peru in the 1980s. Its off-shore oil platforms were expropriated and the company obtained a $100+ million payout from an insurer. The insurer then turned to the Peruvian government for payment, since it was subrogated to the investor's assets. The government, of course, did not have that kind of money to spare, so the insurance company and government agreed that payment would occur over a number of years via revenue derived from the government's sale of oil to the international markets.

The expropriation of half of the Kuwaiti Airways fleet by Iraq at the beginning of the Gulf War in August 1991 is another example of the value of the insurance. Fortunately for the Kuwaiti government, it had a PRI contract protecting it against aircraft repossession, which resulted in reimbursement for approximately $230 million within 30 days of the action. The insurer was later able to secure repayment through acquisition and sale of the aircraft after the war was over.

There are four major types of expropriatory actions:

- *Formal:* this type of expropriation occurs when a government seizes an asset and does not adequately compensate the investor. This typically happens when a change of government occurs and the new government acts either to retaliate against interests aligned with the previous government or to make good on promises to attack foreign investors. The political or economic situation in a host country may also encourage an existing government to seize foreign-owned assets. In the earlier example, if a foreign-owned mine is about to terminate several thousand workers because economic conditions prevent the mine from operating profitably, a government may expropriate the mine to prevent the loss of jobs.
- *Forced sale of assets:* a foreign investor may be forced to sell its assets because economic or political conditions make it difficult to control or operate the investment. The host government may take an action making it impossible to operate the investment profitably. It could also pass a law requiring the sale of foreign-owned assets.
- *Selective action/deprivation:* an action or a series of actions interfere in the investor's fundamental ownership rights. This could be anything from a discriminatory action affecting only foreign investors to host government cancellation of an import license, which prevents a firm from importing the critical raw materials it requires to operate a manufacturing facility.
- *Other types:* events such as tax disputes or blocked bank accounts can trigger the coverage in certain instances.

Expropriation coverage addresses a law, order, decree, or administrative action made by a governing authority or a nongovernmental authority in de facto control of a portion of a country where the expropriatory action occurred. For example, in the 1980s in El Salvador, it was widely acknowledged that the guerrillas fighting the government of El Salvador controlled the eastern third of the country. If the guerrillas seized a foreign-owned factory in that part of the country, most insurers would have considered that to be an insurable event. The same could be said of the Tamil Tigers (until they were defeated in 2009) in northern and eastern Sri Lanka or the former

Maoist rebels in most of Nepal (now, of course, the Maoists are the dominant legitimate political force in Nepal).

However, it is not just an outright seizure of an asset (known as "direct expropriation") that will trigger coverage. Interference in a company's ability to control or operate an investment, as described before, will also trigger coverage (this is referred to as "indirect" or "creeping" expropriation). The caveat here is that many insurers have lengthy waiting periods (the period of time one must wait after an event of loss has occurred before filing a claim, to determine whether the action is permanent and/or whether it may be resolved without filing a claim). Waiting periods may typically range from 90 to 365 days. Most underwriters believe that if an action has lasted for a full year, it is likely to be permanent. Depending on the host country, it is usually possible to obtain the coverage without a waiting period.

It is common for underwriters to compensate an insured for the net book value of the investment in question on the date prior to the expropriatory event. Some underwriters go through a more elaborate calculation to determine the amount of a claim payment (such as the original equity investment plus any retained earnings, inventory, and production equipment owned by the parent company; shareholder loans and loan guarantees between the parent company and subsidiary; and the net of accounts payable and receivable). Coverage is available also for mobile assets, inventory, and production equipment on a stand-alone basis. Claim payments are often based on the lesser of fair market value or replacement cost.

Expropriation coverage is widely available in the private sector on a 100% insured basis for amounts as large as $1 billion. Its cost is generally in the 0.25% to 1.0% per annum range for up to 5 years. Public sector underwriters charge a similar price for investments, but may provide coverage of no more than 90% of the investment's value.

There are a host of differences between the private and public sector underwriters; the biggest difference between the expropriation coverage provided by the private sector versus the public sector used to be the length of coverage. For many years, the private sector could provide coverage for no longer than 3–5 years at a time, due to reinsurance constraints.[3] A number of private sector underwriters now provide coverage of up to 15 years. Public sector underwriters have provided coverage up to 20 years routinely, primarily because they conclude agreements with host countries that protect both investor and insurer, making longer term coverage possible.

Forced Abandonment/Key Operator's Endangerment

These coverages are "add-ons" to basic expropriation coverage. Forced abandonment involves the insured being forced to leave its equipment in circumstances prejudicial to the safety and well-being of project staff, often following an order to leave a host country by a home country government. The coverage compensates the insured for the value of the equipment left behind. Key operator's endangerment coverage addresses the forced withdrawal of specialist personnel, without whom the venture cannot operate, as a result of the occurrence of war or strikes, riots, or civil commotion. It reimburses the insured for the cost of the asset in question, plus the cost of personnel evacuation.

Financed-Asset Nonrepossession

This specialized variant of expropriation coverage is available to protect financiers or lessors of assets such as commercial aircraft or shipping, where the asset is a fundamental part of the security package and an inability to repossess the asset is a serious problem. If the financier or lessor is concerned about country risk where the equipment is being used, nonrepossession insurance can mitigate the cross-border risk by providing coverage against acts of the foreign government (including expropriation) and interference or lack of assistance when the lessor or financier attempts to enforce its contractual right of repossession following a default under the loan or lease contract. Where repossession attempts are successful, coverage is also available against the failure of the foreign government to de-register or de-flag the asset.

Deprivation/Contingent Deprivation

Deprivation is an action taken by a host government that prevents the reexport of physical goods, inventory, production equipment, or other assets. Although these items may not have been seized by the government, the inability to relocate them makes them worthless. Should a host government fail to issue a license to reexport these assets, deprivation coverage would provide compensation for the value of the assets. Contingent deprivation takes this one step further. Should you be successful in exporting the assets, but the country where you wish to import the goods refuses to allow you to import them due to the cancellation of an import license or the imposition of an embargo, contingent deprivation coverage would provide compensation equivalent to the value of the assets.

Currency Inconvertibility/Nontransfer

If you are making an investment in another country, one thing you surely want to be able to do is bring your profits home. Next to expropriation coverage, currency inconvertibility (CI)/nontransfer coverage is the most commonly purchased form of investment insurance. CI protects against the inability to convert dividends, profits, fees, share capital, and loan proceeds from local currency to hard currency and, once converted, to transfer that hard currency out of the host country. CI is considered the riskiest form of investment insurance coverage because there are so many opportunities for a claim to arise.

CI coverage protects against two forms of currency blockage: *active* blockage and *passive* blockage:

- *Active blockage* is a law on the books of a host country that prevents conversion or transfer. A good example of this was Brazil in 1990, when the Collor administration banned all forms of conversion and transfer for domestic and foreign companies in an effort to prevent further decay in the value of the Brazilian currency. This obviously created huge problems for foreign companies, which could not pay their bills outside Brazil, pay their employees in hard currency, bring their profits home, or service their foreign currency debt. Many foreign companies suffered large losses as a result of this action. More recent examples include the Chinese and Malaysian governments restricting conversion and transfer of currency during the Asia Crisis.

- *Passive blockage* takes the form of an excessive delay in converting or transferring currency, either because the central bank (for example) does not process an application for conversion or transfer or because it takes too long to do so. Most insurers consider 90–180 days to be the benchmark for what is considered an acceptable maximum delay. In other words, if you go to the central bank, apply to convert currency, and it takes longer than 180 days to process the request, you would have grounds to file a claim (unless the insurer specifies a longer waiting period). CI does not cover currency fluctuations, devaluations, or preexisting conditions. So in the case of Brazil, if you had applied for the coverage after the restrictions had taken place, you would have been out of luck. (In general, insurers will not provide coverage for preexisting conditions.)

If you apply to convert currency and the government not only declines to convert the currency, but also refuses to give it back to you, you will usually not be able to file a CI claim. The reason is that most underwriters will only provide CI coverage if you can deliver the local currency to them. They will then take the currency to the host government or an outside entity and try to convert it after a claim has been paid. Public sector underwriters, in particular, almost always have an agreement with a host government that permits them to reprocess the local currency. This is possible because the public sector underwriters are owned and operated by the home country government, which may be able to use the local currency to support the operation of its embassy in the host country. In the case of the MIGA or the Overseas Private Investment Corporation (OPIC—the US government's PRI provider), for example, they may be able to use the currency to support a development project in the host country.

Two important points of clarification need to be made:

- If you cannot provide these underwriters with the local currency because the host government entity did not return it to you, they will have no basis on which to enforce their subrogation capabilities and will not pay a claim. For this reason, you should always at minimum insure against expropriation of funds (which protects against the seizure of monetary assets only) in conjunction with CI coverage, to prevent a problem. Using the two coverages in conjunction will protect you against a seizure of the funds, as well as conversion and transfer risk. If you have already taken out standard expropriation coverage, you should automatically be protected against expropriation of funds, but check with your insurance broker or underwriter to be sure.

- You can distinguish between purchasing conversion coverage and transfer coverage. For example, if you are making an investment in China—a country that has the world's largest foreign exchange reserves (in excess of $3 trillion)—you may rightly think that it is highly unlikely that you would ever encounter a problem converting currency there. However, you may not realize that the Chinese government typically does not tap into its foreign exchange reserves to accommodate foreign investors and that foreign investors will usually be responsible for generating their own foreign exchange through their business operations (one reason why China has maintained its place in having the world's highest foreign exchange reserves for more than 20 years). You can reduce the cost of coverage by breaking CI coverage down into its two basic components (conversion and transfer) if you believe this is right for you. If you are convinced there is no transfer problem, take out conversion coverage only because you will save premium cost in doing so.

CI coverage tends to be expensive in the private sector because underwriters generally do not have good reprocessing capabilities. For this reason, the private underwriters may charge 1.0% to 3.0% per annum for the coverage, while the public underwriters may charge 0.30% to 0.80% per annum. The underwriters rarely write this coverage for more than 90% indemnity. In general, CI coverage is more readily available and is less expensive with the public underwriters than with the private sector underwriters. To the extent that you are less concerned about expropriation and more concerned about CI, you may want to consider purchasing CI and expropriation of funds coverage with the public underwriters.

Political Violence

While coverage against physical damage caused by strikes, riots, and civil commotion is a standard component of most property insurance policies, coverage for politically inspired violence may not be provided. Coverage against damage caused by war, civil war, civil disturbance, sabotage, and terrorism must be purchased separately if a company is to be protected against these perils. Political violence (PV) coverage provides protection against the previously named perils in two ways: It covers against physical damage and it also protects against lost income due to business interruption (BI).

In order to trigger coverage under PV coverage in the public sector, the action taken must have been politically motivated; that is, it must have been the result of action taken by an individual or group with an overt political objective. The private sector underwriters do not generally require that the insured demonstrate that an action was politically motivated in order to provide PV coverage. For example, in the public sector a labor disturbance would not be covered unless it could be demonstrated by the insured that the disturbance was motivated not by a pay dispute, but rather by a call for an overthrow of the government. Labor disturbances in South Korea often fit this profile. In the private sector, no such caveat is included. The amount of a claim payment is usually based on the least of the repair cost, the replacement cost, or the fair market value.

PV coverage not only addresses loss due to physical damage, however. An important part of the coverage is loss due to BI. A good example of this would have been trying to do business in Iraq at the height of the Iraqi conflict in 2004 and 2005. If, as a result of the occurrence of PV you cannot operate your business, coverage is generally available. Again, the public sector underwriters will require that you demonstrate that there was a political derivation to the loss and will often require that the interruption has impacted your business for a full year. Waiting periods vary for BI coverage in the private sector.

The amount of PV coverage obtained in either the private or public sector will almost always be equal to the amount and tenor of expropriation coverage obtained, as the two are based on net book value. It would be somewhat unusual for PV coverage to be obtained without expropriation coverage. Private sector insured percentages for PV coverage are often 100% and there is generally a 10% deductible attached. Pricing is inexpensive, generally ranging from 0.01% per annum of the insured value to 0.50% per annum. Public sector insured percentages are, as usual, 90%, with smaller deductibles, similar limits, long-term coverage, and a minimum 90-day waiting period for physical damage (The waiting period for BI is more commonly 1 year.). Pricing may actually be more expensive in the public sector, but the coverage is almost always broader because many underwriters in the private sector are unable to insure fixed land-based assets against war for more than a year at a time, while there is no such restriction in the public sector.

An interesting footnote: While the public sector underwriters have a distinct advantage in a general sense when it comes to subrogation rights because they can rely on the agreements they have made with a host government regarding expropriation or CI losses,[4] this advantage is lost to them with PV coverage because, when an asset is destroyed, there is nothing to become subrogated to, except twisted metal and ashes. For this reason, the public sector underwriters are just as exposed to PV loss as the private sector underwriters. They may therefore be reluctant to agree to insure certain types of risk against PV.

Breach of Contract

The final investment insurance coverage is breach of contract (breach). Some may think that breach is out of place in the investment insurance category because its name does not connote solely investment-related coverage. When some people hear the word "breach," they are inclined to think of a broken trade agreement rather than a broken investment agreement. Coverage is indeed available for breach of a *trade* contract, which is otherwise known as contract frustration coverage (discussed later), but agreements made between investors and governments can also be broken. Breach coverage for investments addresses two basic perils: an inability to access a forum of arbitration and arbitration award default. In simpler language, if you are denied the ability to go to arbitration by a host government or if you go to arbitration, an award is rendered in your favor, but the government refuses to pay that award, breach coverage will provide protection.

This coverage is less used, however, for three reasons:

- The arbitration process can last for many years; the average period is 2 years and sometimes surpasses 5 years. Few companies are willing to continue to pay premiums for that length of time with no guarantee of a favorable outcome because a claim will only be paid if the company wins a judgment.
- The venue of an arbitration becomes very important. Arbitration should always be held outside the host country, preferably in a neutral venue, such as Switzerland. If arbitration occurs in the host country, it may be difficult, if not impossible, to get an award in your favor.
- A claim payment may not necessarily include the cost of legal fees paid to obtain the award, which can cost millions of dollars.

Breach coverage has been a subject of some debate among underwriters for many years, and the topic continues to be debated. Many investors have asked if breach coverage is available for infrastructure projects. The answer for many years was "no" as there were perceived to be too many instances when a loss is caused by an event that cannot clearly be classified as strictly "political." The line between political and commercial risk can be too diffuse. In a power project, for example, how can it be determined with any confidence that a change in the tariff rate was caused by a political action versus a commercial action? Could an investor successfully demonstrate that it was a purely political action? If not, no claim would be paid. However, if you can obtain expropriation coverage for the same project, you can get a claim payment for the same event, as long as you can demonstrate that discrimination was involved in the decision to change the tariff rate (by showing, for instance, that the tariff rate for your project was changed but the rate for a similar power plant 50 miles away was not).

In the majority of cases, breach coverage will not be required or available. If a government breaks a clause in a power purchase agreement (PPA), as long as you can demonstrate that some form of discrimination was involved, you can generally receive payment under expropriation coverage in the public sector, negating the need for breach coverage. This is yet another reason why breach coverage is purchased less often.

Pricing for breach coverage tends to be more expensive as well. Public sector rates for infrastructure projects (which are typically where breach coverage will be considered[5]) range between 1.0% and 1.5% per annum. To the extent that similar coverage is available in the private sector, rates will naturally vary. If modified breach coverage is added on to expropriation coverage, it may be obtained for relatively little additional premium (say, 0.25%–0.50% per annum). Such coverage is not necessarily less attractive in the private sector, even with the shorter period of coverage, because host governments typically tend to change investment agreements with foreign investors in the early years of the investment.

Each form of investment coverage has its own benefits and gaps. You will never be able to insure against every conceivable form of political risk involved in investing abroad. It should be noted, though, that with proper guidance from a knowledgeable PRI broker or risk manager, the majority of political risks associated with investing internationally can indeed be mitigated. If you are in doubt about whether an event or circumstance will be covered under an insurance policy, ask the broker or underwriter to clarify it for you.

An Overview of Trade Insurance

The following descriptions of the trade coverages are by no means intended to be all inclusive. As PRI may be tailored to address almost any scenario, it would be beyond the scope of this chapter to review all of the conceivable forms and combinations of coverage. Rather, what follows is a broad-based description of the most commonly utilized trade coverages.

Exporters and importers confront a dizzying array of home and host country regulations that govern which goods and services may be traded, and under what circumstances an exchange of goods or services may occur. Even if an exporter is complying with home country guidelines for exportation, host country importation guidelines may require compliance with a completely different set of criteria. It is relatively easy to get caught up in a compliance problem. License requirements constantly change and embargoes may be imposed, often without the trader's knowledge.

Contract Frustration

Fortunately, there is a form of PRI designed specifically to address basic trade perils: contract frustration (CF) insurance. CF is the bread and butter of the trade coverages because it is so broad in scope. It addresses six basic perils that can occur when buying from or selling to a government and provides reimbursement up to the full contract value:

- *Unilateral contract termination*: You have a contract with a governmental buyer or seller, you have fully complied with the contract's provisions, and that entity unilaterally cancels your contract.
- *Nonpayment*: You have fully complied with the contract and the governmental entity does not provide payment in accordance with contractual provisions.
- *Import/export license cancellation*: If you have an import or export license and it is canceled, you may pursue reimbursement up to the full value of the contract, provided you can show that your license was obtained legally and was valid at the time of the cancellation.
- *War/civil war*: If, as a result of the occurrence of war or civil war (terrorism, sabotage, or civil disturbance), you cannot ship an export or receive an import, this coverage provides reimbursement;
- *Arbitration award default*: If the governmental entity does not fulfill a contractual obligation, you take the government to arbitration (under the terms of the contract), you win an award, and the government does not honor it, this coverage will reimburse you for the amount of the award.
- *Other governmental acts that can frustrate a contract*: Almost any other governmental act that violates contractual provisions and results in frustration is insurable. This must, however, be spelled out in the contract in advance of its issuance.

CF coverage is also available when trading with private sector buyers or sellers. All of the previously referenced coverages are available in this case except nonpayment coverage (which is viewed as a commercial risk when the buyer is private). Expropriation of the trading partner and the partner's inability to convert or transfer currency (both discussed in more detail later) may be added for private buyers or sellers. Coverage is provided for *preshipment* and *postshipment* risk. The preshipment coverage addresses costs and expenses incurred in performance of the contract, while the postshipment coverage addresses loss in accordance with contractual provisions. Most purchasers of CF coverage buy both forms of the insurance, though it is possible to purchase them separately.

Non-Honoring of Letters of Credit

If a bank fails to honor a letter of credit (LC), this coverage will reimburse you for the amount of the LC. The focus here is exclusively on payment risk. It is an alternative to confirming LCs, which can be cost effective.

Wrongful Calling of Guarantees

Many governments may require that guarantees (also known as standby LCs) be provided by contractors in order to consummate a transaction. Similarly, the posting of bid bonds is often required in order to secure a job or service contract. Wrongful calling of guarantees coverage is intended to protect an insured's counterindemnity (defined as any guarantee given by the insured to its bank or a host country bank in support of a guarantee) when the buyer "calls" a guarantee or the host country bank "calls" a counterguarantee, and the insured is not in default of its obligations under the contract. This coverage is designed to address advance payment guarantees, performance guarantees, maintenance guarantees, bid bonds, and other similar guarantees. The following events will trigger the coverage:

- Embargo
- Cancellation/nonrenewal of import or export licenses
- Arbitration award default
- Not refunding a bid bond
- The imposition of any law, order, regulation, or decree by either the home or host country government that prevents the insured from fulfilling the terms of the contract (e.g., an embargo imposed by either government would trigger the coverage if it prevents you from meeting your obligations)

Coverage for wrongful calling also applies against a *rightful* call of a guarantee due to home or host country governmental action. An example of this would be if the host country government rightfully calls your maintenance guarantee as a result of an embargo because you could not ship parts to the project in question.

Trade Disruption Insurance

Trade disruption insurance (TDI) is a variant of CF coverage that addresses a disruption in your ability to source raw materials or distribute products where no physical damage has occurred, but you are unable to arrange alternative supplies. This extremely broad coverage protects against the political risk perils of expropriation, embargo, license, cancellation, political violence, and government actions that impact product distribution, as well as the nonpolitical risk perils of loss due to nondelivery, fire, flood, explosion, earthquake, volcanic eruption, lightning, derailment, collision, road closure, and third-party blockade.

TDI is intended for supply-related risks that do not fit into other predefined loss categories. For example, if your goods were left in a warehouse and a flood made gaining access to the warehouse impossible, which resulted in missed delivery dates and subsequent penalties, TDI coverage would provide reimbursement for the net loss, including additional costs incurred. If you have a supply risk, TDI should be considered as a form of comprehensive coverage.

Other Categories

One of the hidden benefits of purchasing PRI is that your coverage can be tailored to fit your particular set of needs. Most of the private PRI underwriters will customize coverage for you, including issuing coverage for specific risks. In the case of trade coverages, you can secure protection for the following perils on their own:

- License cancellation
- Embargo
- Arbitration award default
- Failure to supply (on the part of a government)
- Employee repatriation (if an employee is abducted, for example, kidnap and ransom insurance is also available, but is considered a separate line of insurance)
- Virtually any other form of trade coverage

The cost of CF coverage generally ranges between 1.0% and 4.0% per annum (CF is considered to be one of the most expensive forms of PRI). Wrongful calling coverage generally costs between 0.50% and 1.0% per annum. The insurance for both forms usually covers 90% of an exposure for up to 2 years (though coverage from the private sector underwriters is often available for up to 3 years). Waiting periods generally range from between 270 and 420 days. The cost of not honoring LCs and other categories of coverage will vary by transaction, of course.

Export Credit Insurance

Export credit insurance (ECI) is not, strictly speaking, a purely political risk coverage because it is designed to address private buyer payment risk, which, more often than not, is derived from either buyer insolvency or protracted default (meaning that the recipient simply does not pay). That said, ECI generally covers those perils addressed in CF coverage (specifically, import/export license cancellation, war, embargo, expropriation, and CI) and adds in coverage for private buyer payment default. The primary difference between CF coverage and ECI is that CF coverage addresses sales to *public* buyers, while ECI addresses sales to *private* buyers. If you are an exporter and you have not investigated ECI, it should become a top priority, as it could result in a substantial increase in the volume of your exports and an improved payment record.

The principal benefits of ECI are that it protects against unforeseen loss, allows the exporter to extend more liberal payment terms to the buyer, and is a form of credit enhancement (in that the receivables are used as collateral). Its existence in an underlying transaction should make banks more receptive to providing financing, enhance (as opposed to change) existing credit management systems, build confidence when doing business in new places with new buyers, and minimize potential losses. Underwriters tend to provide coverage to experienced sellers who do business with creditworthy buyers based on standard industry-accepted payment terms. An element of good faith is presumed to exist between the buyer and seller.

Coverage can be purchased on a single- or multiple-buyer basis, though it is much more difficult in general to obtain ECI for individual transactions in "difficult" countries (when many exporters explore the availability of coverage). It is much more useful and you will have a much better chance of success if you pursue ECI on a multibuyer basis with a good spread of risk.[6] Coverage may generally be obtained on a short- or medium-term basis (up to 5 years), though a 12- to 18-month period is much more common and longer-term coverage may be available.

Underwriters price ECI coverage based on a number of factors, including the exporter's prior experience with the buyer or buyers, the nature of the payment terms, the exporter's loss history, and the breadth of the exporter's credit control procedures. The type of industry the exporter is involved in, the spread of countries at issue, the quality of the buyer(s), and the insurer's own country capacity can also impact whether coverage will be provided, as well as its cost. The general rate range is 0.25% to 1.0% per annum, based on 90%–100% indemnity. ECI coverage usually implies a 5%–10% deductible, on top of the self-insured retention.

Underwriters and the Underwriting Process

The first PRI contracts were written by government agencies—first in 1919 by Britain's Export Credits Guarantee Department (ECGD), followed by the US EXIM bank in the 1930s. Their objective was to promote national export flows by utilizing government guarantees to encourage foreign traders to expand their international market presence. In the United States, the Agency for International Development (AID) began to participate shortly after World War II by providing investment guarantees to assist in the rebuilding effort in Europe. AID participation eventually led to the creation of OPIC in the late 1960s, which has become a powerful force in promoting the flow of US capital to the developing world.

Although Lloyd's of London has been involved in the PRI business since the 1800s by issuing various forms of coverage, private insurance companies really did not become involved in PRI in any substantive way until the late 1970s. It was the rise of the Sandinistas in Nicaragua and the fall of the Shah in Iran in 1979 that ultimately led to the development of the private PRI industry in the United States and Europe. Demand for PRI soared after these two events because so many foreign companies were expropriated. A number of underwriters, such as the American International Group (AIG—now Chartis), Cigna, and Chubb, developed PRI programs in the 1970s and early 1980s to meet client demand. Though Chartis was for some time the market leader in the United States and Zurich is arguably the largest such underwriter in the United States today, much of all private sector PRI is underwritten through Lloyd's, by Lloyd's underwriters directly, and through the massive Lloyd's reinsurance market,[7] where perhaps 90% of all PRI is either issued or receives some form of support.

The PRI industry experienced some important changes in the 1980s, when it was common for individual private sector underwriters to be able to offer $70 million or more in coverage for a single trade transaction and coverage of $100 million or more was available for most investment coverages. The industry experienced significant losses in the late 1980s as a result of several large CF claims, and reinsurance treaties became more difficult to renew. Lower limits were placed by reinsurers on the types of coverage that could be underwritten, as well as the amount of coverage that could be issued. At that time, the amount of coverage available was a fraction of what it was 10 years earlier. However, there was a resurgence of interest in

PRI in the mid-1990s, prompting reinsurers to provide larger underwriting lines for the private sector underwriters and spurring the creation of several new, important players in the business, such as Sovereign Risk Insurance (Sovereign) and Zurich.

Demand for PRI varied in the first decade of the twenty-first century. Contrary to conventional wisdom, demand for PRI actually fell immediately following 9/11 as trade and investment volumes plummeted, as did risk management budgets in many corporations. PRI was often viewed as a discretionary cost in the past—seen as a luxury by some businesses that could be bypassed when times were tough. This is exactly opposite what businesses should be thinking; rather, in uncertain or difficult economic times, the need for PRI should in fact be higher. Since 9/11, the industry has gradually shifted away from some of the more conventional PRI coverages and toward payment-related coverages. So, sovereign payment risk or nonpayment by private entities with underlying political risk triggers is the new focus.

The Private Sector Players

Although many underwriters are involved in PRI, highlighted next are several of the leading underwriting organizations.

Chartis

Chartis (formerly American International Underwriters) has been the lead private market player since the 1980s. Its specialist PRI company, Global Trade & Political Risks, traditionally held the largest share of the US PRI market and has been in the business since 1974. Despite a history of significant losses, AIG has continued to write this class of business and in the mid-1990s embarked on an impressive enhancement of its political risk capabilities. It has underwriting capabilities across all lines of the business (for trade, investment, and credit) and has underwriting staff in numerous cities around the world. Chartis beefed up its political risk operation by hiring an experienced staff to lead its efforts to tap into the lucrative project finance arena, focusing on large multinational clients. The company initially led the market's transformation from being light years behind public underwriters' capabilities (in terms of tenor) to being one of the first to reach their traditional role as a long-term, large limit insurer. Chartis provides coverage of up to $120 million for investment risks and $75 million for ECI.

Lloyd's

Lloyd's is a marketplace for insurance, much the same way as Home Depot is a marketplace for hardware. More than 80 "syndicates" and 50 managing agents underwrite at Lloyd's, and the Catlin and Kiln syndicates having assumed the lead in this class of business. There is a substantial supporting market composed of more than 20 syndicates, such as Beazley, Chaucer, and Hiscox. In 2011, aggregate per-market capacity at Lloyd's was approximately $630 million for investment insurance, $560 million for trade coverages, and $350 million for credit risk.[8] The primary competitive advantage over its closest competitors that Lloyd's has had over the years has been its ability to pool capacity to insure large exposures. Lloyd's has also traditionally been more innovative with respect to contract wording and has exhibited greater flexibility in insuring "problem" risks. Lloyd's has benefited from the existence of a large and sophisticated brokerage community in London. It is also perceived by many in the business, as well as insureds, to be "user friendly."

Sovereign

Sovereign began operating in 1997 and is based in Bermuda. It is a political risk insurer that offers up to $80 million in coverage per transaction for up to 15 years. Sovereign closely aligns itself with the public agencies, but underwrites stand-alone business as well.

Zurich

Based in Washington, DC, Zurich began operating in 1998 and has quickly become a leader in the PRI and ECI business. Its $150 million capacity per transaction in both investment insurance and trade risk makes it the largest private market player. Zurich's transactional capacity for ECI is $50 million.

Among the other significant private sector underwriters are ACE, Aspen, Atradius, Axis, Coface, and QBE.

Market Capacity
Private Underwriters

The PRI marketplace grew tremendously in the 1990s, having gone from a few large, long-term players to a market filled with new players and capacity. The marketplace previously had a bias in favor of capacity for investment insurance and against trade coverages, the latter being perceived as riskier. In 2011, $500 million of private market capacity was available for a single trade transaction, while $800 million was available for an individual investment project (see Table 17).

The Public Schemes

Long-term coverage of investments (and export credits) was, until the 1990s, primarily the domain of the public sector underwriters, which are

TABLE 17 Private Sector Underwriter Capacity[8]

Insurer	Trade transactions	Investment transactions
Lloyd's	$560,000,000	$632,000,000
Chartis	$120,000,000	$120,000,000
Sovereign	$80,000,000	$80,000,000
Zurich	$150,000,000	$150,000,000
Total (all underwriters)	$1,100,000,000	$1,200,000,000

owned and operated by a government or group of governments. These agencies have the advantage of being able to provide coverage for up to 20 years, which is obviously important for investors and lenders with a long-term orientation. The ability to deter host governments from taking actions opposed to the interests of foreign investors because of an implied or explicit threat of retaliation has helped minimize claim payments for these organizations, though they have paid hundreds of millions of dollars in such claims over the years.

Among the other top providers are ECGD of the UK, the Export Development Corporation (EDC) of Canada, the Export Finance and Insurance Corporation (EFIC) of Australia, MIGA, Nippon Export and Investment Insurance (NEXI) of Japan, and OPIC. A total of 48 organizations belong to the Berne Union[9]—their umbrella organization, which meets quarterly and shares information on investment and insurance trends.

As for ECI, most developed and many developing countries have their own EXIM banks, which promote the exportation of goods from the home country to the rest of the world. By doubling as lenders and insurers, the impact of these banks on the whole export picture is truly significant. They function as "one-stop shops" for the smallest first-time exporter or the largest and most sophisticated trader. The US EXIM bank, for example, has been in operation since 1934 and supported 11,000 financial transactions for more than $65 billion in US exports between 2006 and 2010. There can be distinct advantages to working with an EXIM bank (such as low lending and premium rates); however, there are disadvantages as well (such as lengthy processing periods and domestic content requirements). You should at least consider what your own country's EXIM bank has to offer before making a decision about how to proceed with ECI.

The Underwriting Process

Contrary to how one would imagine political risk assessment would be accomplished (through the use of elaborate quantitative methods), the majority of political risk insurers analyze risk through a combination of quantitative and qualitative means. PRI does not, by nature, encompass a class of risk that is easily categorized; it does not lend itself to actuarial segmentation. Rather, it is one of those unusual areas of insurance that is best assessed through experience and gut instinct, which is why most long-time underwriters can tell immediately whether a transaction is insurable, and at what approximate cost.

In the public side of the business, some underwriters have rating guides that specify rate ranges for certain types of projects and coverages. Typically, the rates will be dependent upon matching a country, project type, and coverage. Such guides are meant to give the underwriter a general idea of how the risk should be priced. Other underwriters, in the private sector, will rely solely on current information about country or sector risk to support their gut instincts. Formal, lengthy, written analysis of transactional risk is not usually undertaken in the private sector. Time constraints resulting from the volume of submissions received by private underwriters (dozens per day in the Lloyd's market) do not allow a formal analysis to be completed. A more thorough review of project documentation is often completed only when a prospective insured has decided to pursue coverage. Even then, no more than a page of written analysis may accompany a rating.

The public sector underwriters operate on a completely different basis. Formal written analyses are integral to the underwriting process. Between analyzing the country risk and the financial, developmental, technical, and environmental aspects of the project, a 20- to 40-page analysis is commonplace. The underwriting process often takes 3–6 months (or more) to complete for a single project. This length of time and depth of analysis could not be accommodated in the private market, which is first and foremost a business. However, some underwriters have enhanced their analytical process by generating five- or six-page written analyses for infrastructure-type projects. This is intended to create a product that satisfies the due diligence process, while not being so administratively burdensome that it would prevent the underwriter from operating in a profitable manner.

PRI is often marketed as a way to manage unforeseen risks. Although underwriting PRI is an art form if done properly, it is also a matter of common sense. Common sense may tell an underwriter that it is probably safe to insure a manufacturing facility in Brazil (a country with a long history of pro-FDI government policies) while insuring a power project in the Dominican Republic, which has a long history of payment-related issues, may not be such a good idea. Only by reviewing hundreds of submissions, and actually underwriting dozens of transactions does the "smell test" become second nature. Once this threshold has been met, it becomes relatively easy to assume liabilities that are unlikely to become claims.

Underwriting Trade Transactions

For investments, the underwriting process involves a fair amount of hypothesizing about what the chances of loss are on a long-term basis, and scenario techniques are often used to determine the likelihood of loss (a case study for underwriting a power project in Indonesia follows). For trade transactions, the underwriting process is somewhat simpler and naturally entails the need to know basic information about the seller, the buyer, and the transaction. As stated previously, much of this is based on common sense, since underwriting is all about synthesizing information to reach a logical conclusion. The underwriting process may take a great deal of time, or very little time, depending on the transaction at hand. What follows is a listing of some of the primary elements that underwriters consider before making a determination about whether or not to assume a risk:

- The applicant
    - What is the applicant's primary business?
    - How many years has it been in this business?
    - What are its total sales and net worth?
    - What experience does the applicant have with the buyer, in the country, and with the type of transaction at issue?

- The buyer
    - Who is the buyer?
    - What does the underwriter know about the buyer?
    - Who owns the buyer?
    - What is the buyer's country of origin?
    - Does the buyer have the full faith and credit of its host government?

- The applicant's experience
    - If the applicant has experience with the buyer, what is the nature of the experience?
    - What are average monthly and yearly sales?
    - What is an average sales amount per transaction?
    - What are the high credit amount and terms?
    - What are the average daily payment delays?
    - Are there any overdue payments from this buyer or in this country?

- The contract
    - What is the total contract value?
    - What is the term of the contract?
    - What is the nature of the contract?
    - Is the subject of the contract standard or custom made?
    - Would the subject of the contract need modification if it were sold to another buyer?
    - If so, how extensive would such modification need to be?

- What are the terms of the termination, arbitration, and force majeure clauses?
- What is the governing law of the contract?
- Have all necessary licenses been obtained?
- How does this contract benefit the host country?

- Payment terms
  - What are the form and terms of payment?
  - If by LC, who is the opening bank, and is it privately or publicly held?
  - What are the LC terms?
  - Is there a guarantor? If so, who is it, and what does it add to the transaction's value?
  - Is external funding being obtained? If so, from whom and under what terms?

- Additional information
  - What coverages, tenor, and limits of liability are being requested?
  - A payment schedule is often requested to show the exact nature of the exposure.
  - Underwriters will generally require a copy of the contract, debt instrument, any guarantee (if applicable), and the applicant's latest available audited financial statement.

What does an underwriter typically do with all this information? Each underwriting organization will have established basic criteria that it will apply to each transaction to make a determination about whether it is a satisfactory risk to insure. These criteria will be unique to each underwriter, tailored to fit its risk management profile, and may include such things as specific client profiles, minimally acceptable payment terms or instruments, or types of goods sold.

An underwriter will typically write a brief risk synopsis of the transaction, which will then be reviewed by senior management. Assuming country capacity is available and the manager agrees with the underwriter's assessment of the transaction, the underwriter will obtain the manager's approval and then draft a contract, which will be approved by legal counsel.

Underwriting Export Credit Transactions

The process for underwriting export credit transactions is not entirely different, except that much more attention is paid to the nature of the exporter's receivables portfolio. Among the most important factors taken into consideration are the following:

- Credit management systems and procedures
- The spread of buyers and markets (the better the spread, the better the perceived risk)

- The value of the underlying good(s) and credit standing of principal customers
- Turnover, terms of payment, and the number of days a sale is outstanding
- Aged debt analysis and overdue collection procedures
- Prior bad debt record

Underwriters tend to focus on the exporter's credit control procedures. They want to have some confidence that the manner in which the exporter normally conducts its business is conservative and that unnecessary risks are not being assumed. This is ordinarily achieved by having the exporter fill out an elaborate application form that seeks to obtain the following types of information:

- Typical payment methods (including whether open account is often used)
- The nature of the sales process
- Total credit losses (including the number of losses and the largest single loss)
- Forecast sales (for the coming 12 months)
- Maximum projected high credit exposures (by amount and buyer)
- How new customers are screened for acceptability
- Collection procedures
- An overview of buyers, sales, payment terms, and how accounts receivable age
- Existence and rescheduling of any bad debt

The existence of efficient credit management procedures and an ability to self-insure predictable losses will permit an underwriter to customize an insurance contract, usually in the client's favor. Although premium rates will vary by contract structure, the most common method of charging premium is a percentage rate applied against turnover. Premium can be charged on a whole turnover or just "named insured" turnover, which allows premium cost to be linked directly with a more precisely defined risk profile.

Premium Rates

Premium rates come in two forms in the PRI business. In the public sector, "base rates" are commonly established, representing what an average risk would be rated for a specific coverage in specific sectors. The underwriter may decrease or increase the rate by as much as 30%, based on an assessment of project-specific risk. For example, one underwriter's base rates used to be as follows:

	Manufacturing	Natural resources	Infrastructure/ oil–gas
Expropriation	0.60%	0.90%	1.25%
Currency inconvertibility	0.50%	0.50%	0.50%
Political violence	0.55%	0.55%	0.60%
Breach of contract	0.80%	1.00%	1.25%

This structure is somewhat misleading in that it implies that CI risk would be rated the same for any type of project and that there is very little perceived difference in PV for a project in the manufacturing and infrastructure sectors. This is not the case in practice; however, it is illustrative of how the issue of premium rates is addressed in the public sector.

In the private sector, PRI capacity is a function of supply and demand (as is any commodity) and rates are very much dependent upon the supply of capacity for a certain country and how much demand for the capacity there is. The following chart illustrates common variations in expropriation rate ranges for three high-demand countries:

Country	Standard rates (%)	Demand-driven rates (%)
Brazil	0.75–1.00	1.50–2.50
China	0.50–0.75	1.25–1.75
Indonesia	0.75–1.00	1.50–2.25

For trade transactions, rates can vary dramatically. For example, contract frustration rates might look something like this:

Country	Standard rates (%)	Demand-driven rates (%)
Brazil	1.00–1.25	2.00–2.25
Mexico	1.50–2.00	3.00–3.50
Argentina	2.00–2.25	3.50–4.00

Rates for expropriation can go as high as 5.0% or 6.0% per annum, and rates for contract frustration can go as high as 25% per annum. Alternatively, when supply is plentiful, demand is low and underwriters are hungry, so rates can drop through the floor. For example, expropriation rates in Mexico may be as low as 0.40%, while CF coverage for Chile may be as low as 0.80%.

The rate applied to a project will depend on a number of factors unrelated to supply and demand of capacity as well. For instance, the sponsor's experience in a given country or sector will weigh heavily on the rating, as will current political events. Whether insuring a transaction enhances or detracts from an insurer's spread of risk is another important factor impacting the insurability of a transaction and an underwriter's willingness to provide coverage. Similarly, current market conditions are factored into the rating process. A good underwriter never underestimates the value of gut instinct, as it is as valid a measure of risk as any other tool.

Pricing Methodology

The rating process can be arbitrary. Few underwriters are inclined to refer to a rating book every time they quote on a risk. The experienced underwriter will not need to reference such a guide in order to price a risk. Although rating guides do exist, they are by definition "dated" as soon as they are produced because country risk conditions change constantly. Rating guides can take many forms; however, they will all have similar elements and they are rarely complicated. For example, an entry for Brazil might look something like this:

Country	Type of coverage	Rate range	Comments
Brazil	Contract frustration	1.50–2.00% per annum	Demand high coverage limited to high-priority items with terms <180 days

Insurance underwriters do not tend to rely on outside sources for pricing information. As stated before, much of how they price risks boils down to the "smell test" and experience. Some underwriters have an in-house country risk "expert" whose sole job is to monitor country risk events and constantly update the firm's rating guide. This is unusual, however. Each underwriter normally does his or her own research and relies on his or her own preferred sources. At the end of the day, that is, after all, what an underwriter is really supposed to do.

Even if there is a rating guide at one's disposal, it is best to utilize information from a variety of sources, identify the central themes that keep reappearing, and make a judgment about the nature of the risk. This should not be done in a vacuum, however. The underwriting and pricing process should be viewed as collaborative, seeking the affirmation of others in the decision-making chain. One indication of how thorough and accurate an underwriting job has been done is what, if any, change is made to the rate being applied to a transaction by senior underwriting management. If little or no change is made, the underwriter could rightly say that he or she had done a proper job of underwriting.

Recoveries

A typical equity investor may need to assign all relevant shares in a project to the insurer before a claim will be paid and recoveries can be pursued.

Subrogation rights are usually pursued after any encumbrance on shares or assets by financial institutions has been released and a claim has been paid. Ideally, subrogation rights for insurers will have been agreed upon in advance by the investor, lender, and insurer, but it often does not work that way, as the lender will have made subrogation a condition of lending. Private sector underwriters normally file suit against the host government to achieve a recovery. In the case of public sector underwriters, an agreement on claims procedures will have been reached prior to any investment being insured in the host country, so the claims process does not involve much guesswork. If a complication does occur, recoveries are usually achieved after several years or a change in government has occurred.

In theory, the public agencies have a huge advantage when enforcing subrogation rights because of their sovereign backing. MIGA, for example, has been able to avoid the occurrence of claims just by flexing its muscles.[10] Other public sector underwriters have benefited from their bilateral relationship with individual countries in order to achieve recoveries. Between 1971 and 2009, OPIC paid 290 claims for a total of $970 million, with a recovery rate of 92%. Although private sector underwriters do not publish their recovery records, it is not uncommon for them to achieve recovery rates above 50%.

Reinsurance

Reinsurance capacity for PRI probably has not been as strong as it is today since the early 1980s, when the private sector PRI market really began to take off. Having been through three crisis periods since the 1980s, reinsurers appear to have regained confidence in the ability of underwriters to operate profitably by covering political risks. The creation of Sovereign's and Zurich's underwriting operations in 1997 and 1998 point to what could be called a trend: Primary insurers and reinsurers that had previously not been involved in the political risk business became interested because they saw a revenue-generating opportunity and because other, more traditional lines of business were not providing desired income due to the continuing soft insurance market. A decade later that trend continued, with the perceived value of PRI rising with the onset of the Great Recession.

Case Study: Assessing the Risk of a Power Plant in Indonesia

To give you a better idea of the analytical process some underwriters engage in to determine if a project is suitable for PRI, the following case study will provide an insider's view of how the underwriting can be done. Underwriters must consider an array of factors when making a determination about whether a risk is insurable, and on what terms. It is not simply a matter of weighing current country risk issues with what may happen in the future. It is more a matter of looking for commonalities that can be identified by reviewing social, economic, legal, and political variables related to a project and a country.

For example, where the project is concerned, the underwriter must consider not only the nationality of the insured, its overseas experience, and its experience of owning or operating a similar project at home and abroad, but also the relative importance to the host country of the sector being invested in and how this impacts the risk profile. An insured's prior loss history is obviously important, but so is its ability to avoid loss. What are its relations with the host government? Does the project earn foreign exchange? If so, presumably it can stand on its own two feet and not require that the host government dip into its coffers to transfer hard currency from the central bank for the benefit of the investor. Does the company have sufficient clout with either the home government or the host government to help ensure that a notice of a claim does not lead to a claim payment? Was corruption involved in securing a contract or maintaining good relations with the host government? If so, is this against the law in the home or host country, and what are its implications? Or, alternatively, does paying a bribe simply put the investor on a level playing field with other foreign investors, in which case it probably does not increase the political risk?

The public sector underwriters will be equally concerned with developmental and environmental issues. What does the host country get out of the investment or trade transaction? How many locals will be employed? How much tax revenue will be generated? Are there any import substitution benefits? What about technology or managerial transfer benefits? These questions are asked because if a project is determined to be important to the country, it can mean one of two things: Either the project brings so much benefit to the country that the likelihood of a host government taking an action detrimental to the project is reduced or a project that valuable makes it a prime candidate for an expropriatory action or an act of political violence. Who is to say which is the case? In times of economic distress, valuable projects tend to become targets. When times are good, host governments are generally inclined to leave well enough alone.

Is there a definable rule of law in the host country? Is it enforceable in an unbiased fashion in a court of law in or out of the host country? More often than not, if a contract calls for arbitration in a court in the host country, the claim is as good as made. How about economic indicators? Does the country have the means to generate hard currency through export sales or by attracting FDI? What is its balance of payments situation? Does it have a large debt burden? Is there a current account deficit? There are two ways to look at poor economic indicators: Either the country is in such a mess that almost any foreign investment or trade transaction is likely to experience a payment problem or the host country is so dependent on foreign trade and investment that the chance of a problem is reduced because the host government knows that foreign money will stop flowing if it starts playing games.

Then there are the purely political risk issues. Who is in power, how did he or she get there, how long has he or she been in power, is he or she likely to last and, if so, for how long? If not, who is likely to succeed him or her? Who opposes the government's rule? Who is likely to oppose it any time in the next decade? These are not easily answered questions. Even if you can make a sensible educated guess to answer questions about the future, does anyone really know what will happen for the next 15 or 20 years? Of course not. All underwriters can do is look at history and current events and hypothesize about what history implies for the future.

Case Study

To facilitate a better understanding of the types of issues that can be involved in PRI underwriting and to enable you to be able to address some of the political risk issues typically associated with an investment project, what follows is a political risk analysis of a hypothetical foreign investor-owned power project in Indonesia. In reading the analysis, bear in mind that the intensity or superficiality of an analysis made by an underwriting organization will largely depend on its operational philosophy and whether or not it is a private or public sector underwriter (implying a streamlined vs. in-depth analytical approach). What follows is intended to demonstrate how broad such an analysis can be and is similar to the types of analyses typically undertaken by the public sector underwriters. It is written as if it were the actual product of an underwriter in 1995, just prior to the Asia Crisis, to illustrate how difficult it can be to make accurate long-term predictions.

The Project

The project involves the construction and operation of two 300 MW coal-fired power generating units that will be built on the Indonesian island of Java. Electricity produced by the project will be sold, under the terms of a 25-year PPA, to the national electricity supplier of Indonesia, Perusahaan Listrik Negara (PLN). The investor, a US-based utility, will invest $100 million of its own money in equity in the project and will seek $200 million in project loans from major US and European financial institutions. The project will comply with World Bank environmental guidelines, so the investor has also sought funding from the International Finance Corporation. The loan will be for 10 years (2 years of construction and an 8-year payback).

The coal will be sourced from the Indonesian island of Kalimantan, which is known for its high-grade coal, under the terms of a fuel supply agreement (FSA) with an Indonesian company in existence since 1966, also for a 25-year term. The project's construction period is 24 months.

Technical/Financial Viability

The investor will design the plant and will provide engineering, procurement, and construction services. It will then assume responsibility for testing, commissioning, and operating and maintaining the plant for the term of the PPA. The technology to be utilized has been employed in dozens of similar plants around the world. The project's financial rate of return is estimated to be 15.6%. Sensitivity analyses indicate that variations in investment costs, fuel price, and production delays would not jeopardize the project's economic viability.

The PPA calls for an indexed tariff rate to be applied to the project. During the project's first 8 years of operation, the per-kilowatt-hour rate to be paid to the investor by the PLN is 8.6 cents, declining to 6.0 cents in the second 8-year period, and reducing to 5.4 cents for the final 9 years of operation. No concessions have been granted to the project by the government of Indonesia (GOI).

Host Country Benefits

All local project employees will be trained by project management to attain the skills necessary to operate the plant. The investor will make every effort to hire local employees and use local suppliers and service providers for all of the project's needs. Families of the project's employees will benefit from an on-site medical facility, recreation facility, and school. Housing will be provided for the families of project management, and transportation will be provided for local area workers to bring them to and from work 6 days per week. The project will make a significant contribution to enhancing the electricity supply of PLN, while generating new tax revenues for the GOI.

Insurance Requirements

The investor has successfully sponsored half a dozen power projects in Latin American and Asia and does not seek PRI coverage for itself. Rather, it wishes to use the insurance as a form of credit enhancement for the benefit of financial institutions from which it seeks funds, so it wishes to reserve capacity for their future use. Given the project loan amount of $200 million, it seeks expropriation, currency inconvertibility, political violence, and breach of contract coverage for that amount for up to 12 years. (The investor seeks coverage for 2 years beyond the contemplated lending period to account for any unforeseen events, such as a delay in start-up or the possible renegotiation of the loan's terms.)

Risk Assessment

Expropriation

1. *The project's importance to the economy.* Given the Indonesian economy's growth rate since the mid-1960s (an average of 7%) and especially in the first half of the 1990s (an average of 8%), the ability of the GOI to deliver an adequate supply of electricity to its populace to support this growth is extremely important. The GOI anticipates a fivefold increase in the number of its citizens that will need to have access to electricity by the year 2000. That the project would add an additional 600 MW of electricity to PLN's supply is important.

2. *The project's size relative to domestic industry.* It is anticipated that private power producers will account for approximately 25% of the 10,000 MW of electricity PLN plans to add to its distribution capabilities by the year 2010. Of this amount, the project would account for approximately 6% of new capacity, which is 24% of the total amount of new capacity to be provided by private power providers.

   a. *The project's contribution to export earnings* is irrelevant, as the project will not export any of its electricity.

   b. *Pertinent aspects of the PPA.* The PPA is a take-or-pay contract whose payment structure is based on generation capacity and actual energy produced. Supplemental payments are due in the event of additional start-up fuel costs attributable to the GOI's actions:

      1. UNCITRAL (United National Conference on International Trade Law) arbitration rules apply. Arbitrators may in certain circumstances be appointed by the International Center for the Settlement of Investment Disputes (ICSID). The arbitration proceedings will occur in Stockholm, Sweden.

      2. The investor will own the grid connection facilities.

      3. The GOI will reimburse the investor for any new taxes that are imposed on the project by any governmental authority.

      4. PLN will purchase all of the project's electricity.

      5. The GOI waives sovereign immunity.

   c. *The project's vulnerability to adverse economic development.* The project would be vulnerable to adverse economic development in that a significant reduction in demand, or a reduction in PLN's ability to pay under the terms of the PPA, could impact the project's economic viability.

d. *The investor's overseas experience.* The investor has owned and operated similar power projects in Venezuela, El Salvador, the Philippines, and Malaysia.

e. *Dissident elements inclined toward expropriatory action.* The Indonesian political system has been dominated for the past 30 years by President Suharto and his family, in close alliance with the military. There are no significant dissident elements known at this time. As long as the president remains in power, there would appear to be little opportunity for dissident elements to have a meaningful voice in the political system. The only dissenting elements within the ranks of the military appear to be at the very top, where jockeying for favorable political position occurs prior to each presidential election, at which time President Suharto chooses a new vice president. It has always been the case that the vice president he selects is a former head of the armed forces or has close ties to the armed forces. When political change occurs, it is unlikely to result in wholesale change.

f. *Existing relationship between the United States and Indonesia.* The bilateral relationship between these two countries has been cordial and friendly for most of the last three decades. However, as has increasingly been the case since 1994, the US Congress has imposed trade and investment sanctions on Indonesia because of worker and human rights concerns. Earlier this year, Congress threatened to remove Indonesia's most favored nation trading status. However, its size and importance in Asia guarantee Indonesia favored treatment on economic and political issues over the long haul. The United States and Indonesia have concluded a bilateral investment treaty.

g. *Indonesia's record of interference in foreign investments.* There is no record of any interference in foreign investment on the part of the GOI since President Suharto assumed power in 1965; however, under the previous president, Sukarno, a large number of expropriations of Dutch investments occurred. Over the past 30 years, the GOI's attitude toward FDI has in fact been almost wholly positive. The Suharto government has encouraged private sector participation in the power sector.

Analysis The GOI has ambitious plans for enhancing its electricity distribution capabilities in the coming decade and the project will make a significant contribution in this regard. The PPA appears to be well drafted from the investor's perspective, with the GOI agreeing to reimburse the investor for any tax increases, the waiver of sovereign immunity, and the UNCITRAL arbitration provision. As is the case with most power projects, this project will not generate any hard currency, which is a source of some concern, given that PLN's balance sheet has not been healthy for many years. That said, there are no known instances of PLN defaulting on its payment obligations and, in any event, the GOI has backed up PLN for this project with a comfort letter from the Ministry of Finance (MOF).

Although the project is vulnerable to adverse economic developments, it seems unlikely that demand will slacken during the coverage period, given the country's outstanding growth rates over the past decade. The investor has had good overseas experience. The GOI has been and continues to be supportive of FDI and investment in the power sector in particular. The US has a solid relationship with Indonesia, despite occasional disagreements over human rights issues. There is no reason to believe this relationship will change during the coverage period. The risk of expropriation is therefore viewed as average.

Critique of the Analysis   While it is certainly useful to point out that Indonesia is going to need more electricity in the coming decade and the PLN has a weak balance sheet, the analysis fails to note that Indonesia will have an oversupply of electricity if all of the independent power projects (IPPs) the GOI has agreed to support in the coming 5 years go forward. This implies that projects with low tariff rates will be the first ones to get paid, while those with higher rates would either have to renegotiate their PPAs or risk not getting paid in full (possibly not at all). This could create a situation where the investor or lender could rightly claim a breach of the PPA by the GOI and could file a claim based on creeping expropriation. If the investor or lender could demonstrate that the GOI discriminated against it by changing the terms of its PPA or canceling it outright while granting payment or operational preferences to other power producers, a claim could be in the making.

Note, also, that the FSA is with an Indonesian entity in business since 1966, the year after Suharto assumed power. It must be assumed that the coal is owned either in part or in whole by a member of the first family (or its cronies) and that a change in power away from the Suhartos could impact the FSA and, ultimately, coal delivery. This could lead to fuel supply problems down the road. Research should have been done to determine the nature of first family involvement in the fuel supply company and the project as a whole.

Currency Inconvertibility

1. *Indonesia's exchange control system.* The value of Indonesia's currency, the rupiah, is determined daily by a managed float. Policies affecting the foreign exchange market are made by the Central Bank, in conjunction with the Ministry of Finance. Commercial banks set their own exchange rates for their own transactions. Foreign exchange transactions are restricted to authorized banks, licensed money changers, and

nonbank financial institutions. Foreign investors may freely repatriate capital and profits. There is no obligation for foreign traders or investors to surrender their export proceeds to the Central Bank.

2. *Transfer delay experience.* It is reported that transfers of foreign currency occur on a timely basis. Foreign banks routinely transfer amounts in excess of $100 million daily.

3. *Country liquidity and economic outlook.* Due to a heavy dependence on the exportation of oil to generate foreign exchange, structural economic reforms were implemented in Indonesia in the 1980s. The result was the creation of a more diverse and efficient economy. The current account deficit exceeded 7% of GNP for most of the 1980s. By the early 1990s, inflation had reached 9% and GDP growth was approximately 6%. Foreign exchange reserves have grown steadily since 1989 and reached approximately $17 billion by 1994.

High interest rates have caused strain in the business community, with rates in excess of 25% making fresh capital unobtainable for many small and medium-sized businesses. Large businesses with large debt burdens are finding it difficult to service their debt. Rising import levels have resulted in increased foreign debt, which reached approximately $100 billion in 1995. The GOI is dependent on overseas aid to help finance development projects and keep pace with its current account deficit.

   a. *Project risk factors.* Although the PPA states that the GOI will bridge the gap between the amount of foreign exchange PLN is able to obtain through foreign exchange (forex) market contracts with banks and the amount it owes the project at any given time (in rupiah or dollars), the government has not granted the project an exemption from PLN's inability to source foreign exchange as a result of any currency transfer restrictions it may impose in a general sense. The project would therefore be at risk of loss due to the imposition of foreign exchange restrictions after becoming operational.

   b. *Potential for recovery.* Even though the project does not generate its own foreign exchange and PLN's balance sheet is weak, the GOI has given its assurance that it will bridge the gap in any shortfall of foreign currency due to the project. The country's foreign exchange situation and its ability to generate foreign exchange from the sale of oil and commodities make the prospect for recovery due to conversion or transfer loss good.

Analysis   Although Indonesia's single largest source of foreign exchange is derived from the sale of oil, the relative importance of oil to the economy has declined since 1985 due to economic diversification and steady growth. It is assumed that the country's foreign exchange reserves will continue to grow as they have since 1989. As with any project that does not earn foreign exchange, there is an inherent risk that the investor or lender could encounter difficulty in converting or transferring currency, since this implies that the government of the host country will have to dip into its foreign exchange reserves to accommodate any project-related transaction. It must be borne in mind that PLN's payment obligations to the project are backed up by the GOI; at the time, there was no known history of payment default by the PLN, and the anticipated repatriations of hard currency should be less than $25 million per year. As such, the risk of loss is considered to be only slightly above average for this project.

Critique of the Analysis Tariff rates had dropped in Indonesia since the project's PPA was negotiated and were likely to drop further. This created a situation where projects with lower rates got paid, while projects with higher rates did not. In fact, what happened in the first half of 1998 (following the economic crisis of late 1997 in Indonesia and the rest of Asia) is that the rupiah lost up to 80% of its value, putting tremendous strain on an already weak PLN. There was no way it could pay the power producers at the prevailing exchange rate, so it told the power producers that it would pay them based on the old rate of 2,450 rupiah to the dollar. The PLN stopped paying many IPPs altogether and even cancelled some PPAs. With the GOI struggling to cope with IMF-imposed economic reforms, which included the removal of some government subsidies of electricity prices, it was forced to choose between obeying the IMF guidelines or angering some public sector PRI underwriters by causing some claims to occur. The IMF guidelines won out. Numerous claims were filed with insurers for power projects in Indonesia in 1998.

This example shows why there is so much risk inherent in currency inconvertibility. Any number of underwriting issues must be taken into account, and any number of possible scenarios can intervene to change the risk climate. No one could have foreseen such a meltdown for the reasons noted in the time frame as described.

Political Violence

1. *Location of the project.* The project is located just north of the central Javanese city of Bandung in a heavily wooded area.
   a. *Dependence on vulnerable transportation links.* The project will be dependent upon a supply of coal from Kalimantan via ship and then by rail from the northern coast of Java to Bandung. The FSA calls for the shipment of 1.2 million tons of coal per year to the project. In Kalimantan, the coal will be delivered

by truck to a barge loading facility and then sent by ship to the northern coastal town of Cirebon, where it will be loaded on rail cars for delivery to the project. The delivery time between Kalimantan and the project should take less than a day. An on-site coal reserve will be maintained for 30 days, in the event of shipment interruption. Should an interruption last longer than 60 days, the project will be free to source coal from an alternative supplier.

b. *Mobility of assets.* The construction equipment and coal will be mobile. Nearly all other physical assets will be fixed.

c. *Vulnerability to damage.* The project is not particularly prone to fire or explosion; however, it would not require much effort to sabotage the turbines or transmission lines.

d. *Security arrangements.* A fence will surround the entire facility and permanent guards will be posted strategically around the site on a 24-hour per day basis.

e. *Strategic importance to the host government and any potential adversaries.* Any power project is important to a host government and would be important to any potential adversaries, both as a potential target for attack or as a strategic asset to be safeguarded for future use.

f. *The project's visibility as a foreign-owned enterprise.* The project's name will be Indonesian. Although it will be a somewhat high-profile project, there is no obvious reason to believe it would be visible as a foreign-owned project.

g. *Existing insurgency, revolution, or other opposition.* The only notable recent sources of political conflict have been located far away from the project site, in the northwest province of Aceh, East Timor, and Irian Jaya. Political violence is not commonplace in Indonesia. Acts of political violence have tended to be sectarian in nature, in major cities, and not directed at foreign investors.

h. *Probability of armed conflict with another country.* Since Indonesia is the strongest military power in Southeast Asia, the likelihood of armed conflict with any of its neighbors seems remote. The GOI has had favorable relations with Australia, Malaysia, and Singapore for a long time.

Analysis The project's physical facilities will be surrounded by a security fence and guards will be permanently assigned to provide protection. The risk of PV for this project rests primarily with the coal supply, however. The coal remains vulnerable from the point of shipment to the project site, as the loading and unloading facilities could be prone to attack. An even greater risk is the rail shipment in Java. Although there is no obvious potential aggressor, it would be relatively simple and inexpensive to sabotage rail tracks. If an aggressor were really serious about causing disruption of coal supply, the project would be vulnerable to attacks from numerous points along the supply route. The transmission lines and power turbines are also vulnerable to attack with relative ease and at relatively small expense. For this reason, the risk of loss must be viewed as above average.

Critique of the Analysis   The analysis is basically sound. It takes account of Indonesia's internal and external security concerns and includes some of the micro-issues associated with the potential for physical damage and business interruption for a power project. It rightly emphasizes where the greatest risk for political violence rests and assumes that even unusual civil commotion would not greatly alter the landscape where this project is concerned. The effectiveness of the project's security force will be all important. It takes just one wrench thrown into a turbine to shut a power project down. It would be important to know how the security force will be trained and what tools its members will have at their disposal to address any unusual episodes in and around the plant.

Breach of Contract

1. *Identification of areas of possible conflict between the host government's obligations and its ability to fulfill those obligations.* The government has agreed to backstop PLN's payment obligations through issuance of a comfort letter from the MOF. Indonesia's fiscal situation is acceptable at this time, and there is no reason to believe it will change any time in the near term. Although Suharto will eventually relinquish power, it is presumed that whoever follows in his footsteps will honor the obligations undertaken by the GOI in this case, given the importance of the project to the Indonesian economy.

2. *Host government's history of compliance with similar contractual obligations.* The GOI has engaged in numerous other similar financial and performance undertakings over the past several decades. We are not aware of any instance in which the government did not honor one.

3. *Legal regime governing the contract.* The contract is governed by Indonesian law, but Indonesia recognizes the New York Convention on Recognition and Enforcement of Arbitral Awards (NY Convention), and Indonesia is a member of the International Center for the Settlement of Investment Disputes.

4. The *venue of arbitration* is Jakarta.

5. *Financial health of the obligor.* PLN is not in sound fiscal condition. It runs chronic budget shortfalls and must be supported by the MOF in order to pay its bills.

Analysis   Although PLN is not in sound fiscal health, the fact that the MOF is backstopping its payment obligations under this contract implies that it should be safe to proceed with the investment. The MOF has offered a comfort letter putting its support for PLN in writing. The fact that Indonesia recognizes the NY Convention and is a member of ICSID should provide additional comfort, as should the fact that Indonesia has not previously defaulted on its payment obligations to other IPPs. Given this, having Jakarta as the venue of arbitration should not matter.

Critique of the Analysis   Alarm bells should have been ringing loudly with this analysis:

- The fact that the MOF only issued a comfort letter, rather than a formal payment guarantee, should have alerted the investor and lender that they should not in fact count on the MOF to come to the rescue if PLN defaulted on its payment obligations. It subsequently turned out to be the case that none of the comfort letters that had been issued to the IPPs were worth the paper they were printed on.

- While it is true that recognition of the New York Convention and membership in ICSID should ordinarily provide comfort that if a dispute turns into arbitration Indonesia will accede to ICSID arbitration and recognize an award, research would have indicated that Indonesia has a checkered past with respect to blocking arbitration proceedings and honoring such awards.

- A foreign investor should never accede to having the host country as the venue of arbitration if it can be avoided. One's chances of getting a fair hearing are greatly reduced as a result.

The Impact of the Asia Crisis and Lessons Learned

Looking back, after the fact, any of the insurers that had agreed to provide PRI for this and other projects might have thought in retrospect they needed to have their heads examined. What was deemed acceptable in 1995, based on common practice and a comfort level derived from conducting business in Indonesia for decades, suddenly became unacceptable just 2 years later. If this transaction had been presented for consideration in 1998, it would not have been underwritten. Consider how dramatically the perception of risk had changed.

The basis for the project functioning on a long-term basis was the assumption of political continuity, which was clearly to become an issue during the life of the project given that Suharto had already been in power for 29 years. At the time, underwriters did not consider the idea of wholesale political change to be likely. Underwriters subsequently learned that the first daughter and Suharto's brother-in-law (Prabowo) owned 2.5% of the project and a no-bid coal supply contract had been awarded to Prabowo. Suharto had approved the deal and Suharto family members received a total of $50 million in benefits. This reeked of political patronage, cronyism, and corruption and should have had alarm bells ringing loudly.

The Crisis had a severe impact on IPPs. The retail rate for electricity fell to between 1.0 and 2.5 cents. Apart from reduced demand for electricity and reduced prices, it became extremely difficult to finance new projects. Investors and lenders learned that transaction structures are subject to sudden changes in the operating environment and that inefficiency costs can add substantially to project costs. They also learned that transparent and affordable pricing gives consumers and producers incentives to behave rationally during periods of insufficient capacity.

The Crisis triggered a severe devaluation in the rupiah from USD1: IDR2,450 down to as low as USD1: IDR16,800. The Indonesian energy program involved approximately 27 IPPs in various stages of development or operation when the crisis occurred. The state-owned utility, PLN, had entered into long-term PPAs with the various IPPs at tariffs ranging from 6 to 8 cents/ kilowatt-hour in order to support the large foreign currency loans obtained by the IPPs to finance the power plants. The IPPs received various levels of support from the GOI, including performance undertakings pursuant to which the GOI agreed that it would ensure that PLN honored its obligations under the PPA. A September 1997 presidential decree divided IPPs into three categories: continued, reviewed, or postponed (depending on the stage of development). Allegations were made that certain IPPs had obtained their original tariffs through corruption, cronyism, and nepotism.

In 1998 PLN began a program of selectively renegotiating PPAs in order to reduce the contractually agreed tariff rates. PLN payment breaches under the PPAs were based on (a) refusal to dispatch a plant followed by a failure to satisfy its take-or-pay obligations, and (b) dispatching to a plant but only paying for electricity using the precrisis exchange rate of USD1: IDR2,500 (see Figure 30). The GOI's breaches under a support agreement included a failure to cause PLN to honor and perform its obligations under the PPAs. Potential expropriatory actions by the GOI included postponement of IPPs without offering compensation and interference by the GOI and the courts of Indonesia in the exercise of the dispute resolution provisions in the PPAs and the GOI support agreements.

If one were to fast forward 13 years, one would find that many of the same concerns that existed in 1997 and 1998 exist today with respect to the market's comfort level with PLN payment risk. Investors and lenders tend to have long memories, and risk managers, credit committees, and boards of directors do not easily forget being burned. Although Indonesia has made

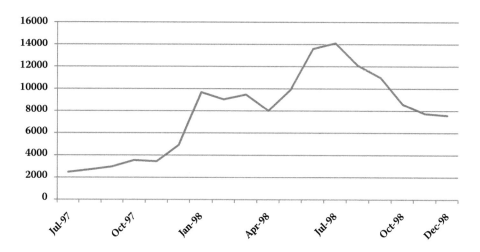

FIGURE 30 **USD/IDR monthly average exchange rate: July 1997 to December 1998. (From http://www.oanda.com/currency/historical-rates)**

great progress since 1998, it has done a poor job of ensuring that the market is able to distinguish between Indonesia then and now. PLN remains unable to stand on its own two feet financially and must still rely on the MOF to backstop its payment obligations. However, since 2003, PLN has not missed any payment obligations, and the Indonesian parliament has not failed to backstop PLN, but the market continues to think of PLN as it was in 1998, rather than in 2003. Indonesia and PLN need to do a better job of advertising the difference, and investors/lenders must do a better job of becoming educated about how obligors and market dynamics may change.

Some will argue that Indonesia has actually not changed all that much from an investment perspective, and they would in fairness have a good argument. After all, corruption remains endemic, the judicial system has not changed all that much, and the perception still exists that Indonesia can be a tough place in which to do business. However, in 1998 a twice democratically elected president was not running Indonesia as he is today, the Corruption Eradication Commission (KPK) did not exist as it does today, and one could not rightly say that Indonesia had a vibrant and free press. In 1997, Indonesia attracted just $4.7 billion of FDI[11]; in 2011, it is expected to attract more than $14 billion of FDI.[12] The market is saying it believes in Indonesia, but still needs convincing where infrastructure investment is concerned.

Notes

1. Political risk insurance guide. International Risk Management Institute, April 1999. Reprinted with permission from IRMI.
2. http://en.wikiquote.org/wiki/Talk:Henry_Kissinger

3. Reinsurance is the insurance that insurance companies purchase on their own liabilities to lay off a portion, or the majority, of the risk.

4. The agreement on expropriation losses will generally require the host government to treat investments insured by public sector underwriters no less favorably than those of local investors. The agreement on CI losses can give public sector underwriters preferential access to foreign exchange in a claims situation.

5. Some public sector underwriters will only offer to provide breach coverage for projects where a concession agreement has been arranged with the host government (such as mining projects). The ability to distinguish between commercial and political risk is easier when a concession agreement exists.

6. Political risk insurers, in general, and export credit providers, in particular, respond well to the "spread of risk" concept, which means combining "good" exposures (in countries with low perceived risk) with "bad" exposures (in countries with high or higher perceived risk). The idea is that the overall risk of loss to the insurance provider will be lower if higher risks are combined with lower risks. If you were to ask an insurer to provide coverage for a single export transaction to a private buyer in a place like Pakistan or Zimbabwe, you are unlikely to receive a positive reply. Take Pakistan or Zimbabwe and combine it with Western Europe, and you will generally obtain a more favorable reply.

7. It is common for a private sector underwriter to lay off as much as 90% of its risk by purchasing reinsurance. Private sector underwriters can generally only underwrite if they have a reinsurance "treaty" (that governs which coverages they can underwrite, under what conditions, for what length of time, and for how much total exposure). Reinsurance treaties are generally renewed annually. Only a few private sector underwriting organizations write PRI coverage without any form of reinsurance.

8. Gallagher, Arthur J. Political Risk Insurance: Report and Market Update, January 2011.

9. Also known as the International Union of Credit and Investment Insurers.

10. This was the case with a project I underwrote in Pakistan while at MIGA in the early 1990s. Notice of a claim was filed. Within 3 months, the problem disappeared because of phone calls having been made to the right people within the US and Pakistani governments, through the lobbying efforts of MIGA's legal department.

11. http://www.aric.adb.org/pdf/aem/mar01/Mar_ARR_special.pdf

12. http://www.reuters.com/article/2010/12/17/indonesia-investment-cbank-idUS-JKB00417620101217

Chapter 6

Tales from the Battle Zone

It's so much easier to suggest solutions when you don't know too much about the problem.

Malcolm Forbes[1]

How Easy It Is to Make Costly Mistakes

What follows are some real examples of foreign investors who failed to do their homework, did not think outside the box, or were simply unlucky. Each of these cases illustrates how easy it is to experience a serious problem as a foreign investor. Through no fault of their own, they became victims of a host country conflict or policy dispute that ended up costing them a lot of money and even shut their operation down. What they have in common is a failure to consider fully the possible impact their operating environment would have on them or their operations would have on their operating environment. If these types of problems can happen to large corporations—and many of them did—any entity operating internationally is vulnerable.

A Telecommunications Company in Pakistan

In the 1990s Company A made a multimillion dollar investment and built the infrastructure necessary to operate a regional mobile phone network in southern Pakistan. Not long after making this investment, the government of Pakistan shut the operation down. At the time, a rebel group (MQM) was operating in and around the southern port of Karachi. The government alleged that MQM was using Company A's network to communicate with one another and that it felt powerless to stop them except by shutting down the entire network. The government alleged that Company A had violated sections of their operating agreement, legitimating the shut down. It also contended that the phone network was effectively a weapon being used against the state. Company A believed that it had complied with all the rules governing the system's operation. The matter was resolved through high-level diplomacy between the governments of Pakistan and of the company, which resumed operation of its telephone system after many months of inactivity.

A Paper Company in Russia

US-based Company B made a $35 million investment to build a paper-box manufacturing facility in Russia in 1989. At that time, Russia was a "B" grade country with a good reputation for paying its bills. The company had secured 18-month bullet payment terms from the local state government where the plant was to be located. The company was to turn over the key to the plant to the state government upon completion, when the company would be paid in full. The facility was completed just as the former Soviet Union collapsed in 1990. Needless to say, the state government failed to make payment. The company's investment was lost and was never repaid.

A Power Company in Brazil

Company C and another company jointly paid $1 billion in 1997 to purchase a 33% ownership stake in a Brazilian power producer, which was majority owned by a state government. An agreement at the time of the purchase by the existing state government gave Company C and its partner operating control of the company. However, the subsequent state government wanted to take back ownership and control of the company and block future privatizations. The two foreign investors believed this claim was illegal and sought a reversal in Brazil's federal court system.

An Arab Oil Company in Saudi Arabia

Japan currently imports approximately 29 million barrels of oil from Saudi Arabia per day. In the 1990s, a Tokyo-based company wanted to renew its drilling rights on a critical oil concession for a field in the neutral zone Saudi Arabia shares with Kuwait. The Saudis hedged on renewing the concession unless Japan agreed to invest more than $2 billion in a Saudi railway project to improve access to remote mining areas. The Saudis also wanted Japan to agree to import a larger percentage of its crude oil in the future. The Japanese offered the Saudis a loan to finance the railway, but the Saudis insisted on a direct investment. Japanese companies owned the majority of the drilling company's shares, with the Saudi and Kuwaiti governments having minority stakes. The drilling company's 40-year concession with Saudi Arabia was to expire in February 2000. The company ultimately lost its concession because it refused to pay the $2 billion, believing the railway would not make money.

An Oil Company in Russia

Company D acquired a 10% stake in a Russian oil company in 1997, investing $484 million in company shares and planning to invest another $3 billion over the course of the next 10 years in a huge Siberian gas field. Its partner in the joint venture was owned by Russia's influential Uneximbank, and Company D thought its partner was capable of maneuvering through Russia's sometimes hostile investment climate. Eighteen months later, the newly merged company became embroiled in a bankruptcy proceeding and takeover fight that threatened to destroy its partner.

As one of Russia's largest foreign investors, Company D had become the victim of actions taken by one of its partner's rivals. Company D accused the rival of tampering with Russia's court system to wrest its partner's main production unit away through an attempt to force the partner to declare bankruptcy, a process that is more often than not used in Russia to strip away assets, rather than pay creditors. Company D ended up writing off $200 million of its investment just 2 years later.

Company D became a victim because it thought that it could master the rules of doing business in Russia and assumed that Western business rules applied to doing business there. While Company D was trying to arrange a refinancing with European financial institutions, its partner's rival purchased $10 million of its partner's debt from a Western bank in which it had an ownership stake. As a result, the rival voted against an amicable settlement with Western creditors, which sent the partner into bankruptcy and increased the rival's chances of acquiring the partner's primary production unit.

One of Company D's key mistakes was agreeing to proceed with an investment that represented such a small percentage (10%) of its partner's ownership stake. It therefore had little decision-making influence. Two key public sector lenders in the transaction were not properly registered as creditors, which prevented them from voting on the election of new managers in the partner company. The partner company's owner, who formerly had top contacts in the Russian government, lost his political influence, leaving Company D to make its own way through Russia's court and legal system.

After many months, the creditors agreed to turn their claims over to the Russian government, which ended up agreeing to resolve the issues surrounding the partner's bankruptcy. While this kept the partner and its subsidiaries intact, the creditors relinquished their rights to the government with no preconditions and little more than a promise by the government that it would act in their collective interests. It was unclear what steps the government might take to save the partner company from bankruptcy. The creditors declined to sell their interests in the partner company to the government, opting instead for an ill-defined future trust agreement. The government made its offer to intervene in an effort to improve its image among the foreign investment community. The creditors ran the risk that an agreement with the current government could be abrogated by a new government. Even a giant oil company cannot avoid becoming a victim in a place like Russia.

A Fast Food Chain in Palestine

In 1999, Company E asked its Israeli franchise holder to remove the company's brand name from a 3-month old hamburger stand in a new mall in Maale Adumim, the largest settlement in the West Bank. The Israeli company that owned the stand refused to do so, defending its right to offer kosher food at the food court in the disputed territory. What Company E thought of as a commercial issue with a franchisee quickly became a political confrontation and a public relations nightmare.

At the beginning of the summer, Arab–American groups protested the establishment of an Israeli-owned fast food company in the West Bank. They led demonstrations at Company E's US restaurants and started a boycott of the company for what they saw as a business act legitimizing Israeli settlement in land claimed by the Palestinians. Their cause was picked up by the Arab League, which threatened to impose an all-Arab boycott of Company E's restaurants. When the company decided to cancel its franchise contract, Jewish groups accused the company of capitulating to Arab pressure. Jewish groups in the US promised their own boycotts if the company did not back down.

For its part, Company E claimed to have been duped by its Israeli partner, which said the address of Maale Adumim was in Israel, rather than the West Bank or occupied territories. Company E did not perform a site visit or do on-the-ground due diligence before approving the application to open the restaurant; a company inspector was sent from Dubai to take a look at the premises, unaware that the restaurant was located in the West Bank. After the owner refused to shut the restaurant down, Company E took its action. When it decided to cancel its franchise contract, Jewish groups in the US, led by the Anti-Defamation League, vowed to take their complaint against

Company E to the US attorney general and Congress. Christian organizations, which vehemently supported Israeli sovereignty over the West Bank, threatened to join the boycott—all because of a failure of effective communication between business partners and a failure to perform proper due diligence.

A Media Enterprise in the Czech Republic

Company F was founded by a well known US entrepreneur, a Czech media organization, and an influential Czech individual who held the broadcast license for a Czech commercial television station 99% owned by Company G. In 1999, the Czech media organization fired the individual partner after discovering he had transferred the TV station's program-buying rights to his own company. Company F then sued the individual partner for the return of $23 million he received as payment for a 5.8% stake in the TV station's operating company, claiming that he had breached a shareholder's agreement. Company F and the individual then waged a war of words through the Czech media, accusing each other of breaking contracts. Both sides filed criminal and commercial complaints in the Czech courts, and both sides denied any wrongdoing.

Soon thereafter, the individual took effective control of the station, filling the schedule with whatever programming he could find. The US investor then turned to the regulatory authorities in hope they would do something, but they failed to act, prompting the US investor to take legal action for violating a bilateral investment treaty with the United States. He accused the Czech authorities of failing to protect his investment. This was the first time a foreign investor had bypassed the country's notoriously slow and cumbersome legal system to invoke an international investment treaty to settle a dispute. The US investor's action was filed in Washington, DC, under arbitration rules of UNCITRAL. The value of his initial stock investment of $40 million had declined to just $3.6 million when the suit was filed.

An Energy Company in Venezuela

In 1998, Company H bid on a $400 million project to inject gas into one of Venezuela's largest oil reservoirs, to enable the state oil producer (Petroleos de Venezuela [PDVSA]) to extract more oil. A 20-year contract was awarded to Company H's consortium, which included US and Japanese firms. After the consortium won the bid, it began to run into problems, largely due to the election the previous month of new President Hugo Chavez. Company H discovered that it could not raise financing for the project. Banks were unwilling to lend funds, so it attempted to secure financing from private investment firms and economic cooperation associations, but without success.

Soon thereafter, PDVSA opened negotiations with the second most competitive bidder on the project (Company I), which signed an agreement to take over where Company H had left off. Company H had not previously obtained financing for a project in Venezuela, but Company I had, although it had not been easy. Since no uncovered bank financing was available for Venezuela at the time, Company H relied on ECAs and the US government (through OPIC) to obtain funding, which was not forthcoming. Company H lost its initial investment in the project as a sunk cost.

A Technology Company in South Korea

In 1997 one of Korea's leading software developers was one step from bankruptcy. Poor management, rampant software piracy, and Asia's financial crisis had all taken their toll on the firm. A US technology company (Company J) proposed to save the company from bankruptcy by investing $20 million in return for the local company ceasing production of its highly popular Korean language word-processing software (which accounted for 80% of the local market) and to start selling Company J's version of the software (which then commanded just 15% of the market).

When the Korean press got hold of the story, the Korean public—well known for its fervent nationalism—was outraged. Rather than proceed with the alliance with Company J, the local company instead chose to accept a $10 million investment from Korean computer-related businesses and associations that had led a nationwide campaign to save the local company, which many Koreans regarded as a national technological treasure, from foreign control.

In the year that followed, the local company's market capitalization increased fivefold. Ironically, both the local and US companies experienced increased revenues, in part because of the country's robust economic recovery, but also because the Korean software piracy rate fell 10% after the debacle, thanks at least in part to the campaign to save the local firm. In the meantime, the battle between the two companies continued, with the local firm filing dumping charges against Company J, accusing it of trying to gain market share illegally.

A Bank in Ecuador

A major US bank had a loss-free history of funding trade transactions in Central and South America. Because business was so good, it wanted to increase the size and scope of its investment in the region. In 1999, it did just that and doubled the size of its exposure in Ecuador to $75 million. Later that year, the combined weight of depressed oil prices, inflation, and damage from El Nino caused the banking system to collapse. The government imposed a mandatory 365-day waiting period before foreign banks could transfer any funds outside the country. The moratorium caused the bank's lines of credit in the country to dry up. Since turnover was short term, its loans could not be repaid, putting $75 million at risk.

A Pharmaceutical Company in Yugoslavia

In 1999, on the eve of Kosovo peace talks in France, Yugoslav President Milosevic ordered the seizure of a Western pharmaceutical company in Belgrade. Company K was owned by a Yugoslav–American and was considered a high profile foreign investment. The company's employees were forcibly removed from the factory and not permitted to return. Troops surrounded the facility. The expropriation occurred because Company K was an American-owned facility, in the hope that it might foment anti-US sentiment among the local populace. The North Atlantic Treaty Organization (NATO)-led war against the government of Milosevic later that year did little to help the plight of the plant's owner, who never recovered the plant.

An Oil Company in Peru

Alan Garcia was elected president of Peru in 1984. One of his first actions was to expropriate the offshore oil platforms owned by Company L, a subsidiary of a major US energy company. The platforms, valued at approximately $150 million, were to become a lucrative source of revenue for the newly elected government. There was little Company L could do, except submit a claim under its PRI policy to its US insurer. It took years for the insurer to be repaid through a negotiated settlement with the government of Peru. Ironically, Alan Garcia was reelected president of Peru again in 2006—this time as a pro-business centrist, which he indeed turned out to be.

A Power Company in Canada

Based on projected demand for electricity use in Quebec and the northeastern US in the 1970s, a government-owned utility in Canada thought it would be justified to build and operate a massive hydroelectric project in Quebec. The project would require the damming of several major rivers in Quebec. Announcement of the plan concerned a number of Canadian aboriginal groups, who had perceived that their rights over the land to be flooded had not been adequately considered. As a result of an agreement between the company and the Indian tribes, land was set aside that would not be affected by the project, and each member of the tribes received cash payments as compensation for what was to occur on the land. Phase I of the project proceeded, as did the separatist movement in Quebec and the environmental movement globally.

By 1989, phase II of the project was ready to commence. The company signed a contract with a US power authority (USPA), worth $17 billion, to generate 1000 MW of electricity for 21 years—the equivalent of 30% of the project's capacity. Some of the Indian tribes, believing that phase II was inevitable, sought concessions from the government of Quebec, including talks on the possibility of self-government. However, others waged a sophisticated media campaign against the project, focusing on the negative environmental impact of the project and criticizing entities in the US for agreeing to purchase power from the project.

By 1991, the USPA had asked for an extension on the no-penalty escape clause in its contract with the company, claiming it had reduced its annual growth estimates. Soon thereafter, Quebec's environment minister called for an environmental assessment of the project. Before long, major environmental groups joined in opposition to the project. The company embarked on a public relations campaign of its own, but it was too late. The USPA pulled out of the project and the company was left with substantial sunk costs on its books and a black mark by its name from environmental groups.

The Failure of a Bank's Country Risk Management Program

Failure to anticipate risk, or simply to use common sense, is not limited to exporters, manufacturers, telecommunication companies, miners, or power producers. I was once asked to conduct a country risk management audit of a regional bank and was shocked at the absence of common sense in its risk management practices. After spending a week at their offices, I learned that 70% of the bank's portfolio of exposure was concentrated in just one country! This was a well-established bank with a risk management department and sophisticated analytical tools at its disposal; yet, it made a common and unforgivable error (especially for a bank): believing that the country in which it had the majority of its exposure was simply too big and important to ignore. Needless to say, the bank got into some trouble by having such a concentration of risk. What follows is what I recommended they do.

One senior person whom I interviewed said, "The avoidance of catastrophic losses is a central tenet of the bank's risk management philosophy and a preoccuption of its board of directors; however, the bank has no stomach for real credit risk." If that were true, then why on earth did they have 70% of their exposure in one country? The only conclusion I could draw was that the bank must have had some tolerance for the possibility of catastrophic loss. In its history, the bank had fortunately never had to absorb a significant loss and it naturally did not want to do so. And yet, the assumption of political and credit risk and the possibility of having to endure a severe loss were positions the bank put itself in every day, just by doing what it was created to do: Lend money to borrowers in other countries.

One of the bank's purposes was to assume the risks associated with promoting foreign trade, which meant that it operated in an environment filled with cross-border risk. The bank's ability to determine which risks should not be assumed, which risks could be safely assumed, and how to manage those risks properly would ultimately determine how successful the country risk management program would be in the long run. The program operated as a small business within a business, within the larger context of the bank's general lending operations. The program had a $900 million portfolio of guarantees with approximately 70% allocated to trade transactions in Country A, 20% in Country B, and 10% split in Countries C to F. As of that time, the bank had never had a loss. That would be an admirable record for any organization, but especially so for a program that had been run by a team of three individuals who did not have the benefit of a structured approach to the issuance of credit and political risk guarantees or the assumption of risk.

What had been the case was that a typical client would approach the team, inform them of a pending trade transaction (often providing very few details), provide them with either a lending agreement or a suggested guarantee wording, and expect that in a short period of time a country risk guarantee would be made available to them on their own terms. Since the program did not have standardized guarantee contracts, it issued political risk guarantees largely based on the client's suggested wording. The net result is that the bank ended up assuming much greater political risk than it might have assumed if it had preapproved, standardized guarantee wordings.

In general, the bank's staff was so accustomed to accommodating the requests and demands of its clients that they were putting the bank in jeopardy. The bank's clients had been spoiled by a system that catered to their interests without due consideration of the impact that the approval process was having on the risk profile of the bank. When a client requested country risk coverage, the country risk management team appeared at times to be under pressure to approve some transactions because of promises that may have been made to the client by other departments within the bank or because of the client's stature in the bank. This created a culture in which program staff did not feel at liberty to reject a request for a guarantee, even if by accepting the risk they could be putting the bank at increased risk of loss.

This needed to change so that only those risks that were truly acceptable to the bank were assumed going forward.

Also, the manner in which country risk guarantee contracts were prepared could in the long run be a large problem for the bank. The documentation process was disjointed and incongruent; it lacked consistency and uniformity. This was in large part due to the habit of accepting client wordings because if wordings vary by client, transaction, or country, each wording will by definition lack basic safeguards that will protect the bank and put conditions on the bank's clients. At that time, the bank's clients were accustomed to getting a "free ride"—that is, an "unconditional guarantee." Since they were used to being able to dictate the terms of coverage, they were not accustomed to having to bear certain responsibilities that they would be required to bear if they were seeking similar guarantees from other institutions or insurance companies.

One of the bank's clients (a US-based bank) had already started to complain that changes being proposed for its master policy made the bank's guarantee "conditional." And yet, the US bank (and other client banks) would not think of approaching PRI providers and demanding that these companies provide PRI based on the clients' own wordings or an unconditional guarantee—which had become routine with the bank. It was important for the bank to remember who it was as an institution, what it represented, its position as a preferred creditor, and its loss history. A guarantee against country risk from this bank was a highly prized commodity, and guarantees should only have been granted to clients that fit strict guidelines and conformed to the bank's risk profile.

The bank's clients had come to rely on its guarantee program in large part because they realized they could not get the product the country risk management program offered anywhere else. The bank's clients were other financial institutions. Since financial institutions are the biggest purchasers of PRI, I was willing to bet that, if it offered a product that was competitive with what the PRI providers offered, the bank's clients would still prefer to continue to do business with it because:

- They had a strong relationship with the bank.
- Obtaining a guarantee from the bank required less time to implement than with an insurer.
- Even a revised country risk management product was likely to be less restrictive than those of the private and public insurers.
- The bank knew the region better than the insurers.

The bank could lose a few clients by transforming its "unconditional" guarantees into "conditional" guarantees, but this should have been acceptable to senior management because:

- It should not worry about losing business from clients who make unreasonable demands.
- The average purchaser of the bank's country risk guarantee already purchased PRI from commercial insurers, so the bank would be an additional market from which they could choose.
- A revised country risk guarantee program that was properly marketed among the bank's clients would significantly increase the number of users of the program.

My position was that the bank's clients had an obligation to share in the risks presented to it, and the bank should not be a "risk dumping ground" for its clients to take advantage of. It was ultimately in everyone's interest that the nature of the country risk management program change.

How the Program Was Revised

The revision of the program involved a wholesale difference in the approach to how risks were underwritten, how the risk management documentation process operated, and how program staff and senior management thought about the program. A useful place to start was to address how to manage the exposures already on the books and how to better manage new exposures that were being assumed. It was necessary to catalogue the exposures already on the books, identify problem areas, and strategize about what could be done to avoid or solve any pending claims.

Existing exposures were separated into three categories: those that

- were benign, where repayment was expected within a 3-month period in countries with no obvious sign of overt country risk
- had the potential to become claims, where repayment was due within a 6-month period and there was some sign of overt country risk
- were likely to become claims (or had become claims) where there was an obvious indication of country risk

Doing so established a watch list. Exposures in the second category would need to be monitored by reviewing country risk data on a monthly basis. Exposures in the third category would need to be monitored by reviewing country risk data weekly, and a dialogue would need to be established with the insured, preferably before the exposure became a claim. The idea was to think about risk mitigation efforts that could jointly be taken to avoid the establishment of a claim.

For example, the bank contacted one country's central bank to gain insight into what the government was thinking about how to address its massive fiscal problems. It learned that the bank was unlikely to be affected by any debt moratorium, particularly as any moratorium was likely to be imposed after payment for the remaining exposure was due. Should an unforeseen development occur on this subject, the bank could then strategize internally or with the client about what measures should be taken to minimize the size or scope of a potential future loss. The decision about whether to assume a proactive role in the claims mitigation process should be made on a case-by-case basis. In other words, where it made sense to try to avert a situation that the bank felt certain will result in a claim, do so, and where there was not enough evidence that a genuine problem existed, refrain from taking any action.

Underwriting Information

The bank subscribed to a variety of publications and substantial informational resources were at its disposal; however, these resources could only benefit the bank if they were utilized in a manner that made sense and provided the information required to make informed decisions. Underwriting information is only good for the risk management process if it can be easily accessed and contains exactly the type of information risk analysts need on a daily basis. The information gathering system must give the end-user the financial, economic, political, and current event information needed to monitor the bank's exposures.

The list of publications to which the bank subscribed was impressive, but the subscriptions appeared to be segmented by department or function. Information available to certain departments of the bank was not made available to other areas of the bank, which meant that unless a given department was subscribing to a particular publication, it would not necessarily benefit from information contained there. There needed to be a way to centralize the information-gathering process so that more people in the bank could benefit from this information. The answer appeared to be to hire someone to manage information acquisition and flow and to synthesize the information into easily digestible products that could be widely disseminated. This person could alert staff about articles or information of interest or produce a summary of the information that would be distributed throughout the bank. Many companies spend a lot of money purchasing multiple subscriptions of the same information product.

Another recommendation concerned the nature of the country risk reports that were produced in house. A team of economic analysts compiled country risk information and wrote reports for the consumption of various teams and individuals in the bank. During my visit, I had an opportunity to read one of these reports, which discussed economic issues in a certain country. I wondered whether commentary about what the data meant was routinely provided, or whether the reader was left to draw his or her own conclusions. Such commentary was not in fact routinely provided, so I recommended the bank consider hiring a country risk expert (as opposed to an economist) to address this issue. Economists can have very useful insights, but they are by nature different from those of someone who is oriented to country risk per se.

Creating an Operational Foundation

The manner in which PRI contracts were prepared was a large potential problem for the bank. As mentioned before, the documentation lacked consistency and uniformity. The best way to rectify it was to create an array of standardized products that could be pulled off a shelf and manuscripted as required to meet transactional needs. The definitions of what constituted expropriation, CI, and PV would remain consistent, or at least reasonably consistent, so that there would not be a need to re-create the wheel at every turn.

It was also important to plug some of the holes that existed in the bank's country risk product. The following is a listing of some of the basic changes that needed to be made to make the bank's product more comprehensive and protective of its interests (some of these may seem rudimentary, but the bank did not have them):

- Create a simple, short *application* form that each client would fill out for each transaction. Doing so would put the burden of information collection on the client (rather than the bank), speed up processing time, and serve as an appendix to each contract (serving as a warranty regarding the accuracy of information provided by the client).
- Create a *submission tracking system* that would enable staff to maintain a listing of new submissions on a monthly basis. The purpose was to identify trends in the number and terms of submissions received, the date they were received, the identity of the applicants, the countries in which they sought coverage, the types of coverage requested, the premium rates applied, and any comments about things that were unusual about the submission.
- Establish a *reference rate of exchange* so that there was no guesswork involved in what exchange rate would be paid to an insured in the event of a CI loss.
- Reference a *payment schedule* in every contract, whether it was a progress payment or a bullet payment.
- Establish an *arbitration provision* so that if there was a dispute between the bank and an insured over a claim payment or a claim denial, there was a mechanism set up to solve the problem.
- Implement *waiting periods* that would apply to all coverages. Doing so would establish clear boundaries for when an insured could submit a claim and what it must do in the interim to minimize loss.

- Insert a *claims determination period* in each contract so that the bank would have time to assess the viability of any claims.
- Create a system that would classify each transaction according to perceived risk. Insurance companies often use a system called *probable maximum loss,* which consists of assigning a rating for each type of coverage, set against reserves, to attempt to manage exposures.

These recommendations should have been implemented whether or not the bank chose to pursue an insurance option as the answer to its intention to create a risk transfer process. As tedious as the creation of and adherence to guidelines can be, there is value in establishing a thoughtful process for managing risk. But the culture of the bank ultimately also had to be changed to make the process meaningful.

Recoveries

When losses occur, a recovery plan must be in place. The plan the bank had drafted was excellent and addressed most of the issues of concern. What it needed was to use the bank's relationship with banking authorities throughout the region to make contingency plans and assist in the actual recovery process. The bank was able to maintain a zero country risk loss ratio in large part because of its relationship with the central bank and ministry of finance in each country, which was far superior to those of private sector financial institutions. The bank needed to use it to its advantage. It was important to establish and maintain sound relations with banking authorities in each newly elected government in the region as they changed. This was the only way to ensure that the bank's ability to recover in the event of unforeseen loss remained reliable. That implied that bank staff needed to devote time to visiting new decision makers, as well as long-standing ones, on a routine basis.

Ultimately, the bank made most of the changes I suggested and dramatically altered its risk management processes and the nature of its exposures. This took time, since so many of the exposures that existed at the time of the audit were put on the books for several years. The country where the bank originally had a 70% exposure experienced a major currency crisis the year after the audit was completed. The bank was able to avoid incurring substantial losses only because it was a multilateral institution, which gave it preferred credit status. This was fortunately a case where the bank had the good sense to address the problem before the problem erupted, and it was able to utilize the relationship it had established and nurtured with the government over the years to extricate itself from a bad situation. Private sector entities do not have that luxury.

As all of these examples illustrate, even the largest, most experienced, and seemingly most sophisticated traders, investors, and lenders can find it easy to walk into a land mine when engaging in cross-border transactions. The best advice I can give to anyone considering doing so, as noted throughout this book, is to take your time, do your homework, get the right types of information, establish sensible risk management procedures and adhere to them, and do not be afraid to say "no, thank you" to transactions that are perceived to be too risky. It is unfortunately not possible to be right every time, but if you use the information contained in this book, you will already be well ahead of the game.

Note

1. http://en.wikiquote.org/wiki/Malcolm_Forbes

Chapter **7**

The Importance of Understanding China and Its Place in the World

China is the first country since the end of the Cold War with the ingenuity, scale and global exposure to shape the world in its image.

Mark Leonard[1]

A turbulent history has taught Chinese leaders that not every problem has a solution and that too great an emphasis on total mastery over specific events could upset the harmony of the universe.

Henry Kissinger[2]

Introduction

No country has influenced the direction of global political and economic affairs in the past decade as much as China, and no country is poised to do so in this decade—and this century—as much as China. Whether it is the future price of commodities, the trade balance of a multitude of the world's countries, or even military spending among the world's great powers, China has the ability to influence the budgets of scores of countries and billions of people's lives beyond its borders. As such, it is useful to spend some time thinking about how China views the world and how the world views China. Doing so will also provide insight into the complexity of bilateral relations between nations, how the global political and economic system functions, and how investors should think about investing in China. The following discussion about China's orientation to geopolitics, FDI, the global economy, its own economy, and foreign investors, attempts to put a frame of reference around the ongoing debate about the wisdom of investing in China and doing business with Chinese companies.

Geopolitics with Chinese Characteristics[3]

The emergence of a new major power in the global arena has often profoundly shifted the geopolitical landscape and caused considerable discomfort among the established order. China's current economic and political resurgence is doing that; however, apart from the inevitable uncertainty and tension associated with any shift in global power, much of the angst in China's case stems from its failure to engage in behavior concomitant with its increased global responsibilities—or even to acknowledge an obligation to do so.

China's rise may be unique, for it has ascended rapidly onto the global stage by virtue of its total economic might, even as it retains characteristics of a developing country by GDP per capita. China seems to want it both ways: It plays geopolitical power games as a force to be reckoned with among equals, yet declines to shoulder the burdens of a great power, and even demands to be afforded the benefits due to a developing country. In this regard, China's leadership often appears schizophrenic, nursing a profound grievance against "colonialists" and "aggressors" as it expands its direct political and economic influence across the globe. China's rulers show bravado when on the world stage, but seem deeply paranoid that their rule at home could all fall apart at any time.

While China's public pronouncements may at times appear mercurial, they are more likely part of a well-conceived strategy. On one hand, China seeks to leverage benefits consistent with being a developing country, plays upon the West's historical guilt over colonialism, and exploits the West's continued belief that economic development will inexorably lead to pluralism. On the other hand, it does not hesitate to attempt to parlay its growing power into influence whenever and wherever it can. This Janus-like strategy gives China leeway and flexibility in crafting its international political and economic policy.

At home, the Chinese Communist Party (CCP) has established "socialism with Chinese characteristics" or, less euphemistically, state capitalism. State capitalism typically involves state powers using markets to create wealth, while ensuring political survival of the ruling class. As a government that now presides over the second largest economy in the world (which should become number one by gross national income by the end of this decade) and that depends intimately on flows of international goods and capital, the CCP no longer simply practices state capitalism at home: It practices it globally.

Although the West has long played mercantilist games, it has gradually migrated toward the belief that liberalization of international markets is mutually beneficial for all countries. But China continues to see international economics as a zero sum game. It finds its developing status a convenient cloak and justification for the application of global state capitalism. It engages in beggar-thy-neighbor policies it deems advantageous and distorts the world's markets according to the dictates of its political demands, while dismissing criticism of such behavior as unfair to a developing country. Similarly, on political issues, China portrays naked self-interest as the reasonable demands of a developing country and displays this behavior in nearly every arena in which it interacts with the world, from foreign aid and investment to multilateral institutions to international relations.

The undervaluation of the yuan is worth reviewing as a representative case and points to further distortions of international markets by China's state capitalism. The Peterson Institute for International Economics estimated in 2010 that the yuan was undervalued by between 20% and 40%, amounting to a massive export subsidy. However, the yuan's undervaluation may be the tip of the iceberg. As importantly, Chinese banks receive a hidden subsidy: a wide spread between the rates paid on household deposits and the rates banks charge for loans. Given that the banking system is largely government run, bankers, who are in effect state employees, funnel the artificially cheap money to state-owned enterprises (SOEs). Since households have no investment alternative to domestic banks, they in effect provide a huge subsidy to Chinese industry.

The CCP's state capitalism mandates growth and employment through exports and investment at all costs in order to ensure its political supremacy. One price of this systemic export subsidy is the distortion of the domestic economy in favor of export-dependent growth. Another, of course, is the distortion of the global economy resulting from China's $1.4 trillion in estimated exports in 2010, combined with foreign exchange reserves in excess of $3 trillion in 2011. Yet China refuses to acknowledge there is a serious problem. Premier Wen Jiabao praised the yuan's stability in 2010 as "an important contribution" to global recovery, adding, "I don't think the yuan is undervalued."[4] Wen then played his rhetorical trump card, alleging that developed countries were seeking to force unfair currency changes for the purpose of increasing their own exports. Wen provides insight into China's strategy when it faces legitimate international criticism by first denying that its state capitalism distorts markets (and therefore that it is playing by different rules of the game than the West) and, second, by obfuscating the issue, depicting it as developed countries picking on developing countries.

Even as China increases its economic presence through investment and greater influence in multilateral institutions, it continues to reap benefits intended to accrue to the world's truly needy nations. By all rights, *China should be a donor nation to multilateral development banks rather than a recipient of aid.* That China is the largest recipient of bank funds from the ADB really is scandalous because it comes at the cost of countries like Bangladesh and Nepal, the poorest of the poor, which truly need the resources. As of 2007, China was ranked in the top 15 of development aid recipients worldwide. In 2009, China received a total of $1.15 billion of overseas development assistance (ODA), according to the Organization of Economic Cooperation and Development (OECD),[5] and more than $2.5 billion in bilateral assistance.[6] In April 2010, China increased its number of voting shares in the World Bank to become the third largest stakeholder, behind the US and Japan. *The US and Japan do not receive development assistance from organizations like the World Bank; at what point does China's absolute strength count for more than its per-capita development? And why should donor countries like the US and Japan allow this double standard to occur?*

China continues to expand its own program of foreign aid (also dubbed ODA), which is closely linked to its outward foreign direct investment (OFDI). Because of the scale of its ODA and OFDI, the two combine as an effective instrument of state policy. This is really no different from how foreign assistance and FDI are deployed by a plethora of other countries, such as Japan, but China's tendency is to "bulldoze" its way into developing countries, providing cash and assistance in order to secure natural resources. China has closely dovetailed ODA with its OFDI, offering infrastructure projects, soft loans, debt relief, and grants as a package deal to resource-rich countries. This projection of Chinese state power and the frequent result (such as a tendency not to hire locals to complete construction projects and a failure to transfer knowledge from China to the recipient nation) have had negative consequences for recipient nations.

China's OFDI is relatively small, but growing at one of the fastest rates in the world. In 2008, OFDI stock amounted to just 3.5% of GDP. Since officially launching its "go global" program in 2001, China has pushed its OFDI growth rate to 116% annually from 2000 to 2006, compared to the average global growth rate of 6% over the same period. SOEs dominate OFDI, and more than half operate in the natural resources sector. In 2006, the top three OFDI investors were China Petrochemical Corporation (Sinopec), China National Petroleum Corporation (CNPC), and China National

Offshore Oil Corporation (CNOOC). Strategic service sector investments to support export and import activity, such as shipping and insurance, account for the largest portion of OFDI to date. The lion's share of Chinese OFDI represents a strategic investment; acquiring firms and footholds in strategic markets and guaranteeing access to commodities necessary to fuel the country's export-oriented economy are the overriding objectives.

Politically, China is an irredentist power that arguably has done more to advance global nuclear proliferation than any other state save Pakistan, while routinely doing business with some of the world's worst governments. Apart from the issues of Taiwan and the Spratly Islands, China lays claim to much of India's state of Arunachal Pradesh and caused major jitters in 2009 with incursions into the territory, combined with strident rhetoric. It has blocked ADB projects approved for India over the issue. It helped Pakistan develop its nuclear arsenal and ballistic missile technology. Currently, the largest recipients of Chinese military aid are India's neighbors, including Burma, Nepal, Bangladesh, and Sri Lanka in addition to Pakistan; India fears that China is engaged in a concerted campaign to undermine and contain it. In addition, China is rapidly developing its "string of pearls" strategy in the Indian Ocean, investing significant resources to develop deepwater ports in the Bay of Bengal, the Arabian Sea, Pakistan, Sri Lanka, and the Seychelles. These appear to be a basis for the projection of a powerful naval presence into what India considers its backyard.

Meanwhile, China blocks action against or actively supports a rogue's gallery of nations, among them Iran, North Korea, Sudan, and Zimbabwe. It claims it has no influence over their actions, based on its policy of noninterference, but China's support clearly requires a quid pro quo, be it natural resource wealth, business ties, or a geopolitically strategic use. China has avoided sanctions from the international community, partly due to the image it has cultivated of itself as a noninterfering developing country. While the West has also projected its power and dealt with equally noxious states, domestic political constraints make such "deals with the devil" increasingly difficult to sell to an electorate attuned to human rights, ethics, and governance.

As long as the CCP continues to govern, China will not change. It will continue to comport itself according to its zero sum vision of the world. At best, the West can hope the CCP's interests converge toward those of the larger globalized world. For the moment, even as China speaks of a peaceful rise within the existing international structure, its behavior, which at times may only be described as ruthless, belies the West's faith in its words. Indeed, the West appears to be running out of patience with China's uncompromising approach to the promotion of its self-interest. President Obama has attempted to engage China on a variety of global issues and, for the most part, found that his proffered hand was met with a clenched fist. The US may soon discard the illusion that China is gradually transitioning to become a responsible global power and may begin to react to China in a manner consistent with what it really is: an emerging global superpower that will stop at nothing to promote its own interests.

China as the Aggressor—The Case of the Spratly Islands[7]

China has become a master at pushing right up to the boundary of internationally acceptable behavior, briefly crossing over the line, retreating, and then doing the same again, until it establishes a "new normal" for what is deemed to be acceptable. This has been seen for some time in a variety of areas, whether it be compliance with World Trade Organization (WTO) rules or applications of international law. Given the saber rattling between China, the Philippines, and Vietnam over national maritime boundaries and the ongoing muscle flexing over the Spratly Island archipelago, it appears China is incapable of speaking the vernacular of international diplomacy in a manner commensurate with the expectations of responsible nation-states.

Located in the southeastern portion of the South China Sea, the Spratly Island group has long been a source of conflict between Brunei, China, Malaysia, the Philippines, Taiwan, and Vietnam. You may wonder why the Spratly and Paracel Islands are so important to China that it would interpret international law to its own satisfaction. The answer is simple: *oil*. Depending on the season and weather conditions, the Spratlys comprise 21 islands and atolls, 50 submerged land atolls, and 28 partly submerged reefs covering an area of 340,000 square miles. The Paracel Islands are a smaller group of islands closer to Vietnam and, unlike the Spratlys, are relatively farther away from Palawan, the major province in the far west of the Philippines. The Spratlys lie at the heart of one of the world's busiest sea lanes and are known to hold rich oil and natural gas reserves. In 2002 a Declaration of Conduct of Parties was agreed between China and the Association of Southeast Asian Nations (ASEAN) to demilitarize the islands, maintain the status quo, and pave the way for joint deep-sea oil exploration.

Among the six claimants, China, the Philippines, and Vietnam have been the most assertive. The Philippines predicates its claim under the theory of occupation and discovery since 1947 and Vietnam through a broader (and less particularized) French title in the 1920s. At first, China attempted to lay claim to the entire "South China" Sea—forming what on a map looks like a long tongue, extending hundreds of miles outside the country's exclusive economic zone and tracing its title, according to the Chinese, back to the Han Dynasty in the 200 BC era. It was only in 1992 that China first attempted to occupy one of the eight islands in the Spratlys—an odd way of addressing a sacred right, given that China is not known for simply ignoring its historical land claims.

Manila accused Beijing of at least six intrusions by Chinese fighter aircraft and vessels in "Philippine territory" and its own "exclusive economic zone" in the first 6 months of 2010. Liu Jianchao, the Chinese ambassador in Manila, called upon the Philippines to halt all oil exploration without Beijing's prior consent. In June 2010, under the guise of naval exercises, Vietnam fired rounds of artillery from its coastline after Chinese vessels allegedly disrupted its own economic activities in the western portion of the Spratlys.

In classic black letter law fashion, the Philippines, a long-time ally of the US, quickly turned to the provisions of its mutual defense treaty with the US. Signed in 1951, the treaty requires the parties to "act to meet the common dangers" in the event of an "armed attack."[8] The treaty's operative phrase, "armed attack," may not qualify as a semantic equivalent of "threat or use of force" under the Geneva Conventions, but couched in antiquated Cold War vernacular, the treaty also stresses that any such "armed attack" should first be reported to the United Nations Security Council (of which China is a permanent member). This implies that multilateral diplomacy and negotiations should be exhausted before the parties may resort to reasonably necessary force. The treaty contemplates an armed attack on a "metropolitan territory" of either party, or one of its "island territories under its jurisdiction in the Pacific Ocean, its armed forces, public vessels or aircraft in the Pacific." In short, ownership over the Spratlys is not clear-cut, and the US may find it inconvenient to take too strong a position in assuaging its ally, the Philippines, whenever treaty obligations are invoked. This becomes more complicated given that China preempted possible US entry into the fray by warning America to stay out of this "regional" conflict.

Whether considered in its entirety or any of its main islands, it is unclear whether the Spratlys can be categorized by the international community or the international courts as a "metropolitan territory" or "island territory" of the Philippines. It is also doubtful whether China, in making its case, can hearken to the sheer nominalism of the "South China" Sea on the map (which India, of course, would not dare do with the "Indian" Ocean). Meaningful bilateral negotiations presuppose equal bargaining power, but this is clearly not the case between China and the Philippines. Can multilateralism be the key? Vietnam tried to take this route via the ASEAN when it served as chair of the organization in 2010—a strategy that China rebuked. Instead, and despite accusations of high-handed unilateralism, Beijing, along with its ambassador in Manila, seems to be disposed to a bilateral approach.

The governing international legal framework—the UN Convention on the Law on the Seas (or UNCLOS), which entered into force in 1994—has been criticized as controversial and its own grievance machinery, ill-equipped.

There is no doubt that no less than six states are jockeying for the largest chunk in the Spratlys with regard to economic interests, which makes the Spratlys an international issue ripe for adjudication under international law. Beyond UNCLOS's built-in grievance system, contestants may turn to the International Court of Justice at The Hague. This will "legalize" the issue and will surely take long to adjudicate.

If the Philippine government wished to field a good case, it should not have presumed that the US would unconditionally support its position. The Philippines had the option to pursue the Spratlys dispute concurrently with the UN Security Council—not under the 1951 mutual defense pact but perhaps under a direct appeal to the UN body. This would have placed China, a permanent member in the Security Council, under heightened scrutiny.

The Spratly issue is ultimately a litmus test for if, or when, China may act not as an 800-pound gorilla that may do as it pleases, but rather as a responsible member of the international community that exercises discretion and judiciousness in its actions. If China were smart, it would play its hand in court, rather than on the high seas. As it continues to get its footing in the international arena, China will come to realize the wisdom of playing the game in an honorable manner consistent with a nation of its stature.

In June 2011, US Secretary of State Clinton and Philippine Foreign Minister Del Rosario held a joint press conference affirming the 1951 Philippines–United States mutual defense treaty. Secretary Clinton was clear that the United States "stands ready to support its ally, the Philippines" amidst escalating tensions over the Spratlys. Both proposed a "rules-based regime" under the parameters of the UNCLOS. Also in June, the US Senate unanimously approved a resolution deploring China's actions against the Philippines and Vietnam.[9] Entitled "Calling for a Peaceful and Multilateral Resolution to Maritime Territorial Disputes in Southeast Asia," Resolution 217 itemized key flashpoints relating to disputed maritime territories of the South China Sea and listed instances of what the Senate deemed unlawful or illegitimate use of force by the Chinese. The Senate likewise expressed support for the 2002 ASEAN–China Code of Conduct in the South China Sea, among a host of international legal norms, in the name of freedom of navigation in the maritime commons of Asia. The text affirmed Washington's commitment to multilateral processes, even as it recognized that the United States was not a party to the disputes.

China should have taken the opportunity to remind itself of the benefits of playing by the rules, adhering to the rule of law, and taking a long-term perspective on regional and bilateral conflicts. It was surely not in anyone's interest (least of all China's, which has the most to lose in the end) simply to do as it pleases and resort to Cold War era rhetoric in this case. That era already seems a century old and out of step with China, a country that is moving swiftly into what is clearly its century. It is difficult to see why China cannot embrace diplomacy as a means of resolving international disputes, and yet the Spratly dispute is a perfect example of what may be expected from it in the future.

Asia Looks Nervously over Its Shoulder[10]

The 2010 signing of a comprehensive economic partnership agreement between India and Japan made each country the other's largest trading partner. Given that Japan is still coming to terms with being supplanted as the world's second biggest economy by China, as well as with China's growing assertiveness in the South China Sea, and that India remains alarmed by China's military links with Pakistan and its growing maritime presence in the Indian Ocean, there were clear political and economic benefits to be gained by India and Japan by forging closer ties. Japan is keen to enhance its accessibility to rare earth metals (REMs), which are vital to the high-tech Japanese economy. Recent maritime conflicts with China and the subsequent disruption in the supply of the REMs have placed diversification of their supply firmly on the Japanese agenda. For India, the removal of Japanese tariffs on tea and other agricultural products is expected to be of enormous benefit, and India eyes Japanese contractors to invest in and upgrade its poor infrastructure network.

The deal was part of an emerging pattern of greater economic cooperation between India and a region looking over its shoulder at China. In addition to Japan, India has over the past several years signed bilateral trade agreements or more comprehensive free-trade agreements (FTAs) with Nepal, South Korea, and the 10-member[11] Association of Southeast Asian Nations (ASEAN). Given an existing agreement with Sri Lanka and ongoing negotiations with Bangladesh, the agreements cover the majority of Asian economies.

China has over the past several years been equally busy signing agreements with ASEAN, New Zealand, and Pakistan, while negotiations are ongoing with Australia and South Korea. China's economic and political presence in Asia, Africa, and Latin America has been growing rapidly. Its penetration in the region—from financing large construction and infrastructure projects to its voracious appetite for natural resources—has worried India, which fears being marginalized in its own backyard. Indian Prime Minister Singh has made enhanced economic and political relations in Asia his foreign policy priority with intent to counter China's growing assertiveness.

The burgeoning Indian–Japanese relationship may ultimately impact China's ability to achieve its own objective of strengthening bilateral ties with a number of countries in the Asia region. India is effectively reinforcing the concept of Japanese centrality in Asian affairs, something that had been waning in recent years. India has also recently engaged in security talks with Malaysia and South Korea and has been courting the region's foremost naval power, Indonesia. Indonesian President Yudhoyono is keen to forge partnerships with India's defense sector, while India sees Indonesia as an important strategic partner in constraining the growing Chinese presence from the Bay of Bengal to the Strait of Malacca. Every year since independence, India has invited a special guest who embodies India's strategic, economic, and political interests at the time; 61 years after Indonesia's first president, Sukarno, was guest of honor, the year 2010 signaled a realignment of the two countries' strategic interests, with President Yudhoyono attending the event.

While being historically suspicious of Indian intentions, Southeast Asia holds a much stronger dislike of China than of India. Chinese machinations in the region are still prominent in popular memory, given China's 1979 invasion of Vietnam, its support of the Pol Pot regime in Cambodia (1976–1979), and accusations of involvement in the 1965 coup that put Suharto in power in Indonesia. Furthermore, China still has unresolved border disputes with several nations in the region, including Bhutan, Taiwan, Japan, Vietnam, the Philippines, and Malaysia, as well as claiming a sizeable chunk of the Indian state of Arunachal Pradesh. Tibet, of course, remains a sore bone of contention in Sino–Indian relations; China's belligerence in relation to a sea collision between a Chinese fishing boat and Japanese patroller in September 2010 caused considerable consternation in the region and prompted many countries to forge or strengthen regional alliances with respect to security.

India's diplomacy has been heavily focused on East and Southeast Asia for more than 20 years. A multifaceted policy, "look East," aims to improve economic and political ties with the region and attempts to carve out a place for India in the larger Asia–Pacific dynamic.[12] One factor helping India in this regard is its own democratic political system, prompting many countries in the region to view India's economic rise to be relatively benign and something to be welcomed. Being the world's largest democracy lends a certain degree of transparency to India's foreign policy motives, something that is worryingly absent from relations with China. A regional order dominated over the past two decades by open markets, international cooperation, and an evolving democratic community backed by Washington's diplomatic and security ties has also facilitated India's growing stature among its regional neighbors.

The stark difference in political systems has at times appeared to be both sides' Achilles heel, however. For India, adherence to democratic norms, checks, and balances has hindered its ability to achieve its larger regional goals. For example, for decades India refused to have any relationship with Myanmar, leaving an opening for China, and long-held political tension with Sri Lanka hindered closer ties between the two countries—a gap that China since has fully exploited. For China, whose leaders have no qualms with benefiting from economic opportunities in countries with distasteful human rights records, opaque decision making has bred mistrust among its regional neighbors, who fear China's intolerance of political pluralism may spill over into its international relations. Almost every country in the region has a sizeable Chinese minority population; this is another factor that has encouraged governments to befriend India as a counterbalance to Chinese influence.

Long viewed by India as firmly within its sphere of influence, India has been concerned by Colombo's active solicitation of Chinese aid and investment. China is now Sri Lanka's number one aid donor (more than US$1 billion per year), main trading partner, and majority supplier of more than half the country's construction and development loans. The construction of the Hambantota Development Zone has been a particular source of concern. China is financing 85% of the zone, which will house an international container port, oil refinery, and international airport, as well as being used as a refueling center for both countries' navies. India claims the zone will increase China's intelligence-gathering capabilities vis-à-vis India, but both Sri Lanka and China have dismissed such concerns, claiming the site is a purely commercial venture. Where India is preoccupied by domestic sensitivities (particularly from its Tamil population, angry at the way Tamils have been treated in Sri Lanka since the 2009 defeat of the rebel Liberation Tigers of Tamil Eelam), China faces no similar issues. The Rajapaksa regime has welcomed Chinese overtures with open arms; India has been scrambling to catch up.

Sri Lanka is merely one front in a broader battle for control of the Indian Ocean. China has steadily built Indian Ocean ports in Bangladesh (Chittagong), Burma (Kyaukphyu), and Pakistan (Gwadar), while also steadily assisting Pakistan's naval expansion, much to the chagrin of India. India has referred to Sino–Pakistani cooperation as detrimental to regional peace. But in the Indian Ocean, at least for the moment, India has the upper hand, having boosted its naval spending to 15% of its total defense budget over the past 5 years in an effort to protect what it views as "India's Lake." With two aircraft carriers under construction as well as modernizing its radar and surveillance hardware, India is keeping pace with China's naval modernization program, though with fewer fiscal resources. India's total defense budget for 2011 was approximately $34 billion, while China's was estimated to be approximately $92 billion. Where India has the benefit of having to focus on only one ocean, China has been preoccupied with securing the Paracel and Spratly Island chains. For the time being at least, there is space for both countries to maintain military supremacy in their own distinct backyards.

For now, India and China will continue their respective economic and political ascent relatively harmoniously, as there is plenty of scope for both countries to flex their muscles in their own neighborhoods. China's main allies in the region have been ill chosen: North Korea, Myanmar, and Pakistan all are perceived as bad boys for one reason or another. India, on the other hand, has aligned itself with countries where it appears to have more to gain than lose (Japan, Indonesia, and Vietnam, among others). India also appears to be making more headway than China in the battle for hearts and minds, which bodes well for the long-term future of Indian relations throughout the region. This suggests that India has the upper hand in the medium term. However, while China's rise has been met with suspicion and in some cases alarm, it remains many Asian countries' largest trade partner, donor, and source of investment.

Anyone who underestimates China's ability to learn quick lessons and adapt to dynamic investment climates will be disappointed. China has proven itself to be a shrewd and cunning competitor in the global economic and political landscape, and its ability and willingness to hurl money at countries yearning for assistance will continue to enhance its influence throughout the region for many years to come.

The Maturing Chinese–Saudi Arabian Alliance[13]

As Washington's influence in the world and the Middle East wanes, Gulf countries are weaning themselves from their traditional orientation toward and dependence on the US. America's postwar political and economic supremacy in the region is now threatened as a result of its own foreign policy, but equally so by the rise in importance of the emerging powers. No country has capitalized on the shifting landscape more than China, which has, consistent with its actions globally, moved assertively to strengthen its ties with the Gulf region generally and in particular with its most important economic and political power, Saudi Arabia.

From the Chinese perspective, energy security is at the heart of the bilateral relationship with Saudi Arabia, as has been the case with many of China's most important strategic relationships over the past decade. China has adopted a multitiered foreign policy designed to acquire and secure long-term energy supplies by diversifying its sources of oil and gas, engaging in "energy diplomacy," and establishing energy reserves. With the world's largest oil reserves, Saudi Arabia was bound to be important to Chinese energy policy.

The kingdom demonstrated its intention to adopt an independent approach to global affairs more than 20 years ago by holding talks between the former Soviet Union and Afghan rebels in 1988. China and Saudi Arabia signed a memorandum of understanding and opened commercial offices in each other's countries that year as well, which led to the formal establishment of diplomatic bilateral ties. Their relationship has steadily grown since then. Just as China has been vociferous in its pursuit of a deeper relationship with the region, Saudi Arabia has been the most assiduous in the region in cultivating a stronger relationship with China. For this reason, Saudi Arabia has, since 9/11, been perceived with suspicion by America, even during the Bush years. King Fahd's first foreign visit upon assuming the throne was to China. President Hu paid two visits to Saudi Arabia in the span of 3 years.

Saudi Arabia cast its eye on Asia with greater fervor over the past decade, recognizing that Japan's thirst for oil, combined with China's and India's economic growth and increasing influence in the global economy, meant that Asia will eventually replace North America and Europe as the largest consumer of Saudi oil. In 2009, Saudi oil exports to the US fell to 989,000 barrels per day—the lowest level in 22 years, down by a third from 2008. By contrast, Saudi oil exports to China doubled between 2008 and 2009 to more than a million barrels per day. The kingdom now supplies a quarter of all of China's oil imports. The importance of each country to the other cannot therefore be exaggerated.

China's oil demand is expected to grow by nearly one million barrels per day over the next 2 years; its overall oil consumption nearly doubled between 2000 and 2009 (to 8.5 million barrels per day). China accounted for one-third of global oil consumption in 2010. So while China's oil consumption is still only half that of the US (at 18.5 million barrels per day), Saudi Arabia knows that it is only a matter of time until China will become the top consumer. The kingdom is reorienting its foreign and energy policy to become consistent with that eventuality.

The kingdom is already China's largest trading partner in the greater Middle East, and China is Saudi Arabia's fourth largest importer and fifth largest exporter in general. Chinese industrial products are increasingly replacing Western goods in Saudi markets; this is impacting Saudi attitudes regarding the relative importance of China—and therefore the West—in long-term strategic relations. If China signs a free-trade agreement with the Gulf Cooperation Council (GCC), China's perceived importance to the entire region will grow.

The truth is that many in the GCC have grown tired of US pressure on fighting terrorism and perceived US interference in domestic affairs. Many Gulf states find their burgeoning relationship with China refreshing, in that China, which itself objects to perceived US interference in its domestic affairs, tends not to do the same with its trading partners. But China's cordial relationship with Gulf states is not without sensitivities. In particular, China's repression of Muslims in Xinjiang Province has complicated its political dialogue with states in the region. Religious activists in the Gulf are bound to draw parallels between Xinjiang, Gaza, and Kashmir. Ultimately, the strength of the region's economic relations with China will dominate its political relations with China, and any disagreements over state political policy will take a backseat to ensuring that regional and bilateral relations remain cordial and on the right track.

Presuming that the acquisition of oil remains central to China's economic and foreign policy, it will not be long before China will want to take its relationship with Saudi Arabia to another level. It will want to transform its relationship from that of a somewhat bashful suitor toward a more formal engagement. To do so, it must choose between working within the confines of the post-war diplomatic landscape crafted by the United States or challenging that order in bold fashion. Doing so would break the century-long dominance America and its allies have had on Gulf diplomatic relations and enable China to begin truly to mold its bilateral and regional relations in its own image. This choice may come sooner than China, or the West, may imagine, for China's political power has in many respects already outstripped its economic power (something pundits tend not to focus on). For example, China has unleashed a fiscal and diplomatic tidal wave in an effort to secure economic resources in Africa for the better part of a decade.

But would this be something China actually seeks? Breaking the status quo ante and undoing a century of history and influence would entail enormous effort in terms of persuasion, fiscal largesse, influence peddling, and relationship building. Africa was a relatively easy nut to crack because most African nations need the money and infrastructure China has provided and are drawn to China simply by the fact that it has pursued a relationship with them. But the Gulf does not need China's money or its infrastructure and is not generally so easily accommodating to such overtures.

So what would China need to do to accomplish a similar feat in the Gulf? It would need to replace the security umbrella the US has so carefully crafted over the past 60 years. This is clearly not something that will be easily achieved, if it can be achieved at all. China is not a global naval power and has not yet projected its influence militarily outside Asia to any significant degree. But it has projected its military power in the Gulf since the 1980s through missile proliferation and arms sales. Saudi Arabia purchased intermediate range CSS-2 missiles from China in 1988, raising suspicion at the time about the kingdom's nuclear ambitions. China met an important strategic need for the kingdom that America would not agree to meet. The US has continued to measure its military support for the kingdom with its strategic imperatives for Israel—something that China has not and will not do.

For now, Saudi Arabia will keep a foot in both the American and Chinese camps, judging that its own long-term interests are well served by maintaining the comparative advantages offered by both nations. That said, the pendulum is clearly shifting toward the Chinese camp. In time, as the kingdom's economic ties grow firmer with China, their military relationship will expand. As China's military power comes to match its political and economic power globally, it will become Saudi Arabia's strongest military ally.

FDI with Chinese Characteristics[14]

Consistent with so much about China's thrust onto the global stage over the past decade, its OFDI has grown far faster than OFDI from other transitional economies. Chinese OFDI is largely politically driven, aimed at achieving specific nationalistic objectives, such as securing natural resources, acquiring strategic assets in key technologies and service industries, and creating national champion companies. China's approach to OFDI, which is often aggressive and brusque in nature, is increasingly coloring its relationship with recipient nations at all levels of development and income.

China has tailored its approach to OFDI based on the relative economic and political strength of the recipient country in exchange for specific benefits. For example, in highly indebted poor countries (HIPCs), China tends to offer to build infrastructure in exchange for the right to access to raw materials. In developing countries, China may offer to help develop an indigenous industry; in emerging markets, grant greater access to the Chinese market; and in developed countries, expand reciprocal agreements related to cross-border investment. In each case, China weighs the relative costs and benefits associated with expanding its relationship with a given county vis-à-vis what it will receive in return.

Developed countries have cried foul over the perceived anticompetitive financial support granted by the Chinese government to Chinese multinational enterprises (MNEs), most of which are state owned, operating in developing countries. Suspicions persist that much Chinese OFDI is driven by political considerations, since SOEs are under the direct control of the state. Aggressive merger and acquisition (M&A) activity by Chinese MNEs in high technology and strategic natural resources has further heightened tensions. At the same time, many developing countries welcome aid with no strings attached, which often accompanies Chinese OFDI, particularly in the natural resources sector. Yet some governments remain wary that such investment will lead to the "development trap": a flood of cash that results in heightened corruption and largesse without building indigenous capacity, knowledge, management skills, or movement up the global economic value chain. This is increasingly becoming an issue as China ramps up its investment presence in the world's poorest countries.

China's stock OFDI is still small compared with that of developed countries and was approximately equal to that of Austria in 2008. That same year, Chinese OFDI stock was only 3.4% of GDP compared to 20.3% for East Asia as a whole and a world average of 27.3%. Yet until 2000, OFDI from China was negligible. That year, Premier Zhu Rongji officially announced that overseas investment would be one of the main objectives of the government's 10th Five Year Plan (2001–2005), giving birth to a "go global" strategy. Premier Wen Jiabao reinforced the importance of overseas investment in the 11th Five Year Plan (2006–2010). The government-led strategy has proven to be effective. In 2006, yearly OFDI flow was 19 times that of 2000, growing at an average rate of 116% per year—far greater than average world OFDI growth of 6% over the same period.[15] Other emerging economies recorded growth of just 31%. According to the latest United Nations Conference on Trade and Development figures, OFDI flows more than doubled from 2006 to 2008.[16]

Until the late 1990s, the Chinese government discouraged OFDI by the private sector. Apart from a few projects run by SOEs, OFDI remained no more than a sideshow to China's export led growth. The "go global" strategy radically shifted the government's policy toward the private sector to one of overseas investment promotion, in addition to aggressively pushing strategic investment by SOEs. In other words, the "go global" strategy is essentially two pronged: in part a strategic decision to maximize China's political and economic power and at the same time a response to macroeconomic and domestic market factors.

The acquisition of strategic natural resources through investment in the primary sector abroad is at the top of the government's agenda. Such investment is designed to provide supply and price security for China's manufacturing-based economy, whose ravenous appetite for oil, metals, construction materials, and other key commodities makes their supply a national security imperative for the government. Not surprisingly, SOEs conduct OFDI in the primary sector, where investments are dominated by a few giant firms such as Baosteel, the CNOOC, the CNPC, Sinochem, and Sinopec.

A second strategic objective is to spur investment that acquires sophisticated, proprietary technology; technical skills; industry best practices; and established brand names and distribution networks. The government hopes strategic asset acquisition can propel its chosen SOEs into industries at the top of the global value-added chain, while obtaining the latest technology for potential government use. Such investment often takes the form of M&A activity. Lenovo's purchase of IBM's computer unit and Huaneng Group's acquisition of InterGen are representative examples.

China's overall strategy for SOEs is to focus on large acquisitions, aiming to create national champions from large SOEs through extensive government support while giving small and medium-sized SOEs greater exposure to the market. The government hopes to establish global, vertically and horizontally diversified MNEs operating with the most advanced technology and business practices as tools to advance its political and economic objectives. In addition to the primary sector, the government seeks to create and support national champions among some manufacturing, shipping, telecommunications, and financial services companies.

Finally, OFDI serves as a strategic objective at the macroeconomic level, relieving some of the imbalances that have been built up by economic policy that distorts the marketplace. Upward pressure on the yuan can be somewhat mitigated by encouraging greater capital outflows, and OFDI reduces the massive capital stock the government has accumulated. Furthermore, promoting OFDI allows for investment diversification, particularly away from US and other government bonds.

Domestic market dynamics have increasingly factored into OFDI growth and would have fueled its growth even without government promotion, given China's low OFDI relative to GDP. The increasing maturity and sophistication of some Chinese industries has oriented them to profitable natural expansion overseas. Fierce domestic competition has also propelled Chinese business in that direction through organic business development and survival strategies. Establishing overseas production facilities and sales and distribution networks cuts operating costs, permits access to new markets, and provides the ability to avoid tariff barriers. As China's economic growth continues, labor costs, which are already held artificially low, will become more expensive. As domestic investment continues, capital will become cheaper, so firms from low-skilled, labor-intensive industries will increasingly use their domestic knowledge to seek more efficient production markets.

While private sector enterprises exposed to market forces are clearly playing a greater role, SOEs have continued to dominate OFDI, holding approximately 84% of OFDI stock and accounting for approximately the same percentage of OFDI flows from 2004 to 2006. Nearly all of the 30 largest Chinese MNEs are SOEs, and all large SOEs are under the direct control of the state-owned Assets Supervision and Administration Council, which has authority over human resources, budgets, and investment decisions and strategy. Therefore, much of the OFDI can be viewed as an extension of government economic policy.

SOEs receive direct financial support from the government in the form of loans below market rate, direct payments, and other subsidies associated with official aid programs. The China Development Bank and China Export and Import Bank are the two primary government organs that provide support, although other state-owned banks and specially created funds also provide backing. Strategic OFDI receives significant political backing, so while private sector enterprises will gradually expand their share of OFDI, the government will maintain strict control of what it views as strategic industries.

An increased share of global investment is one consequence of China's economic and political rise. Chinese OFDI has the potential to become a large portion of global cross-border investment, but China's obstreperous use of bargaining power creates political obstacles that may inhibit that growth. The blowback China has recently received from some African countries objecting to its one-size-fits-all approach to OFDI (leaving them with a nice football stadium but no knowledge that will help them grow in the long term) has prompted China to reconsider its approach.

Some African countries are no longer simply rolling out the red carpet. In an increasing number of cases, natural resource export earnings must now be deposited into offshore escrow accounts, with the value of the exports determined at the time of export, rather than in advance. Angola has required some Chinese companies to subcontract up to 30% of the work generated by OFDI to local companies and workers and also begun to require that Chinese companies obtain a minimum of three locally sourced bids for every project. The government of Congo is now requiring that up to 12% of any infrastructure project pursued by Chinese companies involve local firms, with no more than 20% of workers being Chinese, and up to 1% of the costs of each project devoted to worker training programs.[17] This is a far cry from how Chinese OFDI started in these countries, when the Chinese simply dictated the terms of engagement.

Developing countries accounted for 95% of Chinese OFDI stock by the end of 2006, with a significant percentage in countries with weak governance and rule of law. Many of these countries have experienced the classic "resource curse" in which valuable reserves of minerals or fossil fuels enhanced corruption and conflict rather than promoting economic development. Chinese SOEs typically step into this environment with the advantages of political backing and government-subsidized and -insured investment, and China has often used significant sweeteners to win contracts. As part and parcel of negotiating OFDI deals in resource-rich poor countries, China usually sends high-ranking officials to negotiate deals alongside official development aid programs. In order to secure investment deals, the government offers infrastructure projects, politically important landmarks, soft loans, and grant programs as a package deal with a proposed natural resource investment. With government financing and political support, Chinese SOEs avoid a plethora of risks that often plague investments in resource-rich poor countries. Political and reputational risks are usually mitigated, and financing uncertainty is eliminated.

For several years, the World Bank has ranked Congo last on its ease-of-doing-business measurement. Congo has a failed legal system, a kleptocratic bureaucracy, and a nearly nonexistent infrastructure, and is consistently rated as one of the most corrupt countries in the world by Transparency International. Yet in 2008, EXIM Bank and China Development Bank (CDB) signed investment deals estimated to be worth up to $14 billion with the Congolese government. The banks agreed to build infrastructure and refurbish mines in exchange for 3.5 million tons of copper reserves.[18]

While Freeport McMoRan, a US firm, controls three times as much copper at its Tenke Fungurume mine in Congo, it took years to arrange the investment. Furthermore, the speed with which the Chinese SOEs reached a deal is striking by comparison to a mine in Katanga Province that Freeport recently opened (Tenke Fungurume Mining Sarl), which took more than a decade to finance and get off the ground. It has already faced significant obstacles, including unforeseen and possibly illegal taxes, jailed employees, and fines running in the millions of dollars.[19] Such risks hinder Western MNEs, which must respect the bottom line, but are of little concern to Chinese SOEs.

China's relationship with other emerging markets is complex. Subsidized Chinese OFDI may crowd out less or unsubsidized OFDI or internal investment from other emerging market countries. At the same time, emerging markets view Chinese investment into their countries, particularly in infrastructure and industrial projects, as a valuable resource for economic development because it comes with few strings attached at a time when FDI in general is stunted. China's strategy has been to negotiate such investment through diplomatic channels, with investments taking the form of partnerships and quid pro quo loans as opposed to being exclusively under Chinese control; emerging markets have more negotiating power than HIPCs, and Chinese negotiators know it.

A series of business partnerships emerged from President Hu's bilateral diplomacy with Brazil's former President da Silva. For example, Brazil's state oil giant Petrobras completed a 900-mile natural gas pipeline in 2010 as part of a joint venture with Sinopec. In 2009, the CDB loaned Petrobras $10 billion to develop offshore reserves in exchange for future oil supply contracts.[20] Yet while Brazil welcomes such investment and negotiates with confidence, it also fears being limited to exporting commodities to China. Brazil imports a wide variety of manufactured products from China, but sends mostly oil, minerals, and agricultural products in the other direction. At some point, Brazil and other emerging markets may take a harder line as their manufacturing firms face subsidized competition from China.

China has not hesitated to use socialist ideology as a comparative advantage to press ahead with investment in the natural resource sector in other strategically important oil-producing countries. In Venezuela, President Hu signed an accord with President Chavez in 2010 to provide $20 billion of financing to support joint investment in the country's oil, electricity, construction, and agricultural sectors. When combined with an existing investment fund created by the Chinese in Venezuela for $12 billion in return for forward sales of oil, the Chinese have committed more than $30 billion in recent years to support the development of Venezuela's petroleum reserves.[21]

In neither Brazil's nor Venezuela's case did China use extra sweeteners to obtain strategic investments; rather, it used diplomacy, ideology, and camaraderie. That tends not to be the case in developed countries, where China finds it is playing on a more even field. When placed in a competitive environment with a formidable opposite number, China tends to use a sledgehammer to get what it wants. For example, in July 2009, Chinese police arrested four employees of the world's third-largest mining firm, Rio Tinto, on charges of bribery and industrial espionage. One of those arrested, Stern Hu, an Australian citizen, was Rio Tinto's lead iron ore negotiator in China. The arrests were believed to be payback for Rio Tinto's tough negotiating stance on the price of iron ore and for a failed $19.5 billion bid by Chinalco (an SOE) to increase its stake in the company. Since Rio Tinto derives approximately 19% of its total sales from China, which is its largest market, the company has since tried to smooth relations, even though Hu was sentenced to 10 years in prison.[22]

In 2005, CNOOC failed in its bid for Unocal in the US because it did not anticipate that US lawmakers would not approve of such a strategic acquisition by a Chinese SOE. The objection to the acquisition was made on national security grounds, but also because SOE involvement implied unfair financing resources and hence not a fair, competitive landscape. An HIPC or developing country probably would not have opposed such an overture because their government officials could be bribed to accept the deal or the Chinese could find some other way to bulldoze the deal through. Such an approach will not work in a developed country because of the legal and regulatory safeguards in place.

Points of conflict with developed countries occur primarily in three areas. First, OFDI by Chinese SOEs is increasingly seen as unfairly competitive with private sector companies. China's support for strategic investments through direct subsidies and official development aid to win contracts allows for project bids that might not otherwise be viable in a free-market context. Government ownership allows for a high tolerance of reputational and operational risk. By virtue of government ownership and backing, Chinese SOEs often operate investments in risky environments where Western multinational companies prefer not to operate and at reduced cost, thereby outmaneuvering Western firms. As Western multinationals generally operate based on market conditions, albeit with advantages from established reputations, technology, and industry best practices, they and their home countries believe the playing field is no longer level. Indeed, China's growing noncommercially motivated OFDI has the potential to distort global markets, leading to long-term loss of productivity and efficiency.

Second, Chinese official aid to unsavory governments in order to lubricate OFDI contracts raises governance and humanitarian concerns and therefore hackles among developed countries' governments. China's general willingness to befriend rogue or distasteful governments, funding projects in countries such as Sudan, Iran, Venezuela, and Niger, creates tension with the developed world. Some of this tension may actually stem from the fact that the exercise of realpolitik by China puts it on top and outmaneuvers Western firms that have had their activities circumscribed in such countries due to sanctions, and reputational or political risk. Finally, Chinese SOEs' attempts to acquire ownership or assets of large developed country MNEs operating under market conditions have unnerved some developed country governments that fear losing market access to strategic resources, as well as their edge in technological and advanced practices.

If it were not for the West's preoccupation with achieving a higher moral standard and adherence to international standards of acceptable behavior, China would not have been as successful as it has been in securing OFDI in the developing and emerging world. China is in the process of beating the West at its own game: identifying what is sees as the West's weakness on the grand chess board and filling in the gaps left behind. If the West played the game the same way, China's investment ambitions would be restricted or at least more expensive. But the West is not going to change its stripes any more than China will be changing its own. In some respects, China is outmaneuvering the West in the "great game" that the West invented.

China is quickly learning the benefits of establishing more equitable and genuinely mutually beneficial bilateral economic relationships. Soon enough it will master that game, too. Once that occurs, China will truly be able to demonstrate why this is the Chinese century. Until then, the developing world will have to figure out a way to encourage China to leave something other than a football stadium behind.

China's Rare Earth Bravado[23]

In September 2010, a Chinese fishing boat purposely collided with a Japanese coast guard vessel in contested waters in the East China Sea. Japan subsequently arrested the captain of that vessel, prompting outrage from the Chinese government and, subsequently, its people. At the same time, China ceased all exports of rare earth minerals (REMs) to Japan, though it claimed no linkage to the dispute. China had been suspending its exports of REMs to the United States and Europe and more generally steadily reducing its exports of REMs since 2005. China produces 93% of the world's known REM supply, although only about a third of the world's reserves are located there. The Chinese government claims it possesses just 15 to 20 years' worth of medium and heavy minerals and thus must preserve its supply. The export quotas apply only to the raw REMs, not the processed minerals. Its most recent reduction cut an additional 30% of supply to the rest of the world in 2011.

Given that 3–5 years are generally required to make new mines operational, substantial alternative sources of REMs are years away. A number of countries, Japan among them, have already arranged to replace

Chinese-sourced REMs with those of other countries, such as Vietnam, Mongolia, Kazakhstan, Greenland, and India. Other countries, such as the US, which has the second largest known reserves of REMs after China, are ramping up their production efforts. Given America's own dependence on Chinese REMs, the US Government Accountability Office produced a report in April 2010 that calculated it will take up to 15 years for a domestic REM industry sufficient to meet its needs to be reestablished.

China's declared motives for implementing the restrictions appear simple enough: As its economy continues to grow at a blistering pace, its needs for increasing amounts of REMs to support the country's economy and export production machine will only grow, and it wants to increase its downstream minerals processing industry. In that regard, China's government is doing nothing different from what almost any other government would do: protect the country's long-term interests. The fact that REMs are in limited supply and are used to produce a wide array of products that are in high demand, are critical to green technology, or have military applications does complicate things, however.

In spite of US and Japanese protestations, China's action has not apparently alarmed the WTO, which announced at the time of the Japan dispute that it would not immediately consider whether China's actions were in violation of WTO guidelines. America's United Steelworkers Union, the EU, and Mexico brought a suit against China stating that when China joined the WTO it committed to eliminate export quotas and taxes on all but a select list of products, and that REMs were not included on that list. As a result, China is violating WTO rules, they claimed. In July 2011, the WTO ruled in the union's favor, stating that China's imposition of quotas and duties was illegal.

China has been challenged numerous times at the WTO and has lost numerous cases, but like any other member of the organization, it knows very well how to push the system to its limit, to its own advantage. Here again, China is no different from many other countries in being a clever member of international organizations that plays within the rules, but up to the very limit. China cannot really be blamed for wanting to protect its interests. It did not, after all, simply stop shipping REMs all at once or without notice. But China has become masterful at using international organizations to its own maximum advantage.

In that regard, it should not really be criticized for doing what other countries, including the US and Japan, do. Perhaps, instead, the rest of the world should be criticized for allowing itself to become so dependent on China for REMs, even in the face of an increasingly assertive China that is rising on the global stage. If there was any doubt about whether every country should similarly look out for its own interests and incorporate foresight and common sense into its future strategic planning, that doubt has now been removed.

China and the Power of the Dollar[24]

China and Russia's agreement in 2010 to allow their currencies to trade on spot interbank markets should be welcomed as a sign that both countries have matured to a stage where they can compete in the global currency markets. Although the official purpose of the move was to promote bilateral trade and reduce conversion costs, it also reduces both countries' reliance on the US dollar as a trading currency and may ultimately supplant the dollar's status as the premier reserve currency for trade between the two countries.

Cash payment for bilateral trade between China and Russia, valued at approximately $40 billion annually, had been denominated exclusively in dollars until then. In effect, both governments were seeking to phase out the dollar as a means of supporting bilateral trade. This is consistent with former President Putin and President Medvedev's long held desire to reduce the volatility of the ruble and establish a ruble-denominated exchange for oil and gas sales. It is also consistent with China's ongoing ambition to eventually make the yuan a global currency and in the process strengthen its ties with its most important trading partners.

Although the dollar remains the premier currency for global trade and foreign exchange transactions, China and Russia's action marks the beginning of an era in which the largest emerging markets are raising the profile of their currencies in an attempt to influence the decades-old, dollar-dominated global trading system. The dollar is being gradually isolated among other important bilateral trading partners in emerging markets. For example, also in 2010, India's central bank proposed alternative methods of payment for crude oil from Iran, which had previously been processed through the Asia Currency Union.

The larger question is whether any other currencies can at this time supplant the dominance of the US dollar. The short answer is "no." In the absence of a major shock to the dollar, there simply is no viable alternative. In spite of the growth of euro-denominated transactions since the currency began circulation in 2002, euro-dominated capital markets remain inconsistent in terms of liquidity availability, and many central banks remain hesitant to hold euro-denominated securities as a result of the ongoing economic convulsions in Europe. This is unlikely to change in the medium term. Also, given the European Central Bank's neutrality on the use of euros as an international currency, European governments would undoubtedly voice objection toward any overture by China to enhance the value of the euro as a global currency.

The only other currency that could conceivably be considered an alternative to the dollar is the Japanese yen. However, more than a quarter of Japan's more than $8 trillion government debt is short term, and Japan has the highest ratio of debt to GDP of any wealthy country. This limits the long-term desirability of the yen as a trading currency.

The Chinese yuan is not yet convertible on the capital account, its capital markets are not yet well developed, and foreigners have no access to Chinese government securities. However, if as anticipated the Chinese government does eventually make the yuan fully convertible and is successful in developing its capital markets to become competitive internationally, the yuan is perhaps best suited to become an alternative to the dollar over the next two decades. China could in theory seek to influence the US financial system in the interim in a variety of ways, but given its own vast holdings of dollars, any significant decline in the value of the dollar would not be in its own interest. There is no cost-free way for China to disengage itself from its own reliance on dollars.

In an effort to reduce its reliance on the dollar, the Chinese government has allowed Chinese companies to use the yuan to settle international trade transactions since 2009. The government is also promoting the practice of state-owned companies using the yuan to make acquisitions. And the government has taken an important step in further internationalizing the role of the yuan by permitting its domestic companies to shift yuan offshore for investment purposes. The attempt to internationalize the yuan is being done while the government is maintaining extensive capital controls—in essence, having its cake and eating it too. This is unsustainable over the long term.

In short, in the absence of any realistic alternative to replace the supremacy of the dollar, it is likely to remain the dominant global currency for many years to come. No other currency is more widely accepted or used. Unless some coordinated action is taken by the world's leading governments to supplant the dollar, China's savvy push to enhance the perceived future value of the yuan is likely to result in enhanced bilateral trading relationships and greater flexibility for Chinese companies, but little else for the foreseeable future. In fact, in the summer of 2011, growing concern about the short-term outlook for the Chinese economy had prompted currency traders to bet against the yuan continuing to strengthen and investors to hedge against further devaluation of the yuan, thus throwing cold water on the idea that the yuan could become a global currency by the end of this decade.

China's Great "Development" Challenge[25]

During the National People's Congress in 2010, President Wen Jaibao characterized China as a developing country with a weak economic basis, citing growing gaps between the rich and poor, and the cities and rural areas. Wen said it may take another 100 years for China to reach developed country status. This attempt to deflate global expectations of China is disingenuous at best, given that its economy continues to grow at 9%–10% per year, it has surpassed Germany as the world's largest exporter, its foreign exchange reserves (the world's largest, by far) exceeds $3 trillion, and it has surpassed Japan as the second largest economy in the world. This is impressive for a "developing" country.

The United Nations Statistics Division notes that the designations of countries as "developed" and "developing" are intended for statistical convenience and do not necessarily express a judgment about the stage reached by a particular country or area in the development process.[26] The World Bank adds that classifying countries by incomes does not necessarily reflect their development status.[27] The truth is that China possesses characteristics of both developed and developing countries and is not simply one or the other.

China has many things—good and bad—in common with a variety of countries. Its recently unveiled sensitivity to the environment, for example, contrasts with a nouveau-riche mentality among China's powerful, notable for its lack of ethical codes commensurate with their status and wealth. This is a natural phase of development, akin to what the US experienced a century ago, as chronicled in Upton Sinclair's *The Jungle*. Sinclair contrasted how, at the beginning of the twentieth century, the presence of poverty, difficult living and working conditions, and hopelessness among the working class contrasted with deeply rooted corruption on the part of those in power, which perpetuated the status quo. It took the Depression to bring America to its senses and change its ways. Something similar will undoubtedly need to occur in China's case, for it cannot continue business as usual indefinitely.

China's stellar economic growth over the past two decades is largely the result of the predominance of SOEs and an economy that remains overly dependent on a seemingly unending cycle of exports and investment. To break this cycle, what China needs is a new economic model that benefits consumers rather than producers—raising per capita spending power rather than focusing heavily on the concerns of SOEs. Paying consumers below-market rates for their deposits while lending SOEs the same money at virtually no cost does little to create a system more conducive to long-term economic health.

It also seems clear that for China to break the cycle of exports and investment it must address the issue of the valuation of the yuan. China's central bank has kept the value of the yuan slowly depreciating from 6.8 to the US dollar since July 2008. Given the nature of the economic relationship China has with the United States, Europe, and Japan (with China having had historically large current account surpluses with each), China's currency policy has hindered their ability to emerge more forcefully from the Great Recession. If the yuan were not undervalued, it would likely have had a significant positive impact on the global recovery; China would at the same time create a more market-driven foundation and realistic basis upon which to achieve future growth.

Like any other country, China does not like to be told what to do and prefers to play by its own rules. Since China has not been responsive to US demands that it revalue the yuan, the United States may have no choice but to change its approach to the subject, get more aggressive, treat the exchange rate issue as an export subsidy or countervailing duty, and take it to the WTO. The US government has been hesitant to do so for fear of a backlash, given that it is so dependent on China to continue to purchase US treasury bonds. There is, of course, a risk that a trade war could erupt, but this seems remote; China has been adept at taking its trade-related grievances to the WTO, and it stands to lose every bit as much as the United States in a trade war.

China has proven itself to be both deft at global diplomacy and ruthless as a business partner. From China's perspective, it is merely looking out for its own interests, as any other country does. But it is different to do so as an 800-pound economic goliath versus a friendly neighborhood ice cream vendor. China is searching for its footing as it tap dances on the global economic and political stage, but it is doing itself a disservice to shy away from its responsibilities so brazenly. It would be far better off embracing its well-earned position as a responsible member of the family of nations and acting like the "developing" global superpower that it is.

China's Real Estate Syndrome[28]

If something looks like a duck, walks like a duck, and quacks like a duck, it is usually a duck—except in China. In China, there can be 30 billion square feet of unused office and residential capacity (the equivalent of 23 square feet for each of China's 1.3 billion people) and the "China can do no wrong" crowd will call it evidence of a permanent long-term boom. In most countries, that kind of excess would be called evidence of an imminent collapse, but not in China.

Western pundits are divided about whether such statistics foretell continuation of China's permaboom or imminent collapse, but China is a country where market forces have less impact than the will of the Chinese government, so the boom should remain sustainable as long as the government says it will or ensures that it is. In a country that needs to grow 9% per annum just to keep up with the ranks of new entrants into the job market and that had an average growth rate of 10.3% between 2000 and 2009,[29] a long-term boom prediction may just be right, even though official statistics may be suspect.

If we have learned anything about China since it adopted "socialism with Chinese characteristics" in 1993, it is that the country has defied all conventional logic and reasonable predictions about how it would grow and come to impact the global economy. One benefit of being an authoritarian government is that it does not have to care what its people or the rest of the world thinks. Thus far, the government has done a stellar job of keeping the juggernaut that is the Chinese economy humming.

It has naturally made mistakes along the way, just as every other government has, but at the beginning of the current economic crisis, the Chinese government acted like a bastion of fiscal conservatism when compared with the US Federal Reserve. Although the Chinese government can certainly be criticized for its heavy hand, it can also be argued that the heavy hand is what has enabled China to weather the crisis relatively unscathed and to continue to do so. The world has become dependent upon China to drive the global economy, so we should all wish the government well in its task.

So is the duck that is the Chinese economy built on sustainable fundamentals or a pile of quicksand? There is much conventional evidence that the foundation of China's fantastic growth is unsustainable, but that has been the case for years, and it continues to grow and grow. For example, bank lending nearly doubled between 2008 and 2009, the sale of residences rose by 44% in 2009, and two-thirds of the country's gross domestic product consists of fixed-asset investment, which is clearly unsustainable. But these statistics mask some hidden strengths, such as that most homes are paid for in cash, urban disposable income has risen an average of 7% per year since 2000, and real output per worker rises between 10% and 12% per year. It could therefore be argued that there are checks and balances in place that enable China's economy to maintain equilibrium.

Minxin Pei, a senior associate at the Carnegie Endowment for International Peace, notes that China's banking system, which is dominated by half a dozen enormous state-owned banks, has almost unlimited access to low-cost credit, enabling it to engage in unbridled real estate speculation and giving the banks an incentive to keep the seemingly endless cycle of high growth going.[30] In 2011 it was reported that there are approximately 65 million empty apartments that Chinese citizens have purchased—not to occupy, but rather to flip at some time in the future. We know how that kind of behavior ended up in the US and elsewhere. But local governments depend on the tax revenue generated from such purchases, so they, too, have a vested interest in keeping the bubble growing.

Some Western economists predict that the housing bubble will need to be punctured before inflation rises to such an extent that it risks causing social disharmony; this is something the Chinese government is rather anxious to avoid. Although inflation officially averaged just 4.25% between 1994 and 2010, by 2011 the government had to acknowledge formally that food and other prices were rising at a much faster level than that at which it had maintained as of 2010 (approximately 5%); by June 2011 it had acknowledged that the official inflation rate was 6.4%.[31] A variety of economists and think tanks are pointing to a hard landing for China's economy, but it has been in this situation before and has repeatedly confounded the critics with either a soft landing or no landing at all.

A thought-provoking article in forbes.com[32] in 2010 claimed there was no bubble and that the amount of leverage typically used to purchase real estate around the world (the reason why so many markets have gotten into trouble) was simply not a major factor in China. Given that such a high proportion of homes are paid for in cash in China, most home buyers can actually afford to buy their homes. The article's author added that the government has imposed restrictions on the size and number of certain types of homes to erode some of the demand and that, as a result of the housing and office space glut, rental prices had dropped, taking some steam out of the equation. So the Chinese government has a handle on the real estate market as only it can.

China's financial system should be seen as a source of strength for the Chinese economy, however imperfect it may be, because of its ability to support the financing of infrastructure and other investments needed to sustain rapid growth. That the banking sector is dominated by state-owned banks that can lend at will at low cost certainly has its advantages, and it is a prime reason why China's economy may be expected to continue to grow in the 9%–10% range for the coming decade and beyond.

Another reason is that China's population is becoming wealthier—and not just in the country's coastal cities. A 2010 report by the Brookings Institution[33] says that China's middle class is poised to rise significantly not only because of the country's economic growth rate, but also because more Chinese are continuing to break out of the ranks of the poor. It is estimated that consumer-driven domestic consumption will account for up to 50% of GDP by 2015, up from 33% last year. This is a guarantee of high growth going forward.

What all this boils down to is that there is every reason to believe that a combination of government economic control, a high degree of liquidity, rising incomes and consumer spending, and the government's ongoing ability to tap on the brakes whenever the economy gets too hot should mean that the housing bubble that has developed is unlikely to burst any time soon. If it does, it can be controlled more meaningfully in China than in most other countries. The doomsayers and pessimists have been wrong every time they have predicted the Chinese economy's imminent demise. These pundits will continue to be wrong.

The Enigma of China's Middle Class[34]

Many international companies have long believed that they must have a presence in China because its 1.3 billion people are all potential consumers; this implies a seemingly endless stream of future revenue. As noted before, the existence of a robust middle class, upon which this vision is based, is clearly growing at an accelerated pace in China; however, an increasing body of research raises questions about who the country's middle class really is and the true meaning of its disposable income. This, in turn, raises questions about whether all those starry-eyed capitalists are deluding themselves in establishing operations in China with the expectation that, if they do so, they will become an instant success.

Defining the middle class with accuracy is challenging at a time when China's economy has grown to be the world's second largest, yet 10% of the population remain classified by the World Bank as poverty stricken.[35] Reputable sources disagree considerably about the size and scope of the Chinese middle class and its purchasing power implications, but there is little doubt that it will be a force to be reckoned with in the current decade.

Recent definitions of what constitutes the middle class in China range from approximately 10% to nearly half of the population. In 2007, Goldman Sachs[36] said it believed 100 million Chinese consumers should be classified as middle class and estimated that by 2015 that figure would jump to 650 million. The ADB[37] suggested in 2010 that by 2020 more than 1 billion Chinese will be classified as middle class. In 2006 McKinsey & Company[38] estimated that the disposable income of China's urban population was $622 *billion*; that same year, the Chinese government declared it to be $562 *million*.

In a study released in 2010, the ADB defined the middle class in China as individuals earning between $2 per day (the low end of lower middle class) and $19 per day (the high end of upper middle class) in income.[37] The bank noted that in 2005, 35% of the Chinese workforce earned just $2–$4 per day, another 30% earned $4–$10 per day, and less than 5% earned more than $10 per day. The bank defined "affluent" consumers in China as those earning more than $20 per day (or $7,300 per year), consisting of 44.8 million in urban areas and 11.1 million in rural areas of the country—approximately 4% of the total population.

According to a 2009 report in *The Economist*,[39] the commonly accepted definition of income for the poverty line in the developing world is $2 per day, implying that individuals above that income are by definition part of the emerging world's middle class. By contrast, the poverty line in America is $13 per day, but it would be difficult to imagine telling someone who makes $14 per day in the United States that he or she is not poor. By the same token, a person making more than $20 per day in China under the ADB's definition would hardly feel wealthy.

Defining the middle class is a relative proposition, but what seems clear is that the number of people belonging to the middle class in China and, more generally, in Asia is rising. The Brookings Institution report[40] suggests that Asia's middle class is projected to increase from 28% in 2009 to 66% in 2030—an increase of 235% in just 20 years (see Figure 31). The report says that China's middle class is poised to rise significantly not only because of the country's economic growth rate, but also because more Chinese will continue to break out of the ranks of the poor. The number of Chinese making more than $10 per day should increase from 11% today to 74% by 2030.

In 2006 the China National Research Association (CNRA)[41] defined six criteria for what constitutes middle class status in China based on education, salary, profession, societal influence, savings, and holidays. At that time, the income benchmark for being a member of the "new" middle class was just renminbi (RMB) 2,000 (approximately US$300) per month (or $3,600 per year). McKinsey notes that as of 2006, 77% of urban Chinese households lived on less than RMB25,000 ($3,676) per year—meaning that, by the CNRA's definition, 77% of Chinese *do not* belong to the new middle class.

A 2009 study by China's National Bureau of Statistics found that even with an 8.8% rise in disposable income that year, per-capita disposable income for the average urban resident was just RMB17,175 ($2,525) and RMB5,153 ($758) for the average rural resident of the country and that urban dwellers earned 333% more than farmers. This is important because, as of 2006, 70.8% of the Chinese population engaged in some form of agricultural work, according to Xinhua in 2008, and 54.3% of Chinese live in rural areas—meaning the majority of Chinese have very little disposable income.

So the idea that the majority of average Chinese consumers will own a home or a car in the near future appears to be mistaken. This represents the paradox of the Chinese consumer market, where, according to the ADB, in 2005 the percentage of "affluent" households owning a radio, television, air

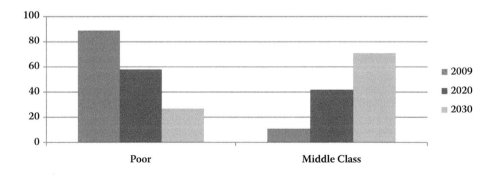

FIGURE 31 Projection of China's poor and middle class (by percent, 2009–2030).[33]

conditioner, refrigerator, or car was lower in China than in the Philippines—a country considered to be much poorer.

At the same time, a 2010 McKinsey study of Chinese consumers[42] points out that in spite of the limited number of affluent consumers and individuals with significant disposable income, in general, Chinese consumers have become more sophisticated and demanding—akin to their counterparts in the developed world. However, Chinese consumers tend not to be brand loyal, but rather are value driven, and they tend to do more research before making a purchase than typical consumers in the developed world. Thus, they generally take more time to make purchasing decisions.

The challenge for any producer of products in China, then, is to transform the average consumer into a loyal consumer, based on value for money. In reality, this is no different from what is required in many other countries. However, as the middle class and middle class consumers find their footing in China, arriving at a definition of what constitutes value for money is bound to be ever changing, as is the definition of what constitutes the middle class.

Investor Beware

China's development has been nothing short of astounding (particularly since 2000) and it has come at great cost in terms of the environment and traditional Chinese culture. China has made tremendous progress with respect to modernizing its business practices and rule of law, but it has a long way to go until it can truly say it is compliant in global best practices. As the discussion in this chapter has demonstrated, China's government is obstreperous, its economy is complicated, its consumers are unpredictable, and the task of analyzing the country with accuracy is challenging, to say the least.

One the things China does very well is to extract from foreign investors knowledge and managerial expertise, without necessarily giving much back in return. It is not uncommon at all for the government to throw its doors open to foreign investors in a particular sector and for foreign firms to rush in with great fanfare and expectations, only to discover quickly that the regulatory environment is stifling, the business climate is highly competitive, and there is no pot of gold at the end of the rainbow.

A good example of this is the insurance sector. China joined the WTO in 2001 and extended equal treatment to foreign insurance entities in 2004. The government wanted to comply with WTO guidelines, but at the same time naturally wanted to promote the development of the domestic insurance industry. As of 2011, after 7 years of "equal treatment" under the law, including a major revision of the insurance law that governs the insurance industry, Chinese insurance companies control 95% of the life insurance market and 99% of the nonlife market. Foreign firms are not treated the same as local firms, either in theory or in practice.

Rather than the percentage of foreign ownership growing, it is actually declining, for a variety of reasons. It can take up to 7 years to get a license to operate as a foreign insurer in China. Foreign firms face restrictions on how, where, and when they may expand their businesses. Foreign firms are restricted from participating in the auto market, which forms 73% of the nonlife marketplace. So many restrictions have been put in place by the China Insurance Regulatory Commission (CIRC) that foreign firms have had to hire full-time staff simply to ensure they are keeping up with the seemingly constant changes to regulations. The CIRC is slowly choking the foreign insurance market. Some laws are clearly discriminatory against foreign firms or are so difficult to comply with that it is becoming difficult for some foreign firms to operate profitably. Several senior executives from major foreign insurance companies have said that it is clear to them the government would prefer that foreign firms simply deposit their knowledge and managerial expertise and leave.

Clearly, China is not an easy place in which to do business; it ranked 151 out of 183 in the World Bank's "Doing Business" series rating for 2011. Another issue is that many firms have discovered—perhaps too late because they did not do their homework before commencing operations in China—that simply importing foreign business practices and transplanting them into China will not work. To be successful, a firm must employ a combination of forethought, insight, adaptation to the local market, realistic expectations, and constant attention to establishing and maintaining good relations with the relevant government entity overseeing regulation of its business. Foreign firms tend to make a variety of behavioral errors when doing business in China. The more common mistakes include inadequate knowledge of local laws, bending the rules, cultural insensitivity, and applying double standards.[43]

One of the biggest errors is not to do proper due diligence on a joint venture partner, and there is no better way to get into big trouble than to select the wrong partner. Doing so can lead to a host of potential problems, ranging from an inability to maneuver through the bureaucracy to running afoul of the law. The best advice is to select a highly experienced law firm to guide you through the process of selecting a partner, establishing the business, and complying with the law.

Individual investors are not the only ones who need to exercise caution when investing in China. Some institutional investors, hedge funds, and sovereign wealth funds have also had their fingers burned. John Paulsen's hedge fund, which famously made billions betting against the US housing market prior to the Great Recession, lost more than $500 million investing in Sino-Forest, a Chinese/Canadian timber and forestry company that was subsequently alleged to have accounting irregularities. Similar concerns about the sanctity of accounting in Chinese companies prompted investors around the world to dump their shares in Chinese Internet companies during the summer of 2011.

In July 2011, Singapore's state-owned investment company, Temasek, announced it had sold $3.6 billion worth of shares in two of China's largest banks: Bank of China and China Construction Bank. Officially, Temasek said it was consolidating its positions in Chinese banks, but news of the sale came amid warnings of a hole in China's public finances and news that Moody's Investor Service had underestimated the debt load of local governments in China by an incredible $541 billion. In its first nationwide audit of local governments, China said that provinces, cities, and counties owed creditors 10.7 trillion yuan (approximately $1.26 trillion). Moody's had upgraded China's sovereign rating only a year before (in 2010) and noted that since the loans had not been properly underwritten in the first place, they could not be properly accounted for as government obligations.[44]

At the same time, investment firm Blackstone pulled out of its investment in Chinese agricultural company Dili Group after being notified that its involvement with the firm complicated its ability to raise its prices. Blackstone sold its position in Dili, the parent company of a Shandong province vegetable trading organization, just weeks before European food firm Unilever was fined in China for announcing a price rise. The Chinese government had been sensitive to price rises, particularly among food products, since it started to try to control inflation in 2010, as rising food prices are viewed as having the potential to create social disorder. The presence of foreign firms in the food space, especially vis-à-vis joint ventures with Chinese companies, complicates the local firms' relationship with the government. The Blackstone move to sell its stake in Dili reflected mutual agreement that Dili would have more flexibility to raise food prices if Blackstone were not a co-investor.[45] If some of the biggest names in global investing and one of the world's leading credit rating agencies can get into trouble, it is easy to see how ordinary investors can get into big trouble investing in China.

Notes

1. Leonard, M. *What does China think?* New York: Harper Collins, 2008, p. 106.
2. http://www.goodreads.com/quotes/show/386900
3. Geopolitics with Chinese characteristics. *The Huffington Post,* May 25, 2010. Reprinted with permission from *The Huffington Post.*
4. http://news.bbc.co.uk/2/hi/8566597.stm
5. http://www.oecd.org/dataoecd/1/21/1880034.gif
6. http://www.businessinsider.com/china-just-became-the-worlds-second-most-powerful-economy-but-its-still-receiving-25-billion-in-foreign-aid-2010-9
7. China's pre-imperial overstretch. *The Huffington Post,* June 15, 2011. Reprinted with permission from *The Huffington Post.*
8. http://en.wikipedia.org/wiki/Mutual_Defense_Treaty_(U.S.%E2%80%93Philippines)

9. http://webb.senate.gov/newsroom/pressreleases/06-27-2011.cfm?renderforprint=1

10. China's and India's battle for influence in Asia. *The Huffington Post*, March 9, 2011.

11. ASEAN includes Brunei, Cambodia, Indonesia, Laos, Malaysia, Myanmar, the Philippines, Singapore, Thailand, and Vietnam.

12. Looking East: India and Southeast Asia. G. V. C Naidu, research fellow, Institute for Defense Studies and Analyses, India.

13. The maturing Saudi–Chinese alliance. *INEGMA,* April 6, 2010. Reprinted with permission from *INEGMA*.

14. FD with Chinese characteristics. *The Huffington Post*, October 12, 2010. Reprinted with permission from *The Huffington Post.*

15. Significant uncertainty underlies official Chinese OFDI statistics. Even after adopting standard accounting procedures, the Ministry of Commerce of the People's Republic of China (MOFCOM, responsible for OFDI statistics) may under-report OFDI stock and flows. The OECD found that its members reported FDI inflows from China to be 40% greater than MOFCOM statistics showed. As OECD and UNCTAD statistics are based on MOFCOM figures, there is a significant possibility that Chinese OFDI flows have been growing at an even faster rate and that stocks are also under-reported. Furthermore, much of Chinese OFDI flows first through offshore financial centers, particularly Hong Kong, the Cayman Islands, and the British Virgin Islands, shielding its final destination. A portion of OFDI therefore becomes "round trip" investment back to China via these centers.

16. Other statistical data are from the latest OECD investment policy review of China, available at www.oecd.org

17. www.foreignaffairs.com/articles/65916/deborah-brautigam/africa%E2%80%99s-eastern-promise

18. www.economist.com/node/10795773?story_id=10795773

19. www.bloomberg.com/apps/news?pid=newsarchive&sid=aINJ3y2J9YDs

20. http://online.wsj.com/article/SB10001424052702304604204575182224127279254.html

21. www.reuters.com/article/idUSTRE63H02M20100418

22. www.businessweek.com/news/2010-03-29/rio-s-stern-hu-found-guilty-in-shanghai-court-update1-.html

23. China's rare earth bravado. *The Huffington Post*, November 3, 2010. Reprinted with permission from *The Huffington Post.*

24. The Chinese yuan versus the power of the dollar. *The Huffington Post*, January 14, 2011. Reprinted with permission from *The Huffington Post.*

25. China's great development challenge. IFR Asia: Asian Development Report 2010, April 27, 2010. Reprinted with permission from IFR Asia.

26. http://unstats.un.org/unsd/methods/m49/m49.htm

27. http://web.worldbank.org/wbsite/external/datastatistics/0,,contentMDK:20420458~menuPK:64133156~pagePK:64133150~piPK:64133175~theSitePK:239419,00.html

28. China's real estate syndrome. *The Huffington Post*, December 10, 2010. Reprinted with permission from *The Huffington Post.*

29. http://www.google.com/publicdata?ds=wb-wdi&met_y=ny_gdp_mktp_kd_zg&idim=country:CAN&dl=en&hl=en&q=gdp+growth+rate#ctype=l&strail=false&nselm=h&met_y=ny_gdp_mktp_kd_zg&scale_y=lin&ind_y=false&rdim=country&idim=country:CHN&hl=en&dl=en

30. Smith, Charles Hugh. Why China's housing bubble will end badly. *Daily Finance,* August 17, 2010.

31. http://www.tradingeconomics.com/china/inflation-cpi
32. Rein, Shaun. Jim Chanos is wrong: There is no China bubble. forbes.com, November 1, 2010.
33. Wolfensohn Center for Development at Brookings. The new global middle class: A cross-over from West to East. Brookings Institution, 2010.
34. China's ubiquitous middle class. *The Huffington Post,* December 21, 2010. Reprinted with permission from *The Huffington Post.*
35. http://www.worldbank.org/research/2009/03/10427760/china-poor-areas-poor-people-chinas-evolving-poverty-reduction-agenda-assessment-poverty-inequality
36. China's illusory middle class. *Business Week,* May 9, 2007.
37. Asian Development Bank. Key indicators for Asia and the Pacific 2010.
38. The value of China's emerging middle class. *McKinsey Quarterly,* June 2006.
39. Who's in the middle? *The Economist,* February 12, 2009.
40. Brookings Institution. The new middle class: Cross-over from West to East, 2010.
41. http://socialismoryourmoneyback.blogspot.com/2011/05/class-is-concept-that-can-be-defined-as.html
42. McKinsey & Company. 2010 Annual Chinese consumer study. *McKinsey Insights China.*
43. Park, Seung Ho and Wilfried Vanhonacker. The challenge for multinational corporations in China: Think local, act global. *MIT Sloan Management Review,* Summer 2007, Volume 8, Number 4.
44. Temasek sells stakes in two of China's leading banks. *Financial Times,* July 7, 2011.
45. Blackstone China stake retreat. *Financial Times,* July 11, 2011.

Chapter 8

Shifting Pendulums, Pressing Concerns, and the State of the World

History is a relentless master. It has no present—only the past rushing into the future.

John F. Kennedy[1]

Introduction

As we have seen throughout the course of this book, the dynamics driving global economics and politics are changing at a dramatic pace. There is every reason to expect the trend to continue in the long term, as the global power pendulum is in the process of shifting between the post-World War II "great" powers and the rising powers of the twenty-first century. One of the things that is happening with greater frequency is that countries that were not previously participants in the global political arena or were peripheral players are now becoming central to its functioning. Two good examples of this are Brazil and Turkey, which have leapt onto the global stage over the past decade. While on one hand this is welcome, as the world clearly needs a new political paradigm in which to operate, on the other hand it comes at a price, with unforeseen consequences and reactions from a variety of places. As you will see here, Brazil's and Turkey's activist approaches to foreign policy have had some successes, but also some notable failures.

In an effort to think critically about current affairs from the perspective of a country risk analyst, other topics that will be explored in this final chapter include whether any of the BRIC (Brazil, Russia, India, China) countries are truly ready to assume a leading role in global economic and political affairs, whether Iraq's democratic experiment can be judged a success, whether the twenty-first century socialism that has gripped parts of Latin America is anything more than lofty idealism, and why India has reason to be concerned as events in Afghanistan and Pakistan spin out of control. Finally, the question of what has changed and what has remained the same since globalization came of age in earnest during the first decade of the twenty-first century will be explored, since there is much that globalization cannot and will not change.

Brazil's and Turkey's Messages[2]

Brazil's and Turkey's alliances with Iran in 2010 on uranium enrichment epitomized the postglobalization realities that are in the process of transforming US foreign policy assumptions, planning, and actions. Two of the pillar concepts of postwar US foreign policy—George Kennan's containment theory and mutual assured destruction—seem ancient and irrelevant in a world where rogue nations deftly manipulate global powers, information zips across the world in a nanosecond, and suicide bombers travel with impunity across borders. Taken together, Brazil's and Turkey's actions, North Korea's and Iran's failures to fall into line, and the West's inability to declare victory in the War on Terror all represent the failure of American foreign policy and the inability of policy makers to grasp harsh new realities.

The bold, assertive foreign policy that emerged from 9/11 became synonymous with preemptive action that knew no boundaries and smug self-righteousness that turned many allies against the US. The combination of unilateral action and interventionism that have prevailed since 2001 have prompted countries such as Brazil, China, Turkey, and Russia to believe that it was America that needed to be contained. To them, America's foreign policy had lost a sense of balance and had become desiccated into so many conflicting strands that it was more reactive, wanton, and reckless than proactive, purposeful, or prudent.

In this context, Brazil's and Turkey's actions were not so mysterious. Both countries are emerging regional powers whose political influence has appeal well beyond their borders. In Brazil's case, apart from its importance as a natural resource powerhouse, former President Lula da Silva was popular globally as a former worker activist turned moderate statesman. Turkey had captured the imagination of moderate Islamic countries and Prime Minister Erdogan had come to symbolize both the power of Islamist parties in politics and opposition to Western influence in the affairs of Islamic nations. But the two countries' own ambitions in the nuclear arena help explain their actions vis-à-vis Iran.

Brazil's and Turkey's Nuclear Ambitions

Brazil first embarked on a nuclear program in the 1930s and pursued a covert nuclear weapons program until the 1970s, when the military government in power went so far as to prepare a nuclear weapons test site. Brazil retains the ability to create nuclear weapons but agreed not to do so under the terms of the Nuclear Non-Proliferation Agreement and as a signatory to the 1994 Treaty of Tlatelolco, which bans nuclear weapons in Latin America. But Brazil continues to have a program to produce enriched uranium for power plants and opened its first uranium enrichment plant in 2006.

In its negotiations with the International Atomic Energy Agency (IAEA) at the time, Brazilian negotiators did not want to allow inspection of its centrifuges, arguing that doing so would reveal technological secrets. Following extensive negotiations, the IAEA relented and agreed not to inspect the centrifuges directly, but rather to inspect the composition of the gas entering and leaving the centrifuges. Brazil won a significant victory and the US was forced to resort merely to stating that it was "sure" Brazil had no plans to develop nuclear weapons.

If Brazil decided to pursue a nuclear weapon today, its centrifuges could be reconfigured to produce enough highly enriched uranium to produce nuclear weapons. In addition, Brazil has ambition to develop a nuclear submarine fleet, having authorized the construction of a prototype submarine propulsion reactor in 2007. So while the world focuses on the potential for nuclear proliferation in Pakistan, North Korea, and Iran, Brazil has similar proliferation capability but is seen as a "team player," getting a green light as one of the good guys from the IAEA and the United States, while actually having manipulated and emasculated both for its own benefit. Seen in this context, Brazil's action vis-à-vis Iran has a potentially sinister connotation in terms of its own proliferation potential.

Turkey first considered embarking on a nuclear power program in 1965 and proceeded with plans to develop its first nuclear power plant in the late 1990s, but did not move ahead due to a series of delays. In May of 2010, Russia and Turkey signed an agreement for Russia to take a controlling interest in the construction of Turkey's first nuclear power plant. It was surely no coincidence that after 45 years of ambition and delays Turkey agreed only in 2010 to proceed with construction of its first nuclear power plant. Doing so is both the satisfaction of a long-held ambition and consistent with the Erdogan government's position vis-à-vis the West's.

Rising Tension with Turkey

Turkish public opinion is divided between pressuring the government to assert itself against Iran, which many see as a competitor to Turkey's own regional political and economic ambitions, and opposing Western influence and security alliances. With both Iran and Russia becoming increasingly aggressive in international relations, Turkey feels pressure to assert itself on the global stage. Given that France, the UK, Russia, and Israel already possess nuclear weapons, and with Iran on an obvious path in that direction, Ankara has made its ambition to obtain nuclear weapons clear through a lobbying effort in Western capitals. The US is torn, on one hand, between succumbing to the seemingly legitimate defense-related requests of an important strategic ally and Iranian neighbor that can act as a counterbalance to a future nuclear armed Iran and, on the other hand, promoting the nuclear proliferation it seeks to prevent.

In 2009 President Obama referred to the US and Turkey's bilateral relationship as a "model partnership," but bilateral relations have been deteriorating since the Gulf War, when President Bush was unsuccessful in facilitating Turkish action against Iraq. Tension had risen for weeks between the two countries over the Iran issue and then the Turkish flotilla to Palestine. Turkey expressed disappointment over Washington's failure to condemn Israel's attack on the flotilla. Anti-US sentiment among the Turkish public was at the time comparable to that of Pakistan—not exactly what Washington would expect from a 60-year postwar alliance.

The Lesson to Be Learned

The Obama administration failed to see Lula's and Erdogan's actions in a broader geostrategic context. The reality is that in the twenty-first century, US allies will no longer automatically side with America on important matters in international affairs, as was the case during the Cold War. Brazil, Turkey, China, India, and Russia are all rising at a time when America's position at the top of the foreign policy pyramid is eroding. The new reality is a shifting geopolitical landscape in which emerging powers may take a position diametrically opposed to US foreign policy, and there is little the US can do about it.

Turkey remains a strong US ally and an assertive Turkey should be viewed positively, as a counterweight to an increasingly aggressive Iran and Russia, rather than simply as an ally that has fallen out of line. The same is true vis-à-vis Brazil, which may be viewed as a counterweight to Hugo Chavez and the socialist tide that has spread across Latin America. As allies, Brazil and Turkey are assets. Until the time comes when they may no longer be seen as allies, the United States should treat them as allies, rather than adversaries.

It is vitally important that US foreign policy not only continue to nurture strong bilateral relations with the twenty-first century's emerging powers, but also acknowledge that America can no longer call the shots going forward. The United States should see Brazil's and Turkey's actions as a harbinger of things to come. As Joseph Nye has noted, the paradox of American power is that in spite of all its might, the US cannot get what it wants by acting alone.

Turkey's Foreign Policy Vision[3]

We are implementing a policy of vision—and that vision is soft power, mediation, engagement and peace. We want a Middle East with high-level political dialogue, a common security environment, a high level of economic interdependency, and multicultural, multireligious coexistence.

Turkish Foreign Minister Ahmet Davutoglu[4]

Much has been written about the meaning of Turkey's newly activist foreign policy. The most logical interpretation is that by exerting its own unique brand of influence in the region, Turkey is rejecting NATO and European leadership in foreign affairs, while at the same time rejecting more extremist influences from the Gulf region. It is not so simple. Foreign Minister Davutoglu considers Turkey's recent initiatives in its neighborhood to be "preventive diplomacy" preventing the exercise of hard power by NATO and the West in the Gulf and Middle East. In his view, the region must find new ways to achieve stability and security through the use of soft power. The foreign minister's public vision of the Middle East is objective, balanced, and simple: Rather than resorting to confrontation, the parties in a conflict should embrace diplomacy and everyone will be happy.

Consistent with this, Turkey's declared objective in joining with Brazil to encourage Iran to willingly process low-enriched uranium (LEU) in France was to prevent an escalation of conflict with the West. Its stated objective in supporting the flotilla to Palestine was to help raise the standard of living of ordinary Palestinians. The trouble is that the manifestations of these two high-profile examples of Turkey's "new" foreign policy vision are a failure to achieve its objectives, severe negative impact on a host of bilateral relationships with its "allies," and the raising of questions about just what Turkey's ambitions in the region are.

If one were to give the government of Turkey the benefit of any doubt and simply agree that its intentions are purely noble, then it is to be applauded for crafting a middle path in foreign affairs in an extremely challenging part of the world. But Turkey's long-term motivations for adopting an activist foreign policy in what is arguably the world's most volatile geographical region, where many of whose governments are among the most bitter of enemies, could also be argued to be a direct challenge to the supremacy of the US at a time when US influence in the region is waning, as well as to the ability of European nations to influence the course of history in the region at a time when the viability of the European Union as an entity is in question.

Turkish Foreign Policy: Moderation in the Extreme

The pillars of Turkish foreign policy since Ataturk created the modern republic in the early 1900s have been security, stability, and peace, with the intention of fostering an environment conducive to cooperation and promoting human development. To achieve this, Turkey has adopted a policy of moderation and has historically attempted to get along with all of its neighbors. The Turkish Ministry of Foreign Affairs summarizes its philosophy as follows:

> Turkey follows a multi-dimensional, goal-oriented, balanced and humanitarian foreign policy with a view to restoring and maintaining peace, enhancing stability and prosperity in the world and particularly in its vicinity. In this vein, Turkey attaches particular importance to its transatlantic ties, actively contributes as a member to the endeavor of the NATO Alliance to maintain international peace and stability, and enhances its relations with countries in the region. Turkey is resolutely headed toward accession to the European Union. It is also helping third [world] countries in solving their bilateral problems and becoming more influential and eminent actors in international politics…Turkey is doing its best to reconcile the West with the East and the North with the South…In a world where international developments become increasingly complex and difficult to manage, Turkey will resolutely continue to pursue a responsible and constructive foreign policy, inspiring confidence in the region."[5]

In short, Turkey would like to be all things to all countries. It wants to embrace EU membership while being a member of the Organization of the Islamic Conference. It wanted a strong bilateral relationship with Israel while at the same time being perceived by Middle Eastern countries as the champion of moderation among Muslim nations. It wants to keep NATO happy by using its air force base at Incirlik to support NATO operations in the region while at the same time embracing Iran.

Turkey's foreign policy vision would work very well if the world were a utopia of peace and harmony and if Turkey existed in the middle of the Pacific Ocean rather than at the crossroads of Europe and Asia. Given that the world is anything but peaceful and harmonious and that Turkey is one of the world's most important countries from a geostrategic perspective, the adoption of such an idealistic foreign policy is bound to upset more countries than it pleases and accomplish far less than it would if Turkey simply chose which side of the coin it wants to be on and promoted a foreign policy consistent with that objective. Trying to be all things to all countries is far more appropriate for a country that does not matter and has few resources, a weak military, and an inability to project its power. For a country such as Turkey, which is none of these things, such an "extreme of moderation" serves only to diminish its place in the world.

Is Turkey Really Rethinking Its Place in the World?

Some pundits fear that the West has "lost" Turkey through a combination of benign neglect and a failure to be more supportive of its ambition to join the EU. They view the Turkish flotilla to Palestine incident and the attempted LEU swap with Iran as evidence of a shift in Turkish foreign policy away from the West and toward the Muslim world consistent with the ruling AK party's Islamist roots. But in fact, for the past 90 years, Turkey's foreign policy has been solidly Western focused; one could argue that this has been at the expense of its Islamic neighbors. Turkey has been a member of NATO since 1952. Its long-term friendship with Israel served as a counterweight to Islamic radicalism in Turkey. And it was actually Prime Minister Erdogan who commenced membership talks with the EU.

At first glance, Turkey's bold embrace of Iran may be seen as nothing more than a power play and brazen attempt to leap onto the global political stage; it is surely in part a muscle flexing exercise, but it is also about "realeconomik." Turkey's economy is heavily dependent on imported gas from Iran. Any military conflict with the West is sure to impact Iran's ability to deliver gas to Turkey and would very likely derail Turkey's strong economic growth (estimated to be 7% in 2011 by the OECD). So apart from the obvious benefit of not having another military conflict in its neighborhood, Turkey's economic health and the political health of the AK Party are hanging in the balance. Seen from this perspective, Erdogan's moderate-in-the-extreme diplomacy is not too much of a surprise, but rather very much in its own interest and not really much different from that of any other country looking out for its economic interests. But if Turkey had to choose between NATO/the West and Iran in a military confrontation, it would surely choose the former.

Similarly, Turkey's support of the aid flotilla to Palestine should not be seen as a break with the past and a stake in the heart of Turkish/Israeli relations. Nations do things that anger other nations all the time; what matters is history, not bluster. Israel and Turkey established relations in 1949 when Turkey became the first majority Muslim nation to recognize Israel. Israel remains a major supplier of arms to Turkey. The flotilla event will not permanently derail bilateral relations between the two countries and Turkey will not turn away from Israel because of realpolitik because, if it wants EU membership, friendship with Israel is one price of admission. Also Israel and Turkey seek the same outcome from the Arab spring—moderate neighbors. Erdogan must be relishing his current hero-like status on the Arab street, but he would undoubtedly relish more being remembered as the man who pushed for EU membership.

Upheaval in the Middle East: An Opportunity for Turkey[6]

Turkey's ongoing economic, military, and foreign policy engagement with the Middle East is multifaceted. Turkey provides noncombat troops for NATO forces in Afghanistan and UN peacekeepers in Lebanon, and it has significant trade relations throughout the region. A multitude of visa-free travel agreements has resulted in enhanced Turkish influence at a societal level, with Turkish pop music and television now widely transmitted throughout the Middle East. Turkey has embraced its neighbors and they have responded in kind, resulting in growing Turkish influence in Middle Eastern affairs.

But it is in the diplomatic arena where Turkey has arguably achieved its greatest success. Turkey has been an active player in attempting to resolve disputes in the Middle East, including the nuclear talks between Iran and the West, the political crises in Lebanon, the Arab–Israeli divide, and proximity talks between Israel and Syria. Turkey also helped to build the Iraq National Movement coalition (which won the most seats of any party in the 2010 Iraqi parliamentary elections) and has forged closer economic and political ties with Iran. Some of these efforts have ultimately failed, but the fact that Turkey was accepted as a mediator is significant.

Turkey has maintained a delicate balancing act in maintaining a generally good relationship with Israel. The cooling of Turkish–Israeli relations following the flotilla incident boosted support for Turkey on the Arab street, which has opened the door to an even more influential relationship with governments throughout the region. It would be wrong to view Turkey's engagement with the Middle East and wider Muslim world as something new or worrying. Turkey's ongoing engagement with the Middle East has developed gradually since the end of World War II. As Turkey's influence has grown, the EU and US have become more suspicious of Turkish intentions; Turkey's regional engagement is viewed as undermining trust in the West and reinforcing anti-Turkish sentiment among some European countries, such as Austria, France, and Germany.

Some analysts contend that competing tendencies—neo-Ottomanism and Kemalism—are driving Turkey's engagement process. Neo-Ottomanism is focused on "soft power," ensuring Turkey is well placed diplomatically, politically, and economically to take on a larger role in the Middle East and beyond. Kemalism seeks to preserve the secular legacy of Turkey's founder

Atatürk and is focused around the Kurdish nationalist threat to Turkey's territorial integrity and regional security. Foreign relations are conducted with the goal of minimizing this threat and preserving the secular foundation of the modern Turkish state.

The Turkish strategy to broaden its influence in the Middle East is being used by other emerging powers seeking a stable neighborhood from which to launch their bids to more global prominence. It is a strategy used similarly by Brazil, India, and South Africa. Turkey's "zero-problems" foreign policy is not dissimilar to the EU's own neighborhood policy of engagement with the "near abroad"—a reason to be skeptical of those portraying Turkey as turning Islamist or to the East.

Until the onset of the Arab Spring, Turkey's engagement with the Middle East was reasonably successful. But how has Turkey's strategy worked in the context of the Middle East upheaval? And is Turkey better placed to mediate regional conflicts with its zero-problems approach to foreign policy?

Turkey was as unable as other nations to steer the course of events in MENA in 2011. It tried unsuccessfully to broker a deal in Libya, and the failure of several diplomatic missions to Damascus has led to growing frustration among Turkish government officials at their seeming impotence to influence the outcome of political change in the region. Though some analysts have described the Turkish response to events as clumsy, to be fair it appears that no country has had any real influence in Syria, and the US and EU looked on equally powerlessly, first at Tunisia and then at Egypt, as violence erupted. US motives are more suspect to many in the Middle East, who view the US as having acted far more duplicitously in condemning repression in Egypt, Libya, and Syria, while ignoring shameful events in Bahrain. And France was lambasted for its cack-handed response to Tunisia and subsequent overeagerness to overthrow strongmen in Libya and the Ivory Coast. Turkey has emerged more favorably positioned than either the US or France in that regard.

Given that Turkey and Syria share a border, Turkey looked nervously over its shoulder regarding the growing repression in Syria during 2011. A new regime granting more rights and freedoms to Syria's own Kurdish minority would not sit well with the Kemalists in the Turkish government and with the military, who were already angry at American support for the significant autonomy granted to Kurds in northern Iraq. The behavior of the Syrian regime forced the Turks to deplore the violence and condemn the government, which had emboldened the Syrian opposition. Turkish fears over increased Kurdish independence in Syria were probably exaggerated, as the protest movement in Syria remained largely nonsectarian and Turkey was meanwhile preparing for an influx of Syrian refugees.

As is the case with any other nation, Turkey's foreign policy is guided by the principle of national interest, with the ultimate aim of its policies being to bring benefits to *Turkey*, rather than to neighboring states. Countries with arguably more influence than Turkey in the region have also had to sit by as the Arab revolutions have played out (such as France in Tunisia and the Americans in Yemen). Turkey is not a global power on the scale of those two nations. Its ability to influence events in the region is growing, however.

In a sense, the Arab Spring came a decade too soon for Turkey. The question is whether Turkey would have been in a better position to exercise influence had it not been engaged more heavily with the region since the mid-1990s. The answer is clearly no. Even if Turkey had exercised more influence on events in the Middle East in the first half of 2011, its diplomatic, economic, and cultural drive for greater integration and cooperation certainly did not hinder its ability to exercise influence.

Ultimately, Turkey turned out to be in the same boat as the majority of Western countries: It did not know how the evolving political change in the region would ultimately turn out, whether successor regimes were likely to be pro-Western or Turkish, or what the impact on the regional power balance would be. However, the soft diplomacy Turkey has been practicing, as well as its reluctance to engage militarily or impose financial sanctions, will stand it in good stead in both eventualities. If more representative governments come to power, Turkey can argue that it participated in military or financial actions against their leaders and that it sought an ongoing diplomatic solution to end the violence. Thus far, there has been no reason to believe that new regimes in Tunisia and Egypt are, or will become, anti-Turkish.

Some analysts have commented that Turkey does not have much to teach the emerging Middle Eastern democracies, when it seems that Turkey is better placed than almost any nation to advise new regimes in Tunisia, Egypt, and, potentially, Libya, Yemen, and the Palestinian territories. Turkey is one of the few Muslim countries that have managed to achieve a meaningful balance between the competing tendencies of Islamism and secularism.

Who then would be better than Turkey—a secular state with an Islamist government—to advise the emerging countries in MENA about how to manage a competing set of ideologies successfully?

The Folly of Brazil's Exceptionalism[7]

Brazil has been referred to as a regional superpower and an emerging global power, and former President Lula da silva had been called the most popular politician in the world by President Obama. But is Brazil's and its former president's status well deserved, and did they live up to their reputations? The answer is "no" to both questions. Rather than having earned its much vaunted position among political and economic pundits, Brazil achieved its status based more on potential than economic performance and, while Lula had certainly earned his popularity in Brazil, on the global political stage he made a mess of things.

To BRIC or Not to BRIC—That Is the Question

Goldman Sachs (Goldman) first coined the term *BRIC* in 2001, instantly catapulting Brazil into emerging regional superstar status; this was puzzling since Brazil was in the middle of a financial crisis at the time. Its $210 billion foreign debt equaled 38% of the country's GDP, per-capita GDP was just $2,800, and its real GDP growth rate was just 2.7% that year. The value of its currency had plunged by 29% from the previous year, and in 2002—the year Lula was first elected president—the country took out a $30 billion financial assistance package from the IMF.

Based on its economic performance, Brazil did not deserve to be placed on the same pedestal as China and India. Goldman undoubtedly threw Brazil into the pot because of its potential as an emerging regional power. However, based on its economic performance, Brazil still does not deserve to be in the same company as the other BRIC countries. Consider this:

- Brazil's average GDP growth rate from 1997 to 2001 was just 2.0%, from 2002 to 2006, just 3.2%, and from 2007 to 2009 just 3.9%.
- Its average GDP per capita actually *fell* from $4,100 between 1997 and 2001 to $4,000 from 2002 to 2006.
- Average annual foreign direct investment to Brazil also *fell* from $27 billion between 1997 to 2001 to less than $16 billion between 2002 and 2006.[8]

The country's GDP growth rate actually exceeded 4% only once between 2001 and 2006, while Russia's, India's, and China's average growth rates for the period were approximately 7%, 9%, and 10%, respectively. Brazil's GDP growth in 2009 was –0.6%. Through 2014 it is projected to revert back to its usual lackluster growth performance (by BRIC standards) of 3% to 4%,[9] while China and India are forecast to continue to try to tame near double digit growth. So it appears that Goldman erred by tossing Brazil into the BRIC pot and must have used different criteria for Brazil than it did for China or India. *This raises a question about the wisdom and validity of having created the term BRIC and the aura that surrounds it.*

A combination of government complacency, an inadequately developed regulatory framework, and a host of infrastructure bottlenecks prevents Brazil from achieving its full potential. Rigid labor laws, a Byzantine tax system, and government domination of long-term credit markets conspire to prevent Brazil from breaking out of its well-established pattern of below average economic performance. Having been lauded by investment banks for a decade and having been rescued by the IMF in crisis after crisis—for more than $40 billion since 1984[10]—Brazil must feel that it can do just about anything and retain its stature in the global arena.

Too Big for Its Britches

Politically, Brazil has simply gotten too big for its britches. The country's obvious regional importance and special status among global policy makers gave President Lula the confidence to leap onto the global political stage. Lula naturally sought to project Brazil's power globally, but based more on his popularity as a friend of the global worker than as a skilled statesman. Although Brazil has admittedly been a pivotal player in forming the G20 and played a significant role in WTO and climate change talks, it appears to have bitten off more than it can chew.

Brazil's foreign policy since 1985 has been based on three pillars of achieving autonomy: diversification of relations with other nations, maintaining a distance from the liberalizing international order, and participation in international forums. For Brazil, independence is paramount, and like Turkey in foreign policy, it wants to be all things to all people. As a result, a tendency to "double deal" with its international partners in order to protect itself has become endemic in Brazilian foreign policy over the past 25 years.[11]

By embracing Iran and attempting to broker with Turkey the LEU swap to France, Lula chose to give priority to Brazil and Iran's $2 billion trade relationship over Brazil's decades-long relationship with Washington. As a result, Lula burned a lot of political capital with Brazil's second largest trading partner (the US). The attempted exchange with Iran demonstrates clearly that Brazil will pursue its own path, even though it is clearly not yet ready to assume a leading role in superpower politics. As Brazilian foreign affairs analyst Matias Spekor has noted, "Foreign policy requires intellectual capital, and Brazil is ill prepared to engage in a globalized world."[12]

Brazil's attempts to play a broker role in Honduras in 2009, when former Honduran President Zalaya was thrown out of power, and in 2010 between the Israelis and Palestinians both failed—the result of Brazil overstepping its bounds and sticking its nose where it did not belong. In his desire to be all things to all people and maintain a diverse range of bilateral relationships, Lula got himself caught on a rather slippery slope and caused potentially long-term damage with some of Brazil's most important allies.

Pursuit of Autonomy versus an Adversarial Role

Brazil's desire to achieve autonomy in foreign affairs is not new, but a number of historical and current examples makes one wonder whether its pursuit of autonomy in foreign affairs makes the country an ally or adversary of the West. As noted earlier, Brazil first embarked on a nuclear program in the 1930s and pursued a covert nuclear weapons program until the 1970s. It retains the ability to create nuclear weapons but agreed not to do so under the terms of the Nuclear Non-Proliferation Agreement and as a signatory to the 1994 Treaty of Tlatelolco, which bans nuclear weapons in Latin America. But Brazil continues to have a program to produce enriched uranium for power plants and opened its first uranium enrichment plant in 2006.

Consistent with its strategy of strengthening ties with poorer countries, Brazil has abstained or attempted to dilute a number of human rights resolutions substantially in the United Nations. In February 2010, Lula visited Fidel Castro, referred to Cuban human rights hunger strikers as common criminals, and defended Cuba's treatment of political opponents. This is ironic, since Lula got into politics as a result of being a union leader and led similar strikes against Brazil's military government in the 1970s. According to Jose Miguel Vivanco, America's director of Human Rights Watch, "outside of non-democratic countries like China, Brazil has become the biggest obstacle nation to advancing universal human rights and freedoms."[13] Is this really the reputation Brazil means to forge for itself over the long term?

Aid Recipient and Provider

As developed countries have done for decades, Brazil is now using its new position in the world to attempt to influence poorer countries by dispensing aid. According to *The Economist*,[14] Brazil now commits more than $4 billion per year in foreign assistance (including disbursements from Brazil's aid agency, the Brazilian Cooperation Agency (BCA), and contributions to individual countries and other aid organizations). That is more than China and about as much as "generous" developed countries, such as Canada and Sweden. In that regard, Brazil is keeping good company.

Spending by the BCA has trebled over the past 2 years and recipient nations are quite happy to receive the aid, since Brazil does not impose Western-style conditions. Unlike China, which focuses its aid on infrastructure and natural resource extraction, Brazil targets its assistance more on social programs and agriculture, which resonates well with local populations. Since Brazil is also a recipient of aid, the country's new role as aid giver has helped blur the distinctions between aid recipients and donors. This is consistent with

Brazil's tendency to want to shake up the *ancien regime* and redefine what it means to be a developing country. But it is entirely possible that, as was the case with China, Brazil's foray into development assistance could come back to bite it later.

Its Own Worst Enemy

In spite of all the hoopla over Brazil as one of the world's globalization poster boys, its worst enemy is itself. Brazil has yet to sustain mid- to high single-digit GDP growth rates as the other BRIC countries have done, and it looks no better poised to do so in the second decade of the twenty-first century than it did in the first. Brazil's inexperience on the global stage, combined with Lula's desire to project Brazilian power, has led to a series of mistakes that are perhaps best described as reckless. By trying to shape the world to reflect its own world view, Lula succeeded in ringing alarm bells in Washington and the capitals of Europe. That cannot help its objective of gaining a permanent seat on the UN Security Council. The Brazilian government would be well advised to steer clear of the established powers' neighborhood until such time as it is genuinely accepted as a member of the club, and can demonstrate that it has something meaningful to offer by becoming engaged in the most sensitive diplomatic issues of the day.

BRICs Form Unstable Foundation for Multilateral Action[15]

The abstention by all four BRIC nations failing to support UN Security Council Resolution 1973 in March 2011, which imposed a no-fly zone in Libya in response to crimes against humanity by Libyan leader Gaddafi and tightened sanctions on the Gaddafi regime, raises serious questions about the future functionality of the multilateral system in which the BRIC countries aspire to have a stronger voice. Effectively, the BRICs sent a message of opposition to allied intervention in countries experiencing fundamental political change. Their vote was an implicit acknowledgment that such collective action often has unintended consequences and can result in one side being given an undue advantage over another. But a less obvious driver for their position is also the notion that one day such a vote could be cast against one of them.

It cannot be said that the collective opposition of the BRIC countries to allied intervention in Libya represents a formal coalition between these countries; indeed, that would seem unlikely, but it cannot be a coincidence that these four members of the fifteen-member UN Security Council all voted in unison. While China and Russia have used their Security Council veto with frequency, aspiring permanent Security Council members Brazil, India, and South Africa are still finding their footing on the global stage and appear hesitant to oppose the collective will of the established five-power permanent members of the Security Council blatantly. What they share is a long-held mistrust of Western-led military action and a more general stance in favor of nonintervention.

One of these countries' major criticisms of the West's decision to intervene in Libya has been the perceived hypocrisy of "selective intervention." While this is a legitimate complaint, several of the BRICS countries (the "S" includes South Africa) risk spouting hypocrisy of their own in the process. For example, China and Russia's willingness to put boots on the ground in foreign countries has been well documented. When, in response to Georgia's invasion of South Ossetia, Russia invaded Georgia in 2008, not a single sanction was imposed by the international community. While Georgia enjoyed widespread sympathy in the West, the action was not judged to be worth a potential rupture in the West's relationship with Russia. China invaded Vietnam in 1979 and backed the Australian intervention in East Timor in 1999 because these actions were viewed in its national interest at the time. In the end, of course, national interest is the ultimate driver of bilateral relations and participation in multilateral action.

India also has a history of armed intervention to protect its national interests. Bangladesh, the Maldives, and Sri Lanka have all experienced intervention by Indian military forces. Likewise, South Africa has intervened numerous times in its history after independence (most prominently in the Angolan civil war in 1975–1976 and in the post-Apartheid era) and participated in multilateral intervention in Lesotho in 1998. After vocally supporting the principle of nonintervention, it eventually voted in favor of allied action in Libya.

With the exception of Brazil, all of the BRICS countries have a history of military interventions, but even Brazil is equally guilty of protecting its own interests. Brazil has strong commercial links to the Gaddafi regime, and major Brazilian companies operate in the country, including Petrobras, Odebrecht, and Queiroz Galvão. It is not surprising, then, that Brazil opted to abstain on the Libya vote. It will be interesting to see how President Rousseff steers the Brazilian ship through international waters. She has signaled her intent by voting in favor of the creation of a special UN Rapporteur for human rights in Iran in the UN Human Rights Council. This is seen as the first major foreign policy divergence between her and former President Lula.

The holy grail of permanent Security Council membership plays a powerful role in guiding these countries' foreign relations with the West. Brazil craves the approval of the US for its Security Council bid, and India, having already achieved this, does not want to jeopardize it. Economically and politically, neither can afford to count the US among its enemies, however unlikely this may seem. Brazil and India would far rather join an international club led by the US and European Union than one led by China or Russia. This reasoning may in part have spurred their abstention in the case of Libya.

The escalation of the Libyan conflict prompted some of the BRICS countries to contemplate what is involved in having a seat at the world's top table. The Libyan case further highlights the limitations of a global order struggling to reconcile principles of national sovereignty with principles of multilateralism. The modern history of the world has shown that there will always be crises that require multilateral action. The question has become when the BRICS will be willing to step up to the plate and place idealism above self-interest—an admittedly lofty ambition for any nation-state. The US and European nations do not have a pristine record in that regard, but they certainly do have substantial economic interests in Libya. The difference is that they have proven willing to sacrifice that interest to participate in sometimes distasteful and necessary political decisions. When was the last time the BRICS countries did that?

Iraq's Democratic Experiment[16]

In 2004 I published an article entitled, "A Western Fix for Iraq? Forget It,"[17] in which I suggested that the United States and its allies would be unsuccessful in transforming Iraq into the Western democracy they hoped it would become. Much of what I wrote then regarding the challenges facing Iraq unfortunately remains true today.

The root of the problem is that human beings are hard wired to be tribal. Iraqis' instincts are to identify with others who share their ethnicity and religion and to be suspicious of those who do not. Iraq continues to struggle with the same fundamental issues surrounding the diversity of its people's religions and ethnicity, as has been the case since the founding of modern Iraq in the 1920s. It takes great liberalizing institutions, decades of time, and much motivation to achieve the kind of integration Iraq requires to succeed as a country. Having been created by the British with boundaries based on geography rather than ethnicity, religion, or history, the country's fate appears to have been sealed.

The net result of the 8-year war—with more than $1 trillion spent by the US government and tens of thousands of lives lost—is a dysfunctional state that functions little better, and in some cases worse, than it did under Saddam. In 2003 there was cautious optimism among average Iraqis that their lives would be better 8 years later. Today, many Iraqis have since sunken into despair. As can be seen in Figure 32, a survey released in January 2010 of 1,015 Iraqi adults noted that 51% believed 2010 would be better than 2009, but 46% believed it would be either the same or worse.

A big reason for the pessimism was a lack of faith in the country's political leaders and the political system itself. While polls confirm that Iraqis clearly prefer democracy, the partisanship and gridlock that has resulted from it have brought Iraq to a political standstill, as evidenced by the lengthy standoff in 2010 between Prime Minister Al-Maliki and former Prime Minister Allawi. The resulting impasse has tested Iraqis' basic political beliefs and created an opening for extremists to return to the arena through violence. Sunnis are not happy that Al-Maliki won the political battle. Extremists among them have promised to object the old-fashioned way.

A survey of 2,228 Iraqi adults taken between March 2007 and February 2009 asked Iraqis to identify the single biggest problem facing the country. Security remained at the top of the list, followed by political, economic, and social issues. Economic and social issues had risen over the 2-year period while political issues remained the same (see Figure 33).

■ Better

■ Same

▨ Worse

■ No Response

FIGURE 32   Do you think 2010 will be better or worse than 2009? (From www.edisonresearch.com/home/archives/2010/01/iiacss_poll_shows_iraqis_mostly_optimistic_as_2010_begins.php)

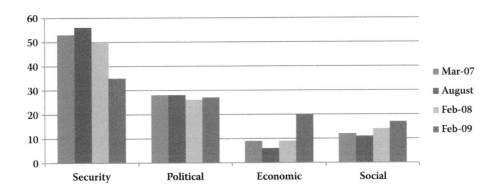

■ Mar-07

■ August

▨ Feb-08

■ Feb-09

FIGURE 33   The single biggest problem facing Iraq. (From the survey conducted by D3 Systems for the BBC, ABC News, ARD German TV, and March 16, 2009: http://abcnews.go.com/PollingUnit/story?id=7058272&page=1)

Although America's combat role has ended, the security environment remains a concern to the average Iraqi, some of whom say the perception of security is actually worse, given that the bulk of the multilateral troop presence has now departed. Although according to Brookings the number of civilian casualties was a small fraction in 2010 of what it was in 2004 (16,800 vs. 1,564 through July 2010), the number of deaths per day from suicide attacks and vehicle bombs was actually higher than it was in 2004 (see Figure 34).

Iraq is at the very bottom in Transparency International's Corruption Perceptions Index, ranked 175 out of 175 countries in 2010. In 2003, Iraq was ranked 113 out of 133—meaning that corruption has gotten significantly *worse* since the end of the Saddam era. Reporters without Borders ranked Iraq 124 out of 166 in 2003 and 145 out of 175 in 2009, which means that press freedom has actually deteriorated since democracy was introduced to the country. And the 2010 Freedom House ranking of political freedom ranked Iraq as "not free," with a political rights ranking of 5 out of 7 and a civil liberties ranking of 6 out of 7 (7 being the bottom).

Another factor contributing to Iraqis' despair is the state of the economy and basic services. Here again, in some respects, the Iraqi economy is worse off than it was during Saddam's rule. According to the *Financial Times*[18]:

- At least 25% of the Iraqi population currently lives in poverty.
- 300,000 Iraqi youths aged 10–18 have never attended school.
- The youth unemployment rate is 30% (double the overall rate).
- 65% of Iraqi youths do not know how to use a computer.
- 42% of electricity demand cannot be met (this figure was 15% in 2003).
- 40% of Baghdad's sewage flows directly into the Tigris River (following the destruction of a prime treatment plant by extremists).

Baghdad residents receive just a few hours per day of electricity in spite of the United States having spent more than $5 billion to upgrade the power sector since 2003. Although electricity generation peaked at 6700 MW in June of 2010, total demand exceeded 11,000 MW. In the 2009 poll, the

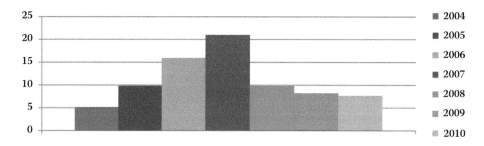

FIGURE 34 Average deaths per day from suicide attacks/vehicle bombs. (From www.iraqbodycount.org/database)

availability of clean water, medical care, and fuel was rated lower in 2009 than in 2004 (see Figure 35).

Iraq's oil ministry announced in 2010 that the country's oil reserves were estimated to be 25% higher than previously thought, at 143 billion barrels. That should be cause for celebration, but taken in context with the plethora of ills that continue to plague Iraq, it is hard to be optimistic about Iraq's long-term future. When Iraqis hear proclamations like this from their government, the depth of their disillusionment only rises because they know the government will in all likelihood not be able to transform the country's potential oil wealth into a better life for most of the country's 30 million people.

According to the International Energy Agency,[19] Iraq's monthly oil exports were 2.484 million barrels per day (mbpd) in February 2003—the month before Saddam was overthrown. At its postinvasion peak (February 2010), Iraq's monthly oil exports were 2.475 mbpd. So it took 7 years to bring the country's oil production capability to a par with what it was prior to the invasion. Monthly oil revenue reached a peak of $7 billion in July 2008 and retreated to approximately $2 billion in January 2009, where it has remained. It is projected that Iraq's oil production will peak in 2022, based on known reserves and exploitation capabilities.[20] If true, Iraq's ability to fund its future development will be more limited than many anticipate (see Figure 36).

Given the number of years that have passed and the resources expended by the US and other governments to attempt to transform post-Saddam Iraq into something better for the majority of its people, on the basis of comparative performance of the indicators addressed here, *Iraq's democratic*

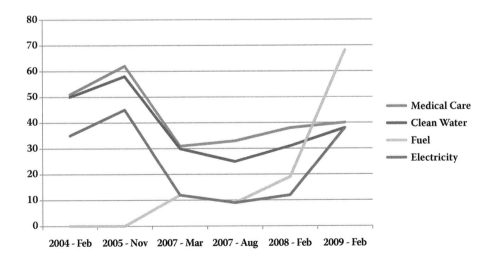

FIGURE 35 **How do you rate the availability of services in your area? (% in favor; fuel is for cooking and driving. Figures for fuel were not available in 2004 and 2005). (From http://www.brookings.edu/~/media/files/centers/saban/iraq%20index/index. pdf)**

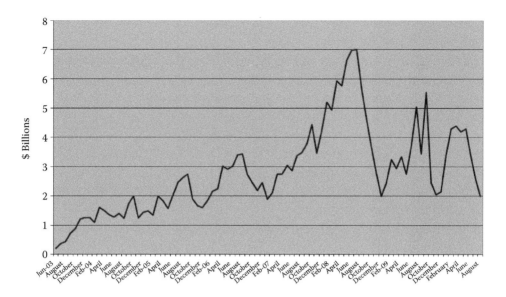

FIGURE 36 **Monthly oil revenues from exports: June 2003–August 2009 (billions of USD). (From For 2003–2008, Iraq Weekly Status Report: www.state.gov/p/nea/rls/rpt/iraqstatus; for 2009 and subsequent years, Iraq Status Report, Department of State: www.state.gov/p/nea/rls/rpt/c28010.htm)**

experiment must be judged an abysmal failure. Many economic and social indicators are worse than they were prior to 2003, the country is more corrupt, and the life of the average Iraqi is little better—and in some instances worse—than it was under Saddam.

As reprehensible as he was, many Iraqis undoubtedly long for the stability and predictability of life under Saddam. Given US withdrawal of its combat troops, a total withdrawal of US forces slated for the end of 2011, the political gridlock the country has experienced over the past year looking set to continue, and a likely return of heightened political violence, the future does not look good for Iraq.

Bolivia, Ecuador, and Nicaragua: Lofty Idealism versus Hard-Nosed Politics[21]

When the leaders of Bolivia, Ecuador, and Nicaragua joined Venezuelan president Chavez in forming a socialist bloc, they intended to transform the life of the common man in Latin America. Bolivia's Morales, Ecuador's Correa, and Nicaragua's Ortega purported to usher in an era that would put an end to the "dark night of neoliberalism," but today the pink tide of twenty-first century socialism looks more like a red tide of authoritarianism and realpolitik. This raises questions about its viability as a political force in the long term.

Ecuador has arguably been the most successful in delivering results, with public perceptions of corruption having dropped dramatically since Correa took power. Correa has successfully broken the cycle of political instability that saw Ecuador inaugurate eight presidents between 1996 and 2006. He has successfully swept out of power the old political class and ushered in a host of opposition figures. Other notable gains include a "revolution tax" wherein Correa was able to boost state tax revenues by 64% in 5 years by improving collection rates,[22] as well as to reduce Ecuador's foreign debt to one of its lowest levels on record. Buoyed by an export boom that has brought a record revenue windfall, the government has implemented costly social spending programs that it will struggle to maintain in leaner times. Correa has preached polarization and exclusion to those who do not share his vision of a new Ecuador. Crime has risen to such an extent that it has become the number one concern of Ecuadorans.

Following the oil and gas nationalizations of 2006, the Morales administration has struggled to maintain production and attract much needed foreign direct investment more generally. Despite much rhetoric, Morales has been far less radical than he initially seemed, though foreign investors continue to view him as radical. He has kept in place the vast majority of Bolivia's neoliberal economic policies[23] that were established in the early 2000s and has concentrated on reforming social, cultural, and judicial structures, with some success. However, domestic politics have occupied much of his time, which has culminated in some embarrassing events, such as when the government was forced to reverse necessary fuel price rises in response to violent protests.

Twenty-first century socialism has perhaps been most disappointing in Nicaragua, where the revolutionary ideals of former Sandinista guerrilla Daniel Ortega have failed to produce many tangible results. WikiLeaks cables released in 2010 reported American suspicions that Ortega's 2006 campaign was financed by drug lords in exchange for releasing captured gang members, as well as alleging that he granted refuge to Colombian drug kingpin Pablo Escobar in 1984 in return for large cash payments. Ortega led Nicaragua into a territorial dispute with Costa Rica with the apparent aim of boosting nationalist support prior to his November 2011 presidential election bid (which he was previously constitutionally banned from contesting). Along with Morales and Correa, he has curried favor with undesirable regimes abroad. Following widely criticized fraudulent municipal elections in 2008, the EU and US suspended most of their development aid to the country.[24] Heavily reliant on Venezuelan subsidies, Ortega has made little effort to create new sources of revenue for his country amid dwindling foreign support and sluggish growth.

The populist backbone of the political movements that propelled these leaders to power is also where many of their common afflictions may be found. The most striking example was the attempted coup d'état in Ecuador in September 2010 when President Correa was held hostage by police and security forces. After his *Alianza Pais* ruling, Correa had been deserted by several top allies who were disillusioned with his style of governance. The military only stepped in to support him when it became apparent that Correa's life was in danger.

Populist leadership styles have historically been accompanied by a reduction in political pluralism in Latin America, as incumbents crack down on political opposition or co-opt certain sectors (such as trade unions, indigenous groups, or the military) into the state apparatus. In all three countries, there have been clear attempts to reduce or eliminate the independence of the media and control the political process. The Economist Intelligence Unit's Democracy Index[25] lists Nicaragua as the second worst offender in the region vis-à-vis media freedom, following Venezuela. The index puts Nicaragua, Ecuador, and Bolivia in the bottom five. Reporters without Borders' 2010 Freedom Index lists Bolivia and Ecuador, which have fallen 87 and 43 places, respectively, as considerably more dangerous for journalists since 2006.

Political freedom has also taken a step backward since the election of these countries' "leaders of the people." The Morales administration systematically targets opposition figures. The Correa government, which still maintains a 60% popularity rating, has rapidly fallen out of favor with trade unions and indigenous movements, which are being excluded from Correa's "national project." In 2010 in Nicaragua, the daily *El Nuevo Diario* reported death threats directed toward its journalists working on alleged government corruption. International observers have deplored the widespread fraud that occurred during the 2008 municipal elections, and the local media denounce the patronage-based style of government supported by Ortega.

All three leaders have failed to deliver on campaign promises to improve the lives of ordinary citizens. In Ecuador, poverty levels have dropped slowly; the government has admitted that this is disappointing, given the vast amount of resources invested in social programs during the Correa administration. Growing lawlessness is complicated by Correa's dysfunctional relationship with the national police force. The northern border area is a source of great concern as an influx of refugees and FARC (Revolutionary Forces of Colombia) guerrillas from Colombia have combined with paramilitary groups involved in illegal activities inside Ecuador.

In Nicaragua, the increasingly dictatorial behavior of President Ortega is at odds with the democratization of politics and decision making at the local level, suggesting that the leadership of the country is proving more of a hindrance than a help.[26] The Ortega administration made progress in improving some social indicators, such as reducing infant mortality and illiteracy and widening access to free health care. But economic growth has been sluggish and slowed consistently since Ortega took office, casting doubt on the government's ability to reduce high rates of poverty in the country.

Under Morales, military spending has increased by 64% in 4 years and now consumes a quarter of government spending, raising questions about the loyalty of the military, given that Bolivia has no palpable threat to its national security. This is particularly worrying as spending on education has fallen consistently under Morales to account for just 3% of government expenditure.

Overall, the outlook for 2011 and the medium term is one of continued tension and uncertainty. Bolivia's need to wean its population off fuel subsidies will cause the popularity of Morales to continue to drop. Nicaragua's pliant judiciary has permitted Ortega to seek reelection in his seventh consecutive presidential election. Opposition figures are sure to attempt to form a coalition with the backing of some in the business sector, and the highly critical media are sure to provoke clashes with government supporters. President Correa appears determined to face down any opposition to his policies and governance style as he forges ahead with his "citizen's revolution." What is less clear is whether he will be able to maintain the support of the army and what strategy he will undertake to tackle security, given that some in his government are already concerned at the level of power and influence the military have come to wield since September 30.

Much of the lofty idealism used to seduce voters to vote for the pink leaders has been replaced by simple hard-nosed politics. In that regard, twenty-first century socialism is no different from other "democratic" movements that have led to authoritarianism.

India's Ongoing Concerns about Pakistan and Afghanistan[27]

There is immense uncertainty and disquiet among the Indian diplomatic and military community, as well as among ordinary citizens, at what Indians see as continuing tacit US approval of Pakistani duplicity in the war on terror. Based on leaked Pentagon memoranda and recollections by those who were once in the inner circle of US interaction with Pakistan, it is clear now that the US tacitly colluded in nurturing Pakistan's Islamic fundamentalists by looking the other way while evidence mounted that elements of the Pakistani government supported the Taliban and other jihadist movements. Pakistan certainly has created its own monster in doing so and is now plagued by the scourge of fundamentalist elements within its borders and government. If Pakistan were the only country impacted by these actions, it would be bad enough, but the entire region has been impacted, with long-term consequences.

Ongoing military aid from the US to Pakistan remains a sore point with India, especially after it became clear that there is no way Osama Bin Laden could have lived as safely as he did in Abbottabad for so long without the complicity and knowledge of senior elements of the Pakistani military. Of course, if it were not for America's need to remain engaged with Pakistan because of the central role it plays in the US war against the Taliban in Afghanistan, as well as Pakistan's status as a nuclear power, US foreign policy toward Pakistan might be different. However, given the harsh realities of the Afpak region, and Pakistan's growing nuclear capability, the US has a rather narrow bandwidth of foreign policy options in dealing with Pakistan. The terrible dilemma which America finds itself in is best summed up by a senior American diplomat, who said recently that for the first time in US history it is dealing with a nation "which is both an ally and an adversary."

As America finds itself in a most distressing dilemma in the Afpak region, a number of Indian security analysts and diplomats can only say, "We told you so," though without the usual relish. American policy toward Pakistan in the post-Cold War years has made little sense to Indians, who cannot see how the United States has been able to advance either of its two professed foreign policy aims: promoting a solidly pro-Western regime in Pakistan and strengthening the country's democracy and liberal values. In the Indian view, successive American regimes have put amazingly misplaced trust in the Pakistani leadership's ability or desire to rein in the Taliban and other militant elements on its soil. In fact, India has been miffed at the United States over its ongoing suggestion that India offer concessions to Pakistan over the vexed Kashmir dispute, particularly since America, which has launched two wars in the name of pursuing the perpetrators of 9/11, displays fleeting similar concern for accountability when India demands it from Pakistan.

At this point in time, any US urging to placate Pakistan seems disingenuous at best and self-defeating at worst. Having gotten over their anger at past US actions that helped prop up the so-called "rogue elements" inside the Pakistani army, Indian officials continue to be very skeptical of the notion that these same entities can somehow be cajoled into jettisoning their pro-jihadist orientation.

At the broader level, however, Indian analysts and diplomats perfectly sympathize with America's huge dilemma in Afghanistan: It can neither leave nor stay without paying an enormous price. For America to leave Afghanistan now or in the near future, even symbolically, while the Taliban are resilient and when large swathes of the country have slipped or are slipping out of government control risks creating the image of a hasty and inglorious exit that could embolden Islamic radicals everywhere. And yet, staying on in Afghanistan for an extended period is likely to confer greater legitimacy on the Taliban as freedom fighters against foreign invaders and will further embroil the United States in a war it really cannot win, let alone have the will and financial resources to continue to fight.

But the most serious aspect is that the complex political and historical strands in Pakistan, already raw and fragile, risk being provoked at any US exit from Afghanistan, no matter how "honorable" that exit is dressed up to appear to be. The impact on Pakistan is very likely to be to push this already unstable and dangerously isolated country further toward chaos.

From India's point of view, Afghanistan can never be made secure for the United States as long as Pakistan remains a safe haven for Islamic jihadist groups. No matter who their declared target is for now, their unbending fundamentalism, which is opposed to any form of cohabitation with other lifestyles and beliefs, will inevitably seek to strike Western targets. As long as armed jihadists can be recruited in large numbers in Pakistan and move freely—as they do—across the Afpak border, Afghanistan will continue to have festering militancy that is deadly to US interests.

Indian diplomatic corridors are full of stories of encounters with Pakistan's liberal elite, who are now running scared. In private south Asian gatherings, senior Pakistanis now readily admit to their Indian counterparts that 60 years of a terribly misguided education system and national policy that has encouraged deep ideological malice, violence, and sense of religious embattlement has been disastrous for Pakistan in every way.

In many Western quarters, Pakistan has now become the equivalent of a seriously dysfunctional and delinquent "special child" who throws violent tantrums, is inherently dangerous to itself and others, and is guided by deeply ingrained habits rather than rational logic. Suddenly, American movies and TV shows have started casting Pakistan as the villainous country in the plot, while the blogosphere is full of less restrained and more openly anti-Pakistan comments. This sudden demonization of its bête noir actually provides no comfort to India because a Pakistan pushed to the wall is hardly in its own interests. India would clearly rather have a fully functional, secure, peaceful, and reliable neighbor.

At the same time, however, US pronouncements remain ambiguous if not worrying. Despite increasing proximity with the US on a host of policy, geopolitical, and cultural issues, there is lingering belief in India that the American foreign policy establishment, which has generously provided the Pakistani army with enormous amounts of aid, equipment, training, and psychological confidence over the past 50 years, has not really learned from its disastrous track record in this region or lost its inclination to play "big power" games. If, in the effort to craft a sensible policy in Afpak, US policy makers choose to involve and rely more on this new friend in south Asia, they will find India more than willing to lend a helping hand.

Globalization Will Not Change Some Things

All country risk analysts can really do is look at history, compare it with the present, and make an educated guess about what it means for the future. Since none of us has a crystal ball, what else can we do? It is only natural for an analyst to assume that history will repeat itself and, sometimes, it does. This is a dangerous brush to paint with, however, since to be accurate, everything else must remain the same, and we know that is not the case. That is one reason why economists and stock pickers so often get their predictions wrong; they assume that because an economy or stock performed one way in the past, it will continue to do so. The trouble is that the global economy is dynamic and, since economics and politics are inextricably linked, politics changes right along with it. But as we will see in what follows, some or our views about the state of the world and our expectations for how it may develop in the future may be wildly off course.

The era of globalization was supposed to level out some of the inequalities in the world we live in and raise the level of income of the majority of the world's people. But if global GDP figures from 1950 to 2008 are any indication, the developed and developing worlds are already *exactly* equal in terms of GDP growth and have been for decades! The average GDP rate for the period was 2.62% per annum for both developed and developing countries, with world average GDP growth at 2.24% for the period. Almost 60 years of statistics shows that, while income disparities certainly exist (with emerging Asia growth at the fastest rate and sub-Saharan Africa the lowest), on average the highest growth countries pulled up the average for the lowest growth countries, and the world has grown at a respectable rate since 1950.[28]

My expectation is that these rates of growth will remain more or less the same on a regional basis in coming decades, despite globalization, because growth patterns are already established. Asia has been leading the train and sub-Saharan Africa has been lagging behind for quite some time already. I see no reason to believe that Asia is likely to slow down or that sub-Saharan Africa is likely to experience a surge in growth in the short or medium term. Longer term, this may be possible. What I would expect to change is the equality of GDP growth rates between developed and developing countries, as it seems clear that, overall, developed countries will continue to experience slower growth and developing countries will experience accelerated growth.

If we compare global GDP with populations living on less than $2 per day and where conflicts are ongoing, a striking correlation appears between the relative level of wealth and the degree of conflict in the world. As noted in Maps 6, 7, and 8, the regions with the lowest GDP and highest number of people living in extreme poverty generally correlate with the highest number of ongoing intrastate or interstate conflicts. So the countries and regions

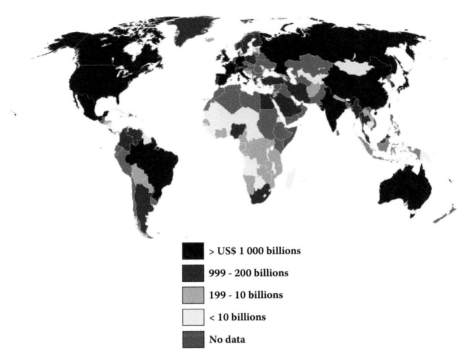

Legend:
- > US$ 1 000 billions
- 999 - 200 billions
- 199 - 10 billions
- < 10 billions
- No data

MAP 6   Global GDP: 2010. (From: http://en.wikipedia.org/wiki/File:World_Normal_ GDP_2010.svg)

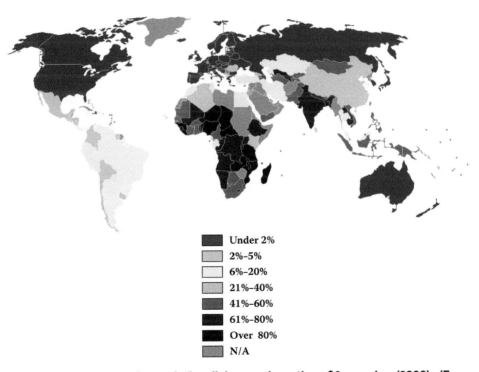

Legend:
- Under 2%
- 2%–5%
- 6%–20%
- 21%–40%
- 41%–60%
- 61%–80%
- Over 80%
- N/A

MAP 7   Percentage of population living on less than $2 per day (2009). (From http://en.wikipedia.org/wiki/File:Percentage_population_living_on_less_than_$2_ per_day_2009.png)

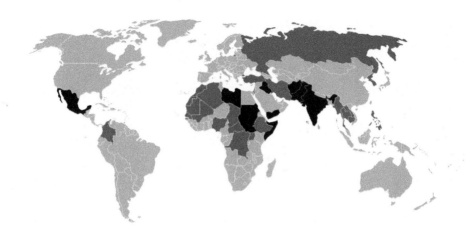

MAP 8   Ongoing military conflicts (as of 2010). Black = major wars (1,000+ deaths per year); blue = other conflicts. (Form http://en.wikipedia.org/wiki/File:Ongoing_ Conflicts.png)

that need to grow the most are least likely to grow as a result of their poverty and instability. Regrettably, that, too, is unlikely to change in the short or even medium term.

A comparison of developing and BRIC countries reveals some surprises regarding the percentage of people living under the poverty line. Figure 37, which is a sampling of nations but includes the world's lowest and highest rates of poverty, shows that, at 3% as of 2008, *China has the lowest percentage of people living below the poverty line,* while the Democratic Republic of Congo has the highest at 71%. This is an astonishing achievement for China because in 1990 its rural poverty rate was 43%.[29] But to demonstrate that high GDP growth rates do not necessarily correlate to low poverty rates, two other BRIC countries—Brazil and Russia, which each had 5.2% GDP growth rates in 2008—have comparably high poverty rates of 22% and 20%, respectively. And Georgia, which ranks number 12 (out of 183) in terms of desirability as a place to do business in the World Bank's "Doing Business" series, has a poverty rate of 55%.

As Figure 38 notes, high rates of poverty also exist among the developed countries. Bermuda, with the highest per-capita GDP rate in the world (approximately $89,000 in 2009), has a poverty rate of 19%. The UAE, with a per-capita GDP rate of $50,000 per year, has a poverty rate of 20%, while the United States, with a GDP per capita of $46,000, had a poverty rate of 12% in 2009[30] (this was revised up to 16% in 2011); thus, *the US poverty rate was five times higher than that of China in 2011.* France has the lowest poverty rate among developed countries (6%). Poverty exists in every country and is rising in many developed countries.

That said, the global Gini coefficient is falling, as noted in Figure 39, largely due to per-capita income gains made in the most populous developing and BRIC countries. Between 1980 and 2006, the degree of inequality among all nations fell by about 8%, from a ranking of 66.5 to a ranking of 61. At the

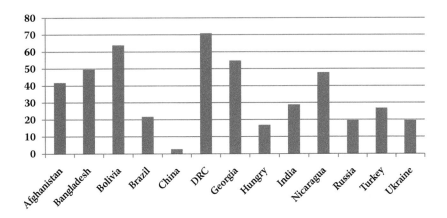

FIGURE 37   Percentage of population in selected BRIC and developing countries living under the poverty line. (From UNDP, Human Development Indices, a Statistical Update, *2008.*)

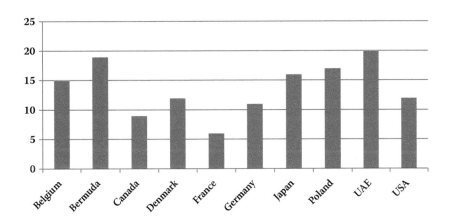

FIGURE 38   Percentage of population in selected developed countries living under the poverty line. (From CIA, *World Fact Book*, February 2011.)

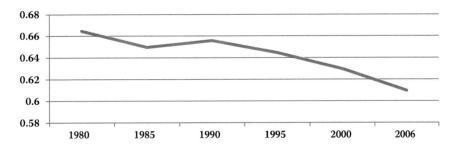

FIGURE 39   Global Gini coefficient: 1980–2006. (From: Columbia University, OECD, World Bank.)

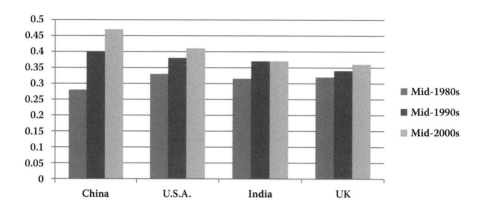

FIGURE 40   Gini coefficient for selected countries: 1980s–2000s. (From Columbia University, OECD, United Nations, World Bank.)

same time, inequality among some developed and BRIC countries is actually rising. Figure 40 shows how the Gini coefficient rose between the mid-1980s and mid-2000s in China, India, the UK, and the United States—evidence that there is a growing gap between those gaining and losing wealth in some of the largest and wealthiest countries. Over time, this will create social tension and rising political risk.

Another factor contributing to social tension and political risk is the rising rate of inflation. It is generally the case that states with the lowest amount of inflation tend to be stronger than those with higher inflation. As Map 9 highlights, the countries with the highest inflation rate also are generally the countries that are the weakest economically, have the highest rates of poverty, or experience the most social and political tension. And as Figure 41 illustrates, inflation translates into high food prices, which require more disposable income from the people who can least afford it. For example, in the US, consumers may spend 6% or 7% of their disposable income on food, but in Pakistan consumers spend nearly half of their disposable income on food. This has all sorts of implications, from less healthy eating habits (which result in higher health-related costs) to rising crime rates and political frustration.

The "youth bulge" is the idea that an excessive percentage of young males in a given society ultimately results in social unrest, a greater likelihood of terrorism, and, ultimately, war. As noted in Figure 42, the sampling of 11 MENA nations shows populations under 30 ranging from 52% to 74% Once again, the places in the world with the youngest populations tend to be the poorest. Parents there tend to have more children in the belief that when the children grow up and become working age, there will be more potential sources of revenue to help them survive collectively. Of course, just the opposite occurs until children are working age, and this strategy often works against the children, the family, and the country, as noted in Map 10.

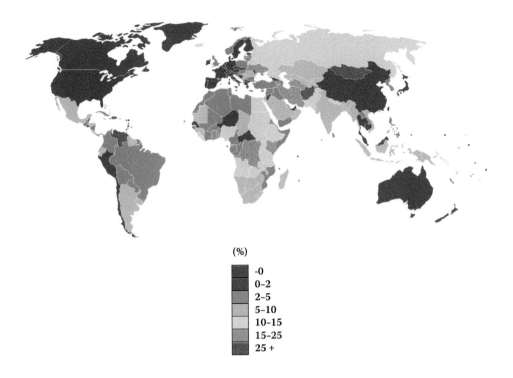

MAP 9 Global inflation rate 2007. (From http://upload.wikimedia.org/wikipedia/commons/6/6e/World_Inflation_rate_2007.png)

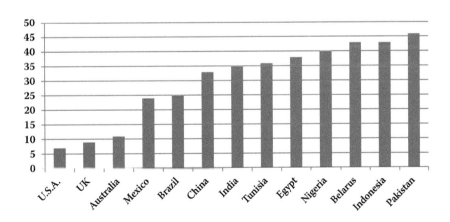

FIGURE 41 Rising grocery bills lead to political unrest. (From the U.S. Department of Agriculture.)

So, putting this all together, we see that some of our preconceptions about fundamental characteristics of an economy or polity fall apart upon closer examination and that globalization has not and will not change some fundamental facts: The poorer a country is, the likelier it is have a higher percentage of youth, suffer disproportionately from the effects of inflation, and have a greater number of intra- or interstate conflicts.

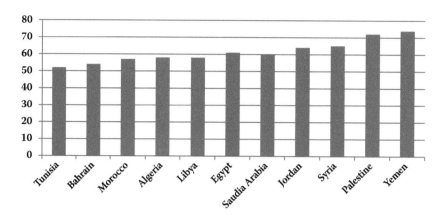

FIGURE 42   Percentage of population under 30. (From: UN Population Division, *The Silatech Index: Voice of Young Arabs,* November 2010; ASDA'A Burson Marsteller Arab Youth Survey, March 2010.)

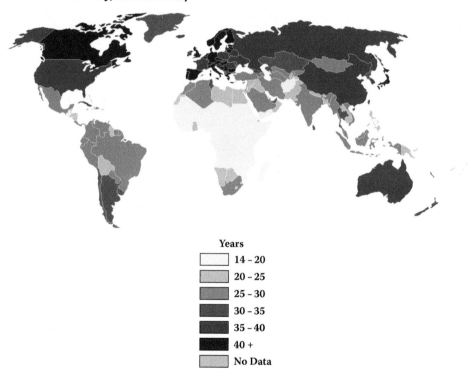

MAP 10   Median age by country. (From: http://upload.wikimedia.org/wikipedia/commons/0/0a/Median_age.png)

We have also seen that GDP wealth is not necessarily an indicator of low poverty rates and that, indeed, in some of the least likely countries in the world, rising Gini coefficients are indications of rising levels of income inequality. As shown in Map 11, the largest concentration of failed states also happens to be largely among the poorest and most conflict-ridden countries in the world.

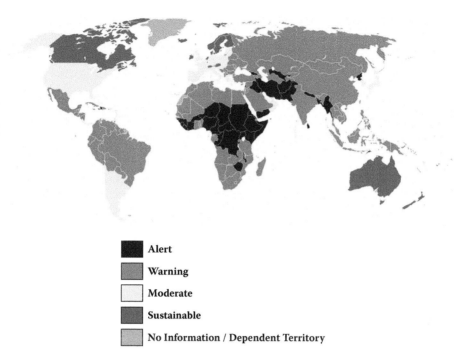

MAP 11 Failed states index 2010. (From: http://en.wikipedia./wiki/File:Failed-states-index-2010.png

The Lee Kuan Yew School of Public Policy in Singapore released a survey in 2011 of prominent leaders in a variety of fields to rate their perception of emerging threats and their relative urgency. Figure 43 shows that growing inequality and rising prices were two of the top three concerns and that the risk of military confrontation was in last place. It seems that what is most on people's minds is ensuring that their basic needs are met—even in developed countries, which is something we would not have seen even a decade ago. Many of the things people in developed countries have taken for granted for decades, such as the payback one will receive from having attended college or the short- and medium-term term payoff from purchasing a home, are rightly being questioned in this time of ongoing economic distress and austerity. If such fundamental tenets of living in developed countries are now being questioned, can any subject really be off the table?

The fact is that the world is facing a host of issues with global impact at the beginning of the second decade of the twenty-first century and there is no single leading nation strong enough to guide the world through it. Weakened US leadership has come at a particularly inopportune time, as diminished resources, along with a greatly weakened capacity and willingness to act at this time of economic dislocation and political upheaval, have potentially negative implications for billions of people. The leading emerging economies of the world—Brazil, China, India, Turkey, and South Africa—are stepping up to the plate and learning to lead by default. We have seen that this can also

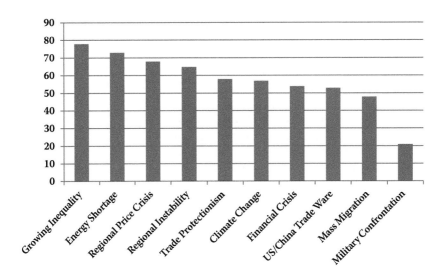

FIGURE 43 Emerging risks and threats by perception of urgency (%). (From Asia Trends Monitoring Bulletin, Imagining Asia in 2020: Future Risks, Future Trends, Lee Kuan Yew School of Public Policy, National University of Singapore, 2011: http://issuu.com/nuslkyschool/docs/atm-8-alt).

have negative consequences and yet, in the absence of their participation in global politics, the world would certainly be worse off, for there would be no country attempting to pick up the slack being left by a weakened US and EU.

What all this means for country risk analysts is that as the new paradigm evolves in this decade and beyond, we must evolve along with it. Many of the conventional ways of thinking about the world, how it works, and how it can be analyzed must now be cast aside. Each transaction must be analyzed, recognizing that it has its own unique risk profile and requires a distinct set of data and analysis to arrive at an accurate interpretation of the nature of the risks associated with it. Armed with the information in this book and some examples of how to think about the ongoing changes in the state of our world, you have the tools you need to get the job done.

Notes

1. http://kennedylegacy.tumblr.com/post/3272372559/history-is-a-relentless -master-it-has-no-present
2. Brazil and Turkey's message. *The Huffington Post,* June 17, 2010. Reprinted with permission from *The Huffington Post.*
3. Turkey's foreign policy vision. *INEGMA,* July 28, 2010. Reprinted with permission from *INEGMA.*
4. The role of transatlantic relations in the new world order. Davutoglu's speech at Chatham House in London, July 8, 2010, pp. 9, 17.
5. Synopsis of Turkish foreign policy. Ministry of Foreign Affairs (http://www.mfa.gov. tr/synopsis-of-the-turkish-foreign-policy.en.mfa).

6. Upheaval in the Middle East: An opportunity for Turkey. foreignpolicyjournal.com (May 21, 2011). Reprinted with permission from foreignpolicyjournal.com

7. The folly of Brazil's exceptionalism. *The Huffington Post,* August 9, 2010. Reprinted with permission from *The Huffington Post.*

8. Political risk services. *Brazil Country Report,* 2010.

9. *Business Monitor International.*

10. Brazil has received eight disbursements from the fund totaling more than $40 billion since 1984 (http://www.imf.org/external/np/fin/tad/extrans1.aspx?memberKey1=90&endDate=2010%2D08%2D08&finposition_flag=YES).

11. Vigevani, T., and G. Cepaluni. Brazilian foreign policy in changing times: The quest for autonomy from Sarney to Lula. Lexington Books, Lanham, MD, 2009.

12. Rogue diplomacy. *Newsweek,* May 7, 2010.

13. Slipping on the global stage. *Wall Street Journal,* March 29, 2010.

14. Speak softly and carry a blank cheque. *The Economist,* July 17, 2010.

15. BRICs form unstable foundation for multilateral action. foreignpolicyjournal.com (April 2, 2011). Reprinted with permission from foreignpolicyjournal.com.

16. Iraq's democratic experiment. *The Huffington Post,* October 5, 2010. Reprinted with permission from *The Huffington Post.*

17. www.irmi.com/expert/articles/2004/wagner04.aspx

18. Uniform unease. *Financial Times,* August 26, 2010, p. 5.

19. http://www.eia.doe.gov/ipm/supply.html

20. http://www.mees.com/cms/2010/07/iraqi-oil-fields-development-profiles-of-production-depletion-and-revenue/

21. Bolivia, Ecuador, and Nicaragua: Lofty idealism vs. hard nosed politics. foreignpolicyjournal.com (February 10, 2011). Reprinted with permission from foreignpolicyjournal.com

22. Lecture at the Institute for the Study of the Americas (ISA) by Guillame Long, PhD candidate at ISA and advisor to the Ecuadorian Minister of Planning and Development René Ramírez Gallegos.

23. Webber, J. Bolivia in the era of Evo Morales. *Latin American Research Review* 45 (3): 248–260, 2010.

24. Millett, R. Nicaragua: The politics of frustration. In *Latin American politics and development,* ed. H. Wiarda and H. Kline. Westview Press, Boulder, CO, 2011.

25. Economist Intelligence Unit. Democracy index 2010: Democracy in retreat (http://www.eiu.com/public/topical_report.aspx?campaignid=demo2010).

26. Information from abstract of paper presented at SLAS Conference 2011, Centralization and decentralization: Municipal political autonomy and democratization in Nicaragua, by Leslie Anderson, University of Florida.

27. India's ongoing concerns over Afghanistan and Pakistan. *The Huffington Post,* July 5, 2011. Reprinted with permission from *The Huffington Post.*

28. Economist Intelligence Unit. Spring tide, 2011, p. 26.

29. http://siteresources.worldbank.org/INTPGI/Resources/12404_TNSrinivasan-Paper2+Tables.pdf

30. http://www.google.com/publicdata?ds=wb-wdi&met_y=ny_gdp_mktp_kd_zg&idim=country:CAN&dl=en&hl=en&q=gdp+growth#ctype=l&strail=false&nselm=h&met_y=ny_gdp_mktp_kd_zg&scale_y=lin&ind_y=false&rdim=country&idim=country:BRA:RUS&hl=en&dl=en

Appendix

Country Risk Management Dictionary of Key Terms

I. Country Risk Concepts[1]

Accountability Risks: Political risks for which no one is accountable. Hence, political risks are ignored, unreported, or inadequately managed.

Appetite: A term used to contrast the different managerial perspectives when choices are made about how or whether to accept political risk. A firm that is willing to assume new risks in response to market opportunities has a higher risk appetite than a firm that chooses to maintain an existing risk profile. A firm's "risk appetite" is made more explicit in an organization that uses techniques, such as risk-adjusted return on capital, that force debate on how much risk is being taken and why, and then evaluating those risks against expected rewards. "Risk tolerance" and "risk threshold" are terms that are often used in the context of describing a firm's appetite for specific risks.

Bilateral Government Relations: As a risk mitigation tool, the political, economic, or security relationships a host government may have with governments other than the investor's home country can reduce vulnerability to political risks for the home country investor. This may influence an investor's choice of joint venture partner from a third country. The involvement of an investor from a third country (other than the home or host country) could serve to ease any difficulties that the home country investor may encounter as a result of a breakdown of relations between the home and host governments.

Business Control: The control processes put in place to manage environment risks and reduce process risks to an acceptable level. These processes include strategic control, operational control, and legal and regulatory compliance control.

Business–Environment Relations Risks: Risks that arise from the interaction of business processes and external forces. These political risks are the result of political decisions that directly target the firm; hence, the actions of the firm will often influence the likelihood and severity of these risks, both positively and negatively.

Business Environment Risks: Risks from external forces that could significantly change the fundamental assumptions that drive a company's overall objectives and strategies or, at the extreme, render its business model obsolete.

Business Model: How companies create value and assume risk through their unique combinations of assets and technologies. Assets fall into five categories for purposes of understanding business models: physical, financial, customer, employee/supplier, and organizational. As individual assets have unique risk and reward profiles, so too does the asset portfolio that makes up each business model. The synergy of assets has the capacity to produce results greater than the sum of the parts, depending on how a company invests and how it manages risk. The reverse is always the case as well, as a portfolio that is concentrated in the wrong assets can dilute value.

Business Process: A process (1) consists of inputs, activities, outputs, and interfaces with other processes; (2) is supported by people and technology; and (3) is designed to achieve one or more specified objectives. Every business can be divided into operating, management, and support processes.

Business Risk: The uncertainties that a firm must understand and effectively manage as it executes its strategies to achieve its business objectives and create value.

Business Risk Management Process: The process used by executive management to manage the risks of a firm and by process/activity owners to manage the risks within their respective business processes and activities. It includes key tasks essential to the risk management environment: establishing goals, objectives, and infrastructure; assessing business risk (identifying, sourcing, and measuring); developing risk management strategies; designing and implementing risk management processes; monitoring process performance; and continuously improving processes. All of these tasks are supported by information for decision making.

Capacity: The aggregate financial ability of a firm to absorb or withstand the cost of risk, expressed in terms of performance variability or loss exposure. For example, firms hold equity in order to respond to unanticipated investment opportunities or to absorb unexpected losses. Since firms cannot predict the future with certainty, they need to hold reserve in the form of equity capital.

Civil Disorder Risks: Events of political unrest, such as general strikes, demonstrations, riots, and social unrest that cause asset damage, endangerment of personnel, or business interruption or otherwise impact assets, personnel, or operations.

Common Language: A risk framework that multiple disciplines within a business can use to initiate and sustain a continuing dialog about risk and processes. A common language is a useful tool for initiating the risk identification process.

Community Protests or Violence Risks: Protests, demonstrations, sabotage, looting, or terrorism directed specifically at a firm because of high levels of antifirm sentiment among the public at large or the local community.

Community Relations: As a risk mitigation tool, educating the general public of a host country about the benefits of foreign investment and the role of the private sector in providing public services. The promotion of schemes to promote social welfare (by building schools and hospitals, for example) and enhancing the rural development process can assist the foreign investor in gaining acceptance of its presence among the local inhabitants of communities at or near a project.

Community Relations Risks: Risks arising from a firm's relationship with the general public. This can range from the public at large (for instance, a firm's reputation in the national media) to the local community where the firm is based.

Competency Risks: Decisions on the commitment of firm resources to politically risky activities or decisions on political risk management techniques are not taken by a qualified person (either because the wrong person is making the decisions or because no qualified person is available).

Comprehensive Risk Management: A term used to convey the firm's risk management coverage of its business risks as broad or complete. A comprehensive risk management approach covers many or all of the significant risks across the entity, which may be a business unit or division or even the enterprise as a whole.

Country Risk: A term used more broadly than "political risk" to encompass the political, economic, social, legal, and cultural risks associated with trading and investing outside one's home country.

Country-Specific Political Risks: Political risks that exist in a general sense in a given country, are not directed at individual companies, and can vary by country. Examples include a government's decision to suspend currency convertibility or the outbreak of a civil war within the host country. Country-specific political risks may not necessarily directly affect individual foreign companies, but can have an impact on their profitability.

Crisis Planning: Risk assessment and management tools are normally used to set a firm's ongoing, strategic posture toward political risk. However, when political risk crises arise, a firm will have to respond with speed and precision to minimize losses to its people, property, reputation, and information. To be effective, crisis response plans must be designed and ready for implementation before a political risk emergency strikes. Crisis planning therefore entails developing procedures for aggressively responding to political unrest, violence, terrorism, and punitive government actions.

Devaluation: A government action designed to reduce the purchasing power or value of its currency against convertible currencies by reducing the value of the domestic currency.

Developing Country: A nonindustrialized country with a low level of material well-being.

Direct Investors: Companies that invest their equity into business ventures, domestically or outside their home country.

Discriminatory Intervention: Interference on the part of a host government in a trade transaction or investment project that discriminates against one corporation in favor of another. Where the foreign trader or investor is concerned, this often means that the host government takes action that is against the interests of the foreign business and in favor of local business interests.

Dispersion: An option for managing risk by distributing financial, physical (facilities or stocks), or information assets deployed by the firm's business model over a wide geographic area, making it less likely or impossible to incur an unacceptable loss. Geographic dispersion of assets needs to be balanced against operating objectives dictating the concentration of assets to achieve needed efficiencies.

Diversification: A versatile management tool for shaping a firm's aggregate risk profile. A firm may diversify its portfolio of businesses, its geographic sources of revenue, its product mix, its customer mix, its research and development portfolio, its sources of supply, and its asset allocation by type of financial asset.

Domestic Economic Policy Risks: Macroeconomic policies that damage a country's economy (potentially impacting investors' customers, suppliers, and workers). Types of economic damage include stagnating growth, recession, high interest rates, and rapid inflation.

Drivers (of political risk): The fundamental political and economic variables that determine the risk of political instability and poor economic policy. For example, infant mortality is a measure of distributional equity and literacy is a measure of social investment.

Enterprise-wide Risk Management: A structured and disciplined approach that aligns strategy, processes, people, technology, and knowledge with the purpose of evaluating and managing the uncertainties a firm faces as it creates value. "Enterprise-wide" suggests an elimination of functional, departmental, or cultural barriers so that a truly holistic, integrated approach is taken to managing risk with the intention of creating value.

Evolutionary Political Change: A change in political leadership through the election process (see also *radical political change* and *revolutionary political change*).

Exchange Controls: Procedures established by a government monetary authority to allow conversion of local currency into foreign currency in order to promote policy objectives.

Exchange Rate: A currency rate established by a government monetary authority or the foreign exchange market that determines the amount of currency that can be bought or sold for a specific amount of another currency.

Exposure Monitoring Risks: There is no enterprise-wide awareness of current political risk exposure because reporting procedures are inadequate, changes in risk levels are not accurately assessed, or there is no enterprise-wide oversight function.

Force Majeure: An event outside the reasonable control of the affected party to a contract that could not have been prevented by good industry practices or by the exercise of reasonable skill and judgment. This typically excuses certain negotiated portions of contract performance during the period for which the event impacted the project or transaction in question.

Foreign Exchange Policy Risks: The government makes macroeconomic policy that leads to currency fluctuations, inconvertibility, or an uncontrolled devaluation, impacting the firm's operations. Examples of these hazards include currency crises, balance of payments crises, liquidity crises, capital controls, and foreign exchange controls.

Foreign Trade and Investment Policy Risks: Government policy results in a decline in or cessation of trade or investment, impacting a firm's operations. Examples of these hazards can include home- or host-country embargoes or trade wars, or withdrawal from trade or investment agreements.

Government Contract: As a risk mitigation tool, engaging in a contract with a host government can establish a right to compensation if the government subsequently makes changes in the agreement to the detriment of foreign investors. Alternatively, doing so may allow any changes in taxation or other regulation-related costs to be passed to consumers through tariff adjustments. Enforcement may be assisted by agreement to refer disputes to international arbitration. Governments may also waive sovereign immunity to the enforcement of such awards in national courts.

Government Contract Risks: The government either breaches or forces a renegotiation of a direct contract with the foreign investor. Such contracts can include contracts for purchase of goods/services from government suppliers, sale of goods/services to government buyers, and concession agreements.

Government Intervention Risks: When a host government actively intervenes in a firm's operations for opportunistic, regulatory, or ideological reasons. This intervention is targeted directly and specifically at the firm (not necessarily at all firms or all foreign firms). In practice, this intervention can be positive or negative and can include restrictions on foreign hiring, local sourcing requirements, export requirements, price controls, or profit repatriation; denial of import/export licenses; denial of infrastructure services; and denial of foreign exchange. This intervention can be triggered by a firm's relationship with the government, by demands from the public, and/or by demands from the firm's labor force.

Government Relations Risks: Risks that arise from the firm's relationship with the government. This includes local and national government bodies and all branches of government, including politicians, bureaucrats, and judges.

Government Risks: Those risks that arise from the exercise of governmental authority, whether that power is used legally or not. A legitimately enacted tax hike and an illegal extortion ring led by a local police chief can be examples of government risks. Indeed, many government risks, particularly those that are firm specific, contain an ambiguous mixture of legal and illegal elements.

Holistic: A term used in risk management that emphasizes the strengthening of the linkages, coordination, and interrelationships between individual risks (or groups of related risks) and the components of an organization that contribute to managing risk. A holistic risk management process is therefore, by definition, one that is not fragmented into functions and departments and is organized with the intention of optimizing the performance of a process, unit, or enterprise in managing a single risk or aggregate group of related risks.

Host Country: The country in which the infrastructure or other project is taking place.

Impact Management: Operational decisions that reduce costs may introduce exposures to political risks. Impact management leads firms to structure their operations so that if political risk crises occur, their vulnerability to losses is reduced. A principal impact management method is to use real options to structure development and investment decisions.

Incentive/Goal Alignment Risks: Incentives for managers are misaligned with the goals of the enterprise. For instance, managers are compensated solely on the basis of returns and hence have an incentive to take on greater political risks.

Information Credibility Risks: Management does not trust internal evaluations of political risk management performance, or it does not trust internal assessments of political risk.

Information/Information Process Control: These control processes address the risks relating to the flow of information from the acquisition of relevant business facts through their ultimate inclusion in financial and management reports.

Information Risks: Risks that arise when a firm's information gathering or information flows do not support its intended response to political risks, leading to errors or inefficiencies in risk management.

Infrastructure/Government Services Risks: Because of corruption, incompetence, or a lack of funds, a host government is unable to provide expected services, such as police protection, sewage, and electricity, to a foreign enterprise and its personnel.

Integrated: A term used in risk management to describe an approach or methodology that aggregates and organizes data, information, measures, and analyses into a larger framework for decision making that contributes rigor and robustness to the process.

Investment Evaluation Risks: Evaluations of investment projects fail to account for political risk or do not measure these risks accurately.

Investors:

    Equity Investors: Must be concerned with how political developments will affect a country's overall business conditions and, by extension, its equity markets. Political crises often have a very sharp impact on a country's equity markets, particularly those markets with immature institutions.

    Fixed-income investors: Primarily interested in political events that can move debt prices. Typically, this translates into political pressures for changes in monetary and fiscal policy. These investors stand to lose the most from debt default, but they also must carefully consider how political dynamics will impact interest rates, inflation, and other indicators.

    Portfolio Investors: Invest in a pool of assets and are concerned with political events that move markets. The political events that constitute risks for portfolio investors will depend on the investor's portfolio positions (i.e., whether the investor is long or short on the security in question). In general, however, political risks for portfolio investors are political events that will depress market prices. Portfolio investors can be broken down into fixed-income and equity investors.

Labor Relations Risks: Risks arising from a firm's relationship with its labor force. These become political risks when the relationship leads to political actions by the workforce (such as riots) or when the relationship triggers intervention by political actors (such as new regulations by labor ministry bureaucrats).

Legal Action Risks: Members of the public at large take legal action against the firm in either local or foreign courts, reflecting antifirm sentiment. The objective of the legal action is to force the investor to leave the country (as opposed, for instance, to a product liability suit).

Legal System Risks: When a legal system is biased against foreign investors; subject to political influence; not well established; or excessively slow, arbitrary, or corrupt and, as a result, a foreign trader or investor has a lack of legal recourse or suffers unfair legal action against it.

Local Private Interests: As a risk mitigation tool, pursuing local joint venture partners can benefit foreign investors by gaining inside knowledge of the local political scene and exercising influence over government policy making. More importantly, governments may be less likely to act to the detriment of foreign enterprises if doing so would harm significant local interests. It may also be desirable to promote widespread local ownership, either directly through local share offerings or indirectly through private pension funds.

Local Stakeholders: Individuals and/or groups from the host country who have a stake in a foreign affiliate's existence as a unit of a parent multinational corporation. Potential stakeholders include, but are not limited to, consumers, suppliers, the subsidiary's local employees, local bankers, and joint venture partners.

Loss Exposure: Uncertainties arising from physical phenomena (weather, earthquakes, fires, floods, etc.) hazardous materials or conditions, accidents or malicious acts (sabotage, terrorism, etc.) that could cause loss or damage of physical assets, injury or death to employees or other people, business interruption, or loss of reputation. These risks are often labeled as "downside risks" because the distribution of potential future outcomes is heavily skewed toward adverse consequences. Simply stated, every foreseeable outcome results in a negative cash flow.

Loss Limits: A determination of how much loss of investment equity a firm can afford to bear in a given project based on its expected returns. These limits are used as thresholds when implementing risk management guidelines.

Macropolitical Risk: See *country-specific political risks.*

Micropolitical Risk: See *project-specific political risks.*

Monitoring: The activities of managers as they oversee and review process performance, changes in the environment, changes in internal processes, and compliance with established policies and limits.

Multilateral Financial Institutions: International organizations such as the International Finance Corporation and Asian Development Bank, which are wholly government owned and lend money to governments or private investors to promote the development process. As a risk mitigation tool, participation by multilateral financial institutions may reduce vulnerability to arbitrary action on the part of host governments. Their participation can also help to reduce the risk of opportunistic government behavior because of the leverage such institutions have over future lending to the country in question and their role vis-à-vis other donors.

National Identity: An empathy for or participation in a national struggle in order to protect one's way of life, national pride, and independence.

This can translate into a bias in favor of compatriots and concern for the general welfare of a national population.

National Interest: An element of nationalism that reflects all governmental intervention that aims for the accomplishment of the social, cultural, political, and economic objectives of the nation.

National Sovereignty: The desire of nations to control their own development. That control can be threatened by perceived interference or influence from other nations through subsidiaries of their multinational companies as well as by the potential economic power that foreign corporations possess within the host country's borders.

Operational Risks: Related to political risk, government interventions that directly constrain the management and performance of local operations in production, marketing, finance, and other business functions.

Operations: Political risk events that affect the firm's ability to execute decisions internal to the firm, often including those related to production, marketing, distribution, support functions, and management:

Control Regulations: Designated seats on a board and veto rights vested in the government.

Employment Regulations: Hiring, firing, and wage regulations.

Flow of Funds Restrictions: Dividends, royalties, interest payments, profit, repatriation, tariffs, nontariff barriers, quotas, sanctions, embargoes, and boycotts.

Legal System: Enforcement of laws and private contracts; consistency of rulings.

Licensing regulations: Permits, licenses, and approvals.

Local Participation Regulations: Content, refining, shipping, and reinvestment requirements.

Personnel: Political risk events that affect the firm's ability to employ, protect, and manage its labor force.

Political Violence: Riots, strikes, civil commotion, sabotage, terrorism, revolution, guerilla war, civil war, and cross-border war.

Production Regulations: Production floors and ceilings.

Staffing Regulations: Advancement of locals and training requirements.

Transfer: Political risk events that affect the firm's ability to transfer capital, equipment, payments, profits, products, technology, and persons into and out of the host country.

Organization Risks: Risks that arise when a firm's organization does not support its intended response to political risks, leading to errors or inefficiencies in risk management.

Performance Monitoring Risks: There is no enterprise-wide awareness of current political risk management performance because reporting procedures are inadequate or because an enterprise-wide oversight function is absent.

Performance Variability: Uncertainties affecting the quality and sustainability of future earnings that are inherent in the firm's normal ongoing operations. Firms manage these risks to reduce their potential impact on business performance to within an acceptable range (or tolerance). If these outcomes are driven by external forces, they are usually uncontrollable and must be managed through a strategic response that configures the firm's risk profile consistent with its risk appetite. If they are driven by internal issues, the firm's internal operating processes may be effective in reducing variability in quality, cost, and time performance to within an acceptable range.

Pervasive Management Controls: These risk controls are implemented across the firm's units and processes to ensure that managers and employees are focused on the right objectives and activities, have the requisite knowledge and skills, do not perform incompatible duties (authorization, custody, and record keeping) in the same function, and protect physical and financial assets and information integrity. They provide a vital frontline of defense, protecting the integrity of business processes.

Policy Compliance Risks: Policies are not followed as specified; hence, exposure limits are exceeded and political risk levels exceed tolerances.

Policy Effectiveness Risks: Policies are insufficient or unspecified; hence, exposure limits are exceeded and political risk levels exceed tolerances.

Policy Risks: Risks that arise when a firm's risk management policies do not support its intended response to political risks, leading to errors or inefficiencies in risk management.

Political: Power relationships that allow one actor or set of actors to alter the behavior of another actor or set of actors.

Political Instability Risks: Risks that arise from "rough" political actions, such as riots and coups. These actions are often, but not always, illegal or violent or involve struggles over political power or resources.

Political Institutions Risks: Political institutions are the "rules of the game" that govern the conduct of political activity. Political institutions risks arise from the state of political institutions in the host country, such as the legal system, the bureaucracy, and the electoral system.

Political Risk: The uncertainties that arise from instances of political instability (such as riots and coups), of poor public policy (such as inflation and currency crises), and of weak institutional frameworks (such as discriminatory regulations and ineffective legal systems).

Political Risk Assessment: A three-part process that catalogues the nature and severity of all significant political risks confronting a project, transaction, or firm. Since political risk assessments can be systematically derived only with regard to specific projects or transactions, a firm's overall political risk exposure will be an aggregate of these individual assessments. The three elements of political risk assessment are:

Identification: The firm identifies a roster of political risks likely to have a significant impact on a project's performance. To verify the significance of the risks on this roster, they are then subjected to *source* and *measurement* analyses:

Source: The firm establishes where the political risks identified may come from.

Measurement: The firm establishes the likelihood that each of these risks might occur and their likely impact on the project in question.

Political Risk Classification Schemes: Dividing classes of political risk by (1) the degree of selectivity or discrimination, (2) the types of actors that generate them, (3) the structural or functional elements of an organization, and (4) the specific functional aspects of a business organization.

Political Risk Events: An event derived from a government action that impacts a foreign enterprise. Political risk events affect *assets, commerce, operations, personnel,* and ability to *transfer*:

Assets: Political risk events that affect the firm's ability acquire, protect, employ, and divest itself of physical assets and intellectual property.

Forced Divestiture: Confiscation, expropriation, nationalization, deprivations, and creeping expropriation.

Intellectual Property Regulations: Patents, copyrights, trademarks, and trade secrets.

Legal System: Enforcement of laws and private contracts; consistency of rulings.

Ownership Regulations: Participation by locals and governments.

Policy-Driven Economic Conditions: Interest rates and inflation.

Political Violence: Riots, strikes, civil commotion, sabotage, terrorism, revolution, guerilla war, civil war, cross-border war.

Political Risk Forecasting: A process of analyzing the nature of the non-commercial risks facing a foreign enterprise that involves (1) understanding the type of government currently in power, its patterns of political behavior, and its norms for stability; (2) analyzing the enterprise's products and operations to identify the types of macro- and micropolitical risk likely to be involved in trade and investment outside the home country; (3) determining the sources of political risk—for example, if the risk is expropriation, whether its source is due to the philosophy of the government or the nature of its leadership; and (4) projecting into the future the possibility of political risk in terms of probability and time horizons.

Political Risk Frameworks:

The Actor/Source Approach: The sources of political risk events are (a) competing political philosophies (nationalism, socialism, communism), (b) social unrest and disorder, (c) vested interests of local business groups, (d) recent and impending political independence, (e) armed conflicts and internal rebellions for political power, or (f) new international alliances.

The Bargaining Power Approach: A foreign enterprise's bargaining power with a host government is derived from the type and nature of its technology, management skills, and exports. A host government's bargaining power with a foreign enterprise is derived from its capability to replace the foreign enterprise and its ultimate control over the company.

The Government Type Approach: The risk of radical political change (i.e., high political instability) depends on the form of government in a host country. Political instability or risk is associated with a typology of political models: (1) the traditional (state-centric) model of national politics, (2) the pluralistic model of national politics, or (3) the bureaucratic model of intragovernmental politics.

The Product/Venture Type Approach: Because of their very nature, different products or industries have different degrees of sensitivity or vulnerability to political risk.

The Relative Deprivation Approach: A high level of national frustration is the key catalyst of host government action contrary to the interests of a foreign enterprise.

The Structural Approach: The vulnerability of an industry, an organization, or a project to political risk is mainly dependent on structural characteristics such as size, localization of management and employment, the level of technology available to perform various business activities, project ownership structure, and host country dependence on the international trading system for its livelihood.

Political Risk Gap Analysis: Assessing a firm's existing political risk management policies and comparing them with best practices to determine where improvements need to be made.

Political Risk Management: The development of processes, structures, and knowledge that allows firms to deal effectively with political risk.

Political Risk Process Design: Essential to political risk management. Many firms with effective risk assessment and management skills nevertheless have sustained severe damage because of organization and process failures. To optimize a firm's political risk process, organizational design and comprehensive executive training are integrated: (1) *Executive training* workshops are used to train firm management in how to identify, assess, and manage political risks, and (2) *organizational design* integrates risk management into the overall strategic planning process, clearly defining and distributing risk management responsibilities, aligning incentive and performance appraisal systems, and ensuring the appropriate flow of risk assessment information to management.

Political Structure: Institutionalized power relationships.

Political Terrorism: Violent actions (such as kidnappings, bombings, or assassinations) undertaken for a political purpose by a person or group seeking to overthrow an existing government.

Political Violence Risks: Violent political events, such as war, civil war, terrorism, and sabotage that cause asset damage, endangerment of personnel, business interruption, or otherwise impact assets, personnel, or operations (see also the definition for *political violence*).

Process and Information Risks: Arise when business organization, processes, policies, and information flows do not achieve the objectives they were designed to achieve in supporting the firm's business model.

Process Risk: Arises when business processes do not achieve the objectives they were designed to achieve in supporting the firm's business model.

Project-Specific Political Risks: Risks directed at a particular firm that are, by their nature, discriminatory—for instance, the risks that a government will void its contract with a given firm or that a terrorist group will target the firm's executives are both firm specific.

Propensity: The extent to which a firm exposes it capital, earnings, and cash flow to performance variability or loss exposure. In other words, propensity is the willingness of a firm to assume risk. Firms that have a low propensity to take risk are "risk averse," while firms that have a high propensity to take risk are "risk takers."

Public Policy Risks: Risks that arise from government policies that encourage, discourage, prohibit, or prescribe the behavior of public or private actors.

Radical Political Change: The ascendancy to power of a person or group holding a different political philosophy from that of the person or group that is replaced. The resulting political change can be evolutionary or revolutionary (see also *evolutionary political change* and *revolutionary political change*).

Regulation/Taxation Risks: Government changes in regulations, laws, or tax codes affecting all firms in the economy, an industry, or all foreign firms (but not the foreign investor's project specifically) in a way that impacts firm operations, personnel, or assets.

Regulatory Assessment Risks: Because of a lack of clarity in legal codes, the existence of unwritten rules, and/or a failure on the part of the firm's regulatory assessment processes, the firm fails to understand the regulations in force accurately, leading to government intervention.

Regulatory Compliance Risks: Whether intentionally or unintentionally, a firm, while understanding existing regulations, fails to comply with these regulations, leading to government intervention.

Regulatory Relations Risks: Arise from the firm's relationship with regulatory authorities, including government ministries and antitrust authorities.

Regulatory System Risks: When a regulatory system (including local, regional, and national bureaucracies) is biased against foreign investors, subject to political influence, not well established, excessively slow, corrupt, or arbitrary and as a result a firm suffers repeated and/or unreasonable regulatory interference.

Relationship Management: A risk management technique used to reduce risks arising between the firm and other stakeholders in the firm's operations. Based on the perspective that these relationships are best seen as ongoing bargaining efforts, firms use this technique to reduce political risks through the estimation and alteration of each party's objectives and bargaining power (see also *business–environment relations risks* and *political risk frameworks, the bargaining power approach*).

Residual Risk: The level of risk remaining after the effective implementation of all risk management strategies (other than a strategy to retain risk). Sometimes used to refer to the level of risk before considering risk transfer strategies.

Revolutionary Political Change: A change in political relations that results in alteration of the social structure of a country (see also *evolutionary political change* and *radical political change*).

Risk: The uncertainty over whether an event or scenario that can have either positive or negative consequences will occur in the future within a given time horizon.

Risk Acceptance: Accepting risk involves a conscious, rational, and often-times supported decision to accept a risk because the firm's processes are effective in managing the risk, the risk is inherent in the firm's day-to-day business, the firm has sufficient equity capital or operating margin to absorb the financial impact if an undesirable risk incident (see separate definition) should occur, and/or the firm possesses sufficient information to understand the risk well enough to retain it.

Risk Analysis: Occurs when managers accountable for managing risk apply their judgment to the information obtained during risk assessment (see separate definition) to determine the significance, likelihood, priority, root causes, and/or financial impact of the risk.

Risk Assessment: The set of tasks in which risk is identified, sourced, and measured. Sometimes used in a more limited context to refer solely to risk identification and prioritization.

Risk Avoidance: A decision to divest a business or product or terminate a process or activity to eliminate unacceptable risks, prohibit high-risk business activities, or implement preventive process improvements that make it impossible for a well-defined, undesirable event to occur.

Risk Chain Analysis: A risk assessment method used to assist firm management in considering how a chain of events can contribute to the likelihood that a political risk will lead to loss. Management considers how one event can prompt others to occur.

Risk Control: Processes that are the monitoring activities, pervasive management controls, business controls, and information and information process controls that reduce the likelihood of an undesirable event occurring to an acceptable level. These processes require supervision, enforcement, and periodic reevaluation.

Risk Evaluation: Occurs when managers accountable for managing risk apply their judgment to the information arising from risk assessment (see separate definition) to determine and select the appropriate strategies for managing the risk.

Risk Exploitation: Management decides to take the risks inherent in its choice to enter new markets, introduce new products, or merge with or acquire another firm to exploit other market opportunities, all of which result in shaping the firm's risk profile differently.

Risk Families/Risk Pools: A natural grouping of risks sharing fundamental characteristics (such as common drivers or positive and negative correlations). These categorizations assist managers in understanding the interrelationships between risks for purposes of selecting the appropriate measurement methodologies and management solutions.

Risk Financing: The process by which a firm pays for the outcome of an undesirable risk incident. There are two forms of financing: external and internal. External financing results in a transfer of risk to an independent third party through financial instruments. Internal financing funds risk through such means as self-insurance or repricing.

Risk Identification: The process used to define potential events by determining what can happen that fundamentally threatens the success of the firm's business model; this includes the risks inherent in the pursuit of targeted opportunities for increased growth and return. The focus of executive management when identifying risk is on the environment. The focus of process/activity owners is on the processes and activities that they manage.

Risk Management: The activities of management directed to identifying, sourcing, measuring, and monitoring risk, formulating risk management strategies, and implementing processes for avoiding, retaining, reducing, and transferring individual risks and shaping risk profiles.

Risk Management Capability: The processes, people, reports, methodologies, and systems needed to implement a particular risk management strategy.

Risk Management Infrastructure: Six key components create a risk management infrastructure: strategy, business and risk management processes, people, management reports, methodologies, and systems and data. To maximize risk management capability, all of these components must be aligned effectively.

Risk Management System: The components of the firm's systems that are concerned with measuring and managing risk, including business planning, risk control processes, monitoring and feedback mechanisms, dedicated risk management personnel, technology (including support systems architecture and databases), methodologies, and risk-focused knowledge sharing and communications processes.

Risk Management Technique Risks: Risks that arise when a firm's selection or implementation of risk management techniques does not support its intended response to political risks, leading to errors or inefficiencies in risk management.

Risk Measurement: Rigorous methodologies and techniques used quantitatively or qualitatively to determine the likelihood and consequence (including financial impact) of events over a given time horizon under alternative scenarios and provide information for informed decision making.

Risk Mitigation: Mitigation reduces the pain or limits the adverse effects of a risk incident (see also *risk control* and *risk reduction,* both of which are terms used interchangeably with risk mitigation; mitigation is sometimes used in a broader sense to include *risk transfer*).

Risk Reduction: Taking action to reduce the risk to an acceptable level, as defined by management's risk tolerance. Approaches to reducing risk vary, but are generally focused on decreasing either (a) the likelihood of an undesirable event occurring or (b) its impact on the business if it should occur. For (a), risk reduction is accomplished by controlling the risk through internal processes. For (b), it is accomplished by spreading the risk (e.g., dispersing assets geographically).

Risk Retention: Planned retention of risk is a purposeful, conscious, and intentional decision to accept the consequences in the event an undesirable risk incident occurs. Unplanned retention of risk occurs when the firm does not know of its existence.

Risk Tolerance Levels: Management's determination of how much political risk it is willing to bear in exchange for increased expected profits, in general, and on a project-specific basis. A firm's risk tolerance level may be categorized as very low, low, medium, high, or very high.

Risk Transfer: Transfer of risk occurs when the firm passes a risk through to an independent, financially capable third party at a reasonable economic cost. Transfer can be accomplished many ways (e.g., through the insurance markets, by hedging risk in the capital markets, by sharing risk through joint venture investments or strategic alliances, through an outsourcing arrangement accompanied by a contractual risk transfer, or by indemnifying risk through legally enforceable contractual agreements).

Risk Treatment: A term normally used in the context of the specific strategy selected for managing a risk. While often used to refer to risk reduction strategies, it is sometimes broadly applied to encompass risk transfer and other strategies.

Scenario-Based Planning: By reviewing plausible, compelling scenarios of political risk events that might beset a firm's current or anticipated operations, the need to address political risks systematically is emphasized. Scenario-based planning can help senior management systematically assess risks and design mitigation strategies.

Source (Sourcing): The process of determining why, how, and where risks are created, either outside the organization, or within its business processes. Risk sourcing is the process of understanding a risk and its interrelationships with other risks as well as its drivers or root causes.

Strategy Option Inventory: When making critical business decisions such as how to enter a new market, firms typically choose from among a portfolio of options. Though these strategies will have differing political risk implications, decision makers will often ignore political risk when choosing among them. Conducting an inventory of a firm's strategy option enables firm management to uncover the political risk consequences of their available strategies and helps them explicitly incorporate these considerations into their strategy selection process.

Tax Holiday: A benefit granted to a project that provides project owners with an exemption from taxation for a negotiated or statutory time period.

Technique Implementation Risks: Political risk management techniques may be appropriate but they are poorly implemented, leading them to be suboptimal (i.e., a more efficient technique exists) or leaving unintended gaps (residual risk).

Technique Selection Risks: The firm chooses political risk management techniques that are suboptimal (i.e., a better technique is available) or that leave unintended gaps in its management (residual risk).

Terrorism: The unlawful use of force by a person or group against people or property with the intention of intimidating or coercing societies or governments, usually for ideological or political purposes.

Time Horizon: The period of time that management considers when assessing the severity or likelihood of a particular risk or group of related risks.

Tolerance: An acceptable level of risk to a firm as defined by management in terms of a loss amount, an error rate, or some form of rating. The term "tolerance" refers to the ability of a firm to accept or withstand performance variability or loss exposure from a given source and it can be expressed in terms of the following question: "What is the firm's tolerance for deviation of actual results from the plan?" Risk tolerances can also be expressed in terms of the acceptable level of loss, as addressed by the question, "What risks are we willing to accept as we pursue our business objectives and execute our strategies?"

Transfer Risks: Possible government restrictions on the transfer abroad (and sometimes into the host country as well) of capital, profits, technology, personnel, equipment, or the actual commodity produced.

II. Political Risk Insurance[2]

AAA: American Arbitration Association.

Active Blockage: Related to currency inconvertibility/nontransfer coverage (see separate definition) wherein the laws of a host country prevent conversion of local currency or transfer outside the country of hard currency by a foreign trader or investor (see also *passive blockage*).

Alternative Risk Transfer (ART): A generic expression used to describe various nontraditional forms of insurance or reinsurance and also various techniques whereby insured risks are transferred to capital markets investors. ART refers to both self-insurance and captives and a new wave of techniques such as finite risk insurance, contingent capital, insurance-linked securities, and insurance derivatives. More broadly, it refers to the convergence of insurance or reinsurance, banking, and capital markets at the wholesale level.

Arbitration Award Default: A variant of breach of contract coverage (see separate definition). Following a breach of a concession agreement and a predefined arbitration procedure, when an award is issued in the plaintiff's favor and the host government does not honor the award, coverage pays the plaintiff for the amount of the award. Whereas breach of contract coverage is broad in scope and can apply when a foreign investor is denied access to a forum of arbitration, arbitration award default coverage applies only when an award has been issued in the plaintiff's favor.

Berne Union: The official organization of most of the world's government-sponsored and private political risk and export credit insurers. Also known as the International Union of Credit and Investment Insurers (see separate definition).

Breach of Contract: "Breach" coverage addresses instances when a host government has violated some aspect of an agreement it has engaged in with a foreign investor. It provides reimbursement for equity, revenues, or loan payments lost as a result of the action. There are two primary means of addressing the subject: through traditional contract frustration coverage (a trade-related peril; see separate definition) or through expropriation coverage (see separate definition).

> Contract frustration implies the existence of a government obligor, but this has historically been utilized primarily for trade-related risks, such as export transactions. It is a purposely broad coverage, but is not necessarily the best way to address concerns about breach for infrastructure projects because of the low limits of liability available, the short tenor of coverage, and the high premium rates.

> Adding breach of contract coverage to expropriation coverage generally makes more sense for large infrastructure projects. The benefit of using this approach is that it, too, addresses payment risk resulting from breach of a contractual obligation by the government, but since it is added on to expropriation coverage, the term of the coverage is much longer than that of contract frustration and is much less expensive. Terms can go to 20 years depending on the carrier, and limits can go into the hundreds of millions of dollars. The coverage is generally structured to respond when a breach of contract has occurred, arbitration follows, an award is issued in the insured's favor, and the host government does not honor the award (otherwise known as "arbitration award default"; see separate definition).

Bridging Coverage: PRI usually obtained from private sector underwriters (see separate definition) for a short period of time while coverage is being underwritten by a public sector underwriter (see separate definition). The coverage can also be applied when temporary

PRI coverage is sought by a trader or investor for instance-specific reasons.

Build–Lease–Transfer (BLT): When a private owner builds an infrastructure facility, leases it for use, and then transfers it to another entity after a specified period of time or use.

Build–Operate–Transfer (BOT): When a private owner builds, operates, and then transfers an infrastructure facility to another entity.

Build–Own–Operate (BOO): When a private owner builds, owns, and operates an infrastructure facility.

Build–Own–Operate–Transfer (BOOT): When a private owner builds, owns, and operates an infrastructure facility and then transfers it to another entity after a specified period of operation.

Build–Transfer–Operate (BTO): When a private owner builds and transfers an infrastructure facility to another entity and then operates it.

Business Interruption (BI): The cessation of normal business operations, often due to physical damage (stemming from political violence) or war, civil war, strikes, riots, or civil commotion.

CEND: Confiscation, expropriation, nationalization, and deprivation. Otherwise known as expropriation (see separate definition).

Chartis: A political risk and trade credit insurer formerly known as American International Underwriters, part of American International Group.

COFACE: French private sector insurer Compagnie Francaise d'Assurance pour le Commerce Exterieur.

Commercial Insurance Market: The private insurance market.

Commercial Risks: Events that have the potential to affect the technical or economic feasibility of a project that are nonpolitical in nature.

Concession Agreement: An agreement between a project company (and the project sponsors, in some situations) and the host government, in which the project company is granted authority to develop, construct, and operate a project for a limited period of time until financing is paid and a negotiated equity return is earned; commonly used in BOT and BOOT projects.

Contract Frustration: The centerpiece of the political risk trade coverages is contract frustration (CF) coverage. CF insurance provides a comprehensive range of coverages designed to protect exporters against risks associated with selling their goods overseas. If an export contract is with a publicly owned buyer, coverage is provided against unilateral contract termination, payment default, cancellation/nonrenewal of import/export licenses, home- or host-country embargo, arbitration award default, and other government acts that can frustrate a trade contract.

If the contract is with a private buyer, these coverages are restricted to government action. In the majority of cases, CF coverage will apply to losses that occur after goods have been shipped. However, coverage can be drafted to address pre-shipment risks, where a government action impacts the transaction after contract signature, but before shipment occurs. Preshipment losses are generally covered for costs and expenses incurred in performance of the contract, while postshipment losses are usually covered for 90% of the contract value.

Cooperative Underwriting Program (CUP): This program of the Multilateral Investment Guarantee Agency (MIGA) encourages private sector underwriters to underwrite investment projects jointly with MIGA. The CUP is a fronting arrangement whereby MIGA is the insurer of record and issues a contract for the entire amount of insurance requested by an investor, but retains only a portion of the exposure for its own account. The remainder is underwritten by one or more private sector insurers using MIGA's contract wording. The premium rates, claim payments, and recoveries are all shared on a *pari passu* (equal) basis. Other underwriters have similar programs.

Creeping Expropriation: A variant of expropriation coverage. An action or series of actions whose net effect is expropriatory, such as the imposition of punitive and selective taxes, which makes a venture commercially unprofitable.

Currency Inconvertibility/Nontransfer: This coverage (commonly referred to as CI coverage) is intended to ensure that dividends, profits, fees, share capital, and loan proceeds are repatriated from a host country in a timely fashion. The conversion of the local currency into hard currency and the transfer of that hard currency out of the host country are covered for both "active blockage" (wherein a law prevents conversion or transfer) and "passive blockage" (in which excessive delays in processing a request to convert or transfer currency by the governing monetary authority prevent repatriation). The amount of currency that could not be converted or transferred is the subject of the coverage.

CI insurance does not protect against currency fluctuation, devaluation, or any preexisting conditions. In order to trigger coverage, most public sector insurers require that the local or hard currency be delivered to the insurer before a claim can be paid. If an investor were to apply for currency conversion and the host government's central bank not only failed to convert the currency in a predefined time period, but also refused to return the local currency to the investor, the investor would not be able to file an inconvertibility claim. In such a case, the currency will have been effectively expropriated. For this reason, CI coverage is almost always purchased in conjunction with expropriation coverage.

Some underwriters will provide coverage for CI on a stand-alone basis. The coverage is often viewed as the riskiest form of PRI because there are so many opportunities for problems to arise in converting or transferring currency and because private sector underwriters have few reprocessing capabilities for local currency. Apart from selling local currency to a local buyer or perhaps investing local currency in a business in the host country, the average private sector underwriter has no way to utilize the currency. This is very different for public sector underwriters (who are owned by home country governments or international institutions), who can (for example) apply local currency toward a local embassy's operations or perhaps invest it in a development project. For this reason, CI coverage is more readily available in the public sector, at reduced cost.

Currency Risk: The difficulties encountered by a foreign borrower or foreign affiliate in making future payments due in a currency other than that in which revenues are earned.

Deprivation/Contingent Deprivation: Deprivation is an action taken by a host government that prevents the reexport of physical goods, inventory, production equipment, or other assets. Although these items may not have been seized by the government, the inability to relocate them makes them worthless. Should a host government fail to issue a license to reexport these assets, the coverage would provide compensation for the value of the assets in question. Contingent deprivation takes deprivation one step further. Should the investor be successful in exporting the assets, but the home country (or country where the investor wishes to import the goods) refuses to allow their importation, due to the cancellation of an import license or the imposition of an embargo, coverage would be available to provide compensation equivalent to the value of the assets.

Event Contingency: Protects against expropriation and political violence for specific project assets and extra expense incurred for event disruption. If, for example, a film company is engaged in shooting scenes in overseas locations, a political event or intervention can cause serious financial loss. Causes of such losses can include withdrawal of filming permits and/or expulsion of personnel from the host country.

Export Credit Insurance (ECI): An insurance coverage that is intended to address private buyer payment risk derived from buyer insolvency or protracted default. ECI generally covers those perils addressed in contract frustration coverage and adds in coverage for private buyer payment default.

Export Development Corporation (EDC): The Canadian government-sponsored political risk and export credit insurer.

Export Finance and Insurance Corporation (EFIC): The Australian government-sponsored political risk and export credit insurer.

Expropriation: The centerpiece of PRI for investments, expropriation insurance, is commonly referred to as confiscation, expropriation, nationalization, and deprivation (CEND) coverage (see separate definition above). Expropriation coverage is designed to protect a foreign investor when its fundamental ownership rights are interfered with by the host government. This may take the form of a direct seizure of an asset (fixed investments or plant and equipment), which is the classic definition of expropriation, or an action or series of actions whose net effect is expropriatory (referred to as "creeping expropriation"), such as the imposition of punitive and selective taxes that make a venture commercially unprofitable.

> Expropriation insurance providers take varying approaches to determining what constitutes an "expropriatory action." Some will say that the action must have been discriminatory against the investor; others will say that the action must have "selectively" or "expressly" restricted the insured's operations. Most underwriters will agree that the governmental action must have resulted in a "permanent" cessation of operational activities. This is because operating conditions routinely change in developing countries, foreign investment laws change, leaderships can change with frequency, and not all of these changes necessarily last for long. If such a change lasts for anywhere from a number of months to a year, underwriters agree that it is likely to be permanent.

> Under international law, a government has the right to seize a foreign-held asset; however, compensation must be provided on a fair, adequate, and prompt basis. When an act of expropriation occurs and such compensation is not provided, expropriation insurance is designed to respond by providing compensation to an investor based on net book value or to a project lender based on the schedule of payments that were missed as a result of the expropriatory action.

Financed-Asset Nonrepossession: A specialized variant of expropriation coverage that is available to protect financiers or lessors of assets such as commercial aircraft or shipping, where the asset is a fundamental part of the security package and an inability to repossess the asset poses a serious problem. If the financier or lessor is concerned about country risk where the equipment is being used, nonrepossession insurance can mitigate the cross-border risk by providing coverage against acts of the foreign government (including expropriation) and interference or lack of assistance when the lessor or financier attempts to enforce its contractual right of repossession following a default under the loan or lease contract. When repossession attempts are successful, coverage is also available against the failure of the foreign government to deregister or deflag the asset.

Forced Abandonment/Key Operator's Endangerment: Forced abandonment involves the insured being forced to leave its equipment in circumstances prejudicial to the safety and well-being of project staff, often following an order to leave a host country by a home country government. The coverage compensates the insured for the value of the equipment left behind. Key operator's endangerment coverage addresses the forced withdrawal of specialist personnel, without whom the venture cannot operate, as a result of the occurrence of war or strikes, riots, and civil commotion. It reimburses the insured for the cost of the asset in question, plus the cost of personnel evacuation.

Foreign Credit Insurance Association (FCIA): The private sector export credit insurer.

Implementation Agreement: A project-specific agreement between the host government and a project developer that provides government assurances and guarantees required for successful project development and allocation of risks that promote equity investments and debt financing.

Independent Power Producer (IPP): This term has become a synonym for any power producer not owned by a government.

International Center for the Settlement of Investment Disputes (ICSID): World Bank Group's center that exists to help solve investment disputes between investors and host countries.

International Finance Corporation (IFC): The World Bank Group's private sector lending subsidiary.

International Union of Credit and Investment Insurers (IUCII): Otherwise known as the Berne Union (see separate definition).

Kidnap and Ransom Insurance: This insurance provides protection to companies through indemnification for expenses incurred in retrieving an employee or dealing with an extortion issue by way of consulting services that are generally included as part of the insurance package. Policies typically cover indemnification for ransom paid in the following situations: (1) kidnappings, hijackings, and personnel detention; (2) threats to kill, injure, or abduct employees; (3) threats to damage property or contaminate products; and (4) threats to divulge secrets or introduce computer viruses. Also covered are (1) loss of ransom payments in transit; (2) death or disablement, medical costs, or psychiatric costs; (3) fees to consulting groups, negotiators, interpreters, forensic analysts, or public relations consultants; (4) associated expenses (advertising, reward money, security guards, and recording equipment); (5) victim rest, rehabilitation, or replacement costs; and (6) corporate liability to employees and their estates when negligence in a kidnap situation is alleged.

> For an additional premium, corporate policies can be extended to cover loss of earnings following property damage, extortion recall, destruction costs, and loss of value following a products extortion emergency repatriation.

> On the consulting side of the coverage, specialist consulting firms provide policy holders with a full range of services, including risk reduction and advice and, in the event of a kidnap-type incident, intelligence and negotiation. These firms have lengthy and successful track records. Their involvement has dramatically improved survival rates.

> Personal policies may be obtained to protect named individuals and family members. For corporations, coverage can be arranged for all employees or for key executives. Global coverage for all employees is the simplest way to cover all of a company's exposures.

License: A governmental grant providing authority to undertake an activity or business.

License Cancellation: The cancellation of previously issued import or export licenses that results in the inability to ship or receive goods internationally.

Lloyd's: The private sector underwriter Lloyd's of London.

Multilateral Investment Guarantee Agency (MIGA): The World Bank Group's political risk investment insurance underwriting arm.

Nippon Export and Investment Insurance (NEXI): The Japanese government-owned political risk and export credit insurer.

Non-Honoring a Letter of Credit: This coverage is a cost-effective alternative to confirming letters of credit (LCs). In comparing the cost of the two, non-honoring coverage is often less expensive than obtaining a confirmation. Coverage is not available for a bank's failure to open an LC, but only for its refusal to honor a previously issued, irrevocable LC.

Offtake Agreement: An agreement to purchase all or a substantial part of the product produced by a project, which typically provides the revenue stream for a project financing.

Offtaker (Offtake Purchaser): The purchaser of a project's output.

Overseas Private Investment Corporation (OPIC): The US government's PRI underwriting organization.

Passive Blockage: Related to currency inconvertibility/nontransfer coverage (see separate definition) wherein excessive delays in processing a request to convert or transfer currency by the governing monetary authority prevent timely and successful repatriation of local or foreign currency (see also *active blockage*).

Political Risk: Government actions that impact the ability of businesses to trade or invest across borders.

Political Risk Insurance (PRI): A specialized line of insurance coverage that protects traders, investors, and credit-based sellers against government actions that impact fundamental ownership rights, interfere in the delivery or receipt of goods internationally, or prevent payment for goods exported. There are two broad categories of coverage within PRI: investment coverages and trade coverages. Investment coverages are oriented toward foreign direct investment and broadly address interference by a host government in fundamental ownership and operation rights. Trade coverages are oriented toward export and import transactions and broadly address host or home government interference in the successful conclusion and payment of the transactions.

Political Violence (PV): This coverage addresses physical damage to an asset as a result of strikes, riots, civil commotion, terrorism, sabotage, war, and civil war. While standard property insurance policies can provide some form of coverage against terrorism, damage due to war is usually excluded. Purchasing PV coverage removes the possibility of a dispute about whether property insurance covered such a loss or not. Coverage usually applies to the lesser of repair, replacement, or fair market value. In addition, coverage for business interruption may also be available, either for net profit lost or for net book value, depending on the underwriter (see also the definition for *political violence* in Section I).

> While private sector underwriters do not generally require that an act of PV be "politically motivated" (meaning that the damage was the result of an action intended to overthrow the host government), public sector underwriters usually require that the insured prove that there was a political motivation behind the action. Public-sector underwriters can write coverage for

war on an unrestricted basis, but private sector underwriters only recently became able to write coverage for war risks on land (because of a long-standing treaty preventing them from doing so previously).

PPA: Power purchase agreement.

Private Sector Underwriters: The primary private sector underwriters are Ace, Aspen, Axis, Chartis, CV Starr, Lloyd's of London, Sovereign, and Zurich. There are a number of other underwriters. Private sector underwriters can write coverage for investment and trade transactions for between 1 and 10 years, have insured percentages of between 90% and 100%, can issue coverage in a matter of days, and have a great degree of flexibility in how the terms of coverage are drafted.

Property Extortion: Coverage provided to foreign investors when criminal groups in a host country threaten to destroy property unless a ransom is paid. Special coverage can be obtained to cover the costs incurred in dealing with such threats.

Public Sector Underwriters: Government owned and operated political risk insurers. Most developed countries and a surprising number of developing countries have their own political risk insurers. Among the best known in the developed world are the Overseas Private Investment Corporation (OPIC) of the United States, the Export Credit Guarantee Corporation (ECGD) of the UK, and MIGA. Public sector underwriters write coverage primarily for investments for up to 20 years, do not normally provide coverage for greater than 90% of the exposure, generally require at least 3 to 6 months to issue coverage, and have only a limited degree of flexibility in how the terms of coverage are drafted.

In general, the 20-year policy period of public sector underwriters will be attractive to long-term foreign investors, though it can take up to 6 months to get the coverage. Private sector underwriters can provide coverage in the interim (see *bridging coverage*). However, private sector underwriters can very often provide coverage of up to 10 years for investments, which may be adequate for many investors' purposes. Private sector underwriters will almost always be the best option for traders because of their rapid response times.

Sovereign: The private sector political risk insurer Sovereign Risk Limited.

Sovereign Guarantee: A government guarantee.

Sovereign Risk: The risk that the host government will default on its contractual undertakings with the project or a project participant, such as under guarantees, indemnity agreements, or input and offtake contracts.

SRCC: Strikes, riots, and civil commotion.

Trade Disruption/Force Majeure (TD/FM): A variant of CF coverage. Should there be a disruption in a trader's ability to source raw materials or distribute its products where no physical damage occurs and alternative supplies of either cannot be arranged, this coverage will respond. TD/FM coverage protects against loss due to nondelivery, fire, flood, explosion, earthquake, volcanic eruption, lightning, derailment, collision, road closure, third-party blockade, CEND, embargo, license cancellation, governmental action, and PV. For example, if goods were left in a warehouse and a flood made gaining access to the warehouse impossible, resulting in missed delivery dates and subsequent penalties, TD/FM coverage would provide reimbursement for the net loss, including additional costs incurred.

United Nations Conference on International Trade Law (UNCITRAL): A forum for the resolution of arbitration disputes.

Wrongful Calling of "On-Demand" Guarantees (WCG): This coverage protects against the wrongful or rightful calling of "on-demand" bid bonds, advance payment guarantees, maintenance guarantees, or performance guarantees and is most often associated with construction projects or service contracts. Coverage is provided when a public buyer draws on a bank guarantee but has no right to do so under the terms of a contract (a "wrongful" call), or when the insured cannot perform its contractual obligations because of a political event (in which case, the host government may rightfully call the guarantee). The insured is compensated for the amount of the guarantee at issue. The coverage is triggered by the following events: (1) any call by the beneficiary where one is not in default, (2) home- or host-country embargo, (3) home- or host-country cancellation/nonrenewal of import/export licenses, (4) arbitration award default, and (5) the imposition of any law, order, regulation, or decree by either government that prevents the insured from fulfilling the terms of the contract.

Notes

1. This section is based on work done jointly by the author and James DeLoach when Mr. DeLoach was with Arthur Andersen.
2. The political risk terms used here are defined specifically as they relate to political risk insurance. Some terms may have different meanings if used in a different context.

Bibliography

Some articles referenced in the book that were authored or coauthored by Daniel Wagner were reproduced in whole or in part with permission from each publisher. Links to the articles authored or coauthored by Daniel Wagner may be found at www.countryrisksolutions.com/publishedworks.html.

Abadie, A., and J. Gardeazabal. The economic costs of conflict: A case study of the Basque country. Harvard University/NBER and the University of the Basque Country, July 2002.

_____. Terrorism and the world economy. Harvard University/NBER and the University of the Basque Country, October 2005.

Agrawal, S., and D. Wagner. The state of Indian-Sino relations. *The Huffington Post,* February 11, 2010.

_____. India's Ongoing concerns over Afghanistan and Pakistan. *The Huffington Post,* July 5, 2011.

Al Arabiya News. Yemen unemployment rates hike and Yemen unrest continues, March 30, 2011 (www.a1arabiya.net/articles/2011/03/30/143616.html).

Asian Development Bank. Key indicators for Asia and the Pacific 2010, August 2010.

_____. FDI confidence index. September 2004, vol. 7.

Australia Department of Foreign Affairs and Trade. Combating terrorism in the transport sector—Economic costs and benefits, 2004.

Bank of International Settlements. *On the use of information and risk management by international banks,* Basle, 1998.

BBC News. Egypt's defiant women fear being cast aside, June 19, 2011. (http://www.bbe.co.uk/news/world-middle-east-13796966).

_____. Egypts suffers post-revolution blues, May 12, 2011. (www.bbc.co.uk/news/world-middle-east-13371974).

Business Week. China's illusory middle class, May 9, 2007.

Chen, A., and T. Siems. The effects of terrorism on global capital markets. Cox School of Business and the Federal Reserve Bank of Dallas, August 2003.

Comptroller of the Currency. Country risk management. *Comptroller Handbook,* October 2001.

Cristiani, D. Turkey-GCC ties: Ankara sets its sights on the Gulf. worldpoliticsreview.com

Deckers, W., and D. Wagner. The evolution of China/EU relations. china.org.cn (February 22, 2010).

The Economist. Who's in the middle? February 12, 2009.

_____. Speak softly and carry a blank cheque. July 17, 2010.

Economist Intelligence Unit. Democracy index: Democracy in retreat, 2010.

Economist Intelligence Unit. Spring tide, 2011.

Enders, W., and T. Sandler. Terrorism and foreign direct investment in Spain and Greece. *Kyklos* (Blackwell Publishing) 49 (3), 1996.

Financial Times. Uniform unease, August 26, 2010.

Freedom House. *How freedom is won: From civic resistance to durable democracy,* 2005.

Human Rights First. Sectarian violence in Egypt, June 11, 2011.

Gallagher, A. J. Political risk insurance: Report and market update, January 2011.

Goldsmith, S., and D. Wagner. A new era for PNG. Project Finance International, May 19, 2010.

_____. Geopolitics with Chinese characteristics. *The Huffington Post,* May 25, 2010.

_____. FDI with Chinese characteristics. *The Huffington Post,* October 12, 2010.

_____. The battle for China's affection. *FDI Magazine,* October/November, 2010.

Gutt, J., and D. Wagner. Country risk management: Removing board blinders. International Risk Management Institute, September 2009.

Jackman, D., and D. Wagner. China's rare earth bravado. *The Huffington Post,* November 3, 2010.

_____. Bolivia, Ecuador and Nicaragua: Lofty idealism vs. hard-nosed politics. foreignpolicyjournal.com (February 10, 2011).

_____. China's and India's battle for influence in Asia. *The Huffington Post,* March 9, 2011.

_____. BRICs form unstable foundation for multilateral action. foreignpolicyjournal.com (April 2, 2011).

_____. Upheaval in the Middle East: An opportunity for Turkey. foreignpolicyjournal.com (May 21, 2011).

Karasik, T., and D. Wagner. The maturing Saudi–Chinese alliance. Institute for Near East and Gulf Military Analysis, April 6, 2010.

Katzenstein, P. J., and R. O. Keohane. *Anti-Americanism in world politics.* Cornell University Press, Ithaca, NY, 2006.

Kearney, A. T. FDI confidence index. September 2003, vol. 6.

Leonard, M. *What does China think?* Harper Collins, New York, 2008.

Leopold, G., and K. Wafo. Political risk and foreign direct investment, Faculty of Economics and Statistics, University of Konstanz, 1998.

Li, Q. (Department of Political Science, Pennsylvania State University). Does democracy promote or reduce transnational terrorist incidents? *Journal of Conflict Resolution* 49 (2), April 2005.

_____. Political violence and foreign direct investment. In *Regional economic integration,* ed. M. Fratianni. Elsevier Publishing, New York, 2006.

Matthews, C. R., and D. Wagner. The future of Iraq. *INEGMA,* April 2009.

McClatchy. U.S. fares poorly in first modern polling of Egyptian views, June 25, 2011. (http://www.mccltchydc.com/2011/06/25/116485/us-fares-poorly-in-first-modern.html).

McKinsey & Company. 2010 Annual Chinese consumer study, *McKinsey Insights China.*

McKinsey Quarterly. The value of China's emerging middle class, June 2006.

Millett, R. Nicaragua: The politics of frustration. In *Latin American politics and development,* ed. H. Wiarda and H. Kline. Westview Press, Boulder, CO, 2011.

Naidu, G. V. C. Looking East: India and Southeast Asia. Research fellow, Institute for Defense Studies and Analyses, India.

Newsweek. Rogue diplomacy. May 7, 2010.

Park, S. H., and W. Vanhonacker. The challenge for multinational corporations in China: Think local, act global. *MIT Sloan Management Review* 8 (4), Summer 2007.

Political Risk Services. Brazil country report, 2010.

Redfern, C. J., and D. Wagner. Will China become the Japan of the 1980s? china.org.cn (September 7, 2009).

Rein, S. Jim Chanos is wrong: There is no China bubble. forbes.com (November 1, 2010).

Rouillard, T., and D. Wagner. Turkey's foreign policy vision. Institute for Near East and Gulf military analysis, July 28, 2010.

Schaub, D., and Q. Li. (Department of Political Science, Pennsylvania State University). Economic globalization and transnational terrorism. *Journal of Conflict Resolution* 48 (2), April 2004.

Sinclair, U. *The Jungle.* Doubleday, Page & Company, New York, 1906.

Smith, C. H. Why China's housing bubble will end badly. *Daily Finance,* August 17, 2010.

Standard and Poors. Sovereign credit ratings: A primer. May 28, 2009.

Tam, J., and D. Wagner. The Chinese yuan versus the power of the dollar. *The Huffington Post,* January 14, 2011.

The Telegraph, Tunisia: Birthplace of the Arab Spring fears Islamist resurgence, October 13, 2011 (http://www.telegraph.co.uk/news/worldnews/africaandindianocean/tunisia/8543674/Tunisia-Birthplace-of-the-Arab-Spring-fears-Islamist-insurgence.html).

Tilley, C. *Democracy.* Cambridge University Press, Cambridge, England, 2007.

Tupaz, E., and D. Wagner. China's pre-imperial overstretch. *The Huffington Post,* June 15, 2011.

_____. China and the mosquitoes. *The Huffington Post,* July 7, 2011.

United Nations Conference on Trade and Development. World investment report 2004.

_____ World investment report 2005.

US State Department. Patterns of global terrorism, 2004.

Vigevant, T., and G. Capaluni. *Brazilian foreign policy in changing times.* Rowman and Littlefield, Lanham, MD, 2010.

Wagner, D. Political risk insurance guide. International Risk Management Institute, 1999.

_____. Defining political risk. International Risk Management Institute website, October 2000.

_____. Political risk in Asia: Fact or fiction? International Risk Management Institute website, November 2001.

_____. A Western fix for Iraq? Forget it. International Risk Management Institute website, April 2004.

_____. The impact of terrorism on foreign direct investment. International Risk Management Institute website, February 2006.

_____. Bolivia's larger message. International Risk Management Institute website, May 2006.

_____. Effective transactional risk management. International Risk Management Institute website, November 2006.

_____. The boardroom vacuum. *Risk Management Magazine,* December 2009.

_____. Expropriation: Pakistan's message to foreign investors. International Risk Management Institute, February 12, 2010.

_____. China's great development challenge. IFR Asia: Asian Development Report 2010, April 27, 2010.

_____. Brazil and Turkey's message. *The Huffington Post,* June 17, 2010.

_____. Country risk management in the C-suite. AlisterPaine.com, July 5, 2010.

_____. Is country risk really rising? International Risk Management Institute, July 2010.

_____. The folly of Brazil's exceptionalism. *The Huffington Post,* August 9, 2010.

_____. Iraq's democratic experiment. *The Huffington Post,* October 5, 2010.

_____. China's real estate syndrome. *The Huffington Post,* December 10, 2010.

_____. China's ubiquitous middle class. *The Huffington Post,* December 21, 2010.

_____. Managing political risk in the new normal. International Risk Management Institute website, January 21, 2011.

_____. Tunisia and implications for political change in the Middle East. *INEGMA,* January 24, 2011.

_____. How political change in the Middle East and North Africa is affecting country risk analysis. International Risk Management Institute, April 21, 2011.

_____. Message to Pakistan: China will not replace U.S. aid. *The Huffington Post,* May 17, 2011.

Wall Street Journal. Slipping on the global stage. March 29, 2010.

Webber, J. Bolivia in the era of Evo Morales. *Latin American Research Review* 45 (3), 2010.

Williams, M. *Uncontrolled risk.* McGraw-Hill, New York, 2010.

Wolfensohn Center for Development at Brookings. The new global middle class: A crossover from West to East. Brookings Institution, 2010.

World Bank. China: From poor areas to poor people. March 2009.

Yew, L. K. Imagining Asia in 2020: Future risks, future trends. *Asia Trends Monitoring Bulletin.* School of Public Policy, National University of Singapore, 2011.

Index